Thackeray
Interviews and Recollections

Volume 1

THACKERAY

Interviews and Recollections

Volume 1

Edited by

Philip Collins

First published 1983 by
THE MACMILLAN PRESS LTD
London and Basingstoke
Companies and representatives
throughout the world

ISBN 0 333 26805 9

Printed in Hong Kong

'Anny is *golden*', said Thackeray of his daughter. Fortunate in having a golden daughter myself, I dedicate this book to her: Rosamund Patricia Collins

Contents

List of Plates

Acknowledgements

It is, as usual, as much a pleasure as a duty to thank those who have helped me. Not often enough, perhaps, do we acknowledge that one of the joys of academic life – certainly in that patch of it which I inhabit – is the opportunity it provides for experiencing the generosity of our colleagues. I cannot recall, indeed, in my thirty-odd years in the profession, being refused help by any of the hundreds of scholars, archivists, librarians, collectors or others to whom I have sent enquiries or requests. Academic authors and their readers are fortunate that such courtesy and camaraderie remain strong in the international community of scholarship.

Like all recent commentators on Thackeray, I owe much to the labours of his editor and biographer Gordon N. Ray, as my annotation will often remind the reader, and Professor Ray has kindly answered enquiries. Many colleagues at the University of Leicester have rescued me when my poor command of languages or history, or other deficiencies in my editorial equipment, were delaying or had floored me, and I thank them: John Hemmings, Anthony Fitton-Brown, Harry Mac-William, Sheila Spire, John Gough, Rupert Evans and John Hampton. K. C. Phillipps, of my own department, most kindly read a draft of my typescript and offered useful suggestions or corrections. Others who helped me include Professor Sylvère Monod, Mr B. Curle (Local Studies Librarian, Kensington and Chelsea Central Library), Mrs B. Freake (Librarian, Charterhouse) and the Headmaster of Charterhouse, Mr Gordon Phillips (Archivist of *The Times*), and Miss Mary Anne Bonney (Librarian of *Punch*). My text has been patiently and elegantly typed by Mrs Sigrid Goddard, Mrs Sylvia Garfield, Miss Anne Sowter and Mrs Pat Taylor. The impulse to edit these volumes came through the BBC's inviting me to write and narrate a documentary feature about Thackeray, and I thank my producers John Theocaris and Margaret Etall for giving me that opportunity.

The editor and publishers wish to thank the following who have kindly given permission for the use of copyright material:

Gordon N. Ray, for the extracts from *Thackeray: The Uses of Adversity 1811–1846*.

Harvard University Press, and Belinda Norman-Butler, literary executor for the Estate of William Thackeray, for the extracts from *The Letters and Private Papers of William Makepeace Thackeray*, ed. Gordon N. Ray, and for the illustrations, which are reproduced as Plates 4, 6 and 7.

Duke University Press, for the extracts from *Nineteenth-Century Literary Perspectives*, ed. Clyde de L. Ryals, copyright 1974.

University of Illinois Press, for the extract from *Letters of the Brownings to George Barrett*, ed. Paul Landis.

Cecil Palmer Ltd, for the extracts from *Letters and Memoirs of Sir William Hardman*, second series, ed. S. M. Ellis.

John Murray (Publishers) Ltd, for the extracts from *Letters of Anne Thackeray Ritchie*, ed. Hester Ritchie, and for the extracts from Lucy Cohen's *Lady de Rothschild and her Daughters*.

Basil Blackwell Publisher Ltd, for the extracts from *The Brontës: Their Lives, Friendships and Correspondence*, ed. T. J. Wise and J. A. Symington.

R. G. G. Price, for the extract from *A History of 'Punch'*.

Every effort has been made to trace all copyright-holders, but if any have been inadvertently overlooked the publishers will be pleased to make the necessary arrangement at the first opportunity.

List of Abbreviations

The following abbreviations are used in the editorial matter:

Adversity   Gordon N. Ray, *Thackeray: The Uses of Adversity 1811–1846* (Oxford, 1955).

Biog. Intros   Anne Thackeray Ritchie, Biographical Introductions to *The Works of William Makepeace Thackeray*, Biographical Edition, 13 vols (London, 1898–9).

LPP   *The Letters and Private Papers of William Makepeace Thackeray*, ed. Gordon N. Ray, 4 vols (Oxford, 1945–6).

TCH   *Thackeray: The Critical Heritage*, ed. Geoffrey Tillotson and Donald Hawes (London, 1968).

Wilson   James Grant Wilson, *Thackeray in the United States 1852–3, 1855–6*, 2 vols (London, 1904).

Wisdom   Gordon N. Ray, *Thackeray: The Age of Wisdom 1847–1863* (Oxford, 1958).

Introduction

This collection of accounts of Thackeray by people who knew or had met him ends with a magazine editor, John Blackwood, who loved 'old Thack', rejecting an anecdotal essay about him, just after his death. It was misleading, he thought, but indeed, as he explained, 'None of the numerous sketches I have read give to me any real picture of the man with his fun and mixture of bitterness with warm good feeling. . . . I feel so truly about him that I am frightened to give a wrong impression of him to one who did not know him' (below, II, 382). Few of Thackeray's friends felt quite so inhibited by this fear of giving the wrong impression. Many of them wrote about him, and collectively their reminiscences will, I hope, help the reader to build up a 'real picture of the man' or to add enriching detail to a picture already formed Many friends, however, shared John Blackwood's feeling that it was difficult to characterise Thackeray rightly, easy to misrepresent him – and that he had been widely misunderstood and misrepresented. The word 'real', used by Blackwood, recurs in many reminiscences: the 'real' Thackeray was hidden except from those who 'really' knew him. Strikingly, the obituary verses on him in the periodical with which he was so much associated, *Punch*, had as the opening words of its first four stanzas one of the accusations most commonly levelled at him by – as the verses imply – ignorant, superficial or malevolent observers: 'He was a cynic', followed by three and a half lines of rebuttal. Evidently it seemed politic to take this slanderous bull by the horns.

> He was a cynic: By his life all wrought
>   Of generous acts, mild words and gentle ways:
> His heart wide open to all kindly thought,
>   His hand so quick to give, his tongue to praise

– and so on (below, II, 376). Thackeray was indeed a controversial and variously reported figure: widely reported, too, because 'everybody' knew him. And 'It was curious', remarked another obituarist, E. S. Dallas in *The Times*, 'to see how warmly his friends loved him, and how fervently his enemies hated him. The hate which he excited among those who but half knew him will soon be forgotten; the warmth of affection by which he was endeared to many friends will long be remembered. He had his foibles, and so have we all.... But...' (below, II, 374). George Venables, a friend since their schooldays, wrote in his obituary assessment, 'By the friends who knew him best, Mr Thackeray was thoroughly beloved, and in due proportion of nearer or remoter intercourse he inspired an affectionate regard in all who shared his conversation' (below, II, 377); and Anthony Trollope, a latter-day friend and colleague, also writing soon after his death, noting his weaknesses as well as his virtues, suggested that 'He was a man to be loved even more than he was liked' (*Wisdom*, p. 425).[1]

Most of the items in this collection were written by people who counted themselves his friends; there is only a limited usefulness in accounts by those who, whether 'enemies' or not, 'but half knew him', though a few such quick glances can be illuminating, as instances of how Thackeray could strike people on brief acquaintance. The plan of volumes in this series of 'Interviews and Recollections'[2] at least provides for 'safety in numbers': many witnesses are called. The book consists indeed of witness rather than interpretation. Biography, wrote one of Thackeray's associates, George Hodder, introducing his account of the novelist, consists not of the knowledge and experience of one privileged person, who perhaps knew the subject personally,

> but of the aggregate contributions of many, who are willing, when occasion offers, to state what they know for the information and benefit of posterity. A hundred admirers of Thackeray might undertake to write a memoir of him, and yet the task of doing full justice to his character and career must necessarily be left to a chosen future historian, who shall zealously gather together all the bits and fragments to be found scattered among books and men, and blend them into a substantial and permanent shape. But it

> must be admitted that there is an exceptional difficulty in
> regard to Thackeray, inasmuch as there were few whom he
> allowed to *know* him, in the true sense of the
> phrase.... (below, II, 229)

'Bits and fragments', from a hundred or so witnesses in my
text and annotation, make up this book; the reader wanting to
see how they, and much other evidence, may be 'blended into
a substantial and permanent shape' will turn, or will already be
familiar with, the two-volume biography by Gordon N. Ray,
who coped admirably with the 'exceptional difficulty' presented by this subject, which George Hodder, like so many
other acquaintances, identified: 'There were few whom he
allowed to *know* him . . .', few who discerned the 'real' Thackeray beneath the surface or beyond the stereotype or
caricature which his literary and personal reputation had
created. Many accounts of him at the time, and later, refer to
the comment of his longtime *Punch* associate – if often his
antagonist – Douglas Jerrold: 'I have known Thackeray for
eighteen years and I don't know him yet.'[3] And many, also like
the author of those *Punch* verses, start by contrasting the
formidable and somewhat unendearing reputation with the
surprisingly agreeable actuality. An American observer, for
instance, John Esten Cooke: 'What impressed me first was the
remarkable difference between the real man and the malicious
cartoons drawn of him by his English critics. . . . I was
quite surprised . . .' (below, II, 256); and Cooke ends his essay
with a restatement of its object: 'to show that the man himself
was not a bitter cynic, but a person of the greatest gentleness
and sweetness, and that no name could suit him better than
that given him by those who knew him best, loving him for his
heart more than they admired him for his head – the name of
"good old Thackeray" '. 'Hug the old boy for me', wrote
another American friend to a fellow-countryman who was
visiting London: 'He has a big heart in his satirical body. . . . I
could never hate W. M. T. as many people do, simply because
he is a satirist.'[4] Not that it was only his enemies, or those who
did not know him well, who charged him with emotional
deficiencies. His lifelong intimate Edward FitzGerald, in two
successive entries below, dated 1832–3, describes him in the
first as being 'as full of good humour and kindness as ever' and

then, within months, in a summary of his character calls him 'very indifferent, almost cold in his feelings' (below, I, 28). Such conflicting opinions from the same person were, it may be remarked, sometimes occasioned by the notorious changeability of Thackeray's moods, a tendency exacerbated in later years by the ups and downs of his health: Blanchard Jerrold is one of the many witnesses to this, and the story of Anthony Trollope's first meeting with Thackeray well illustrates the point (below, II, 357, 342). George Augustus Sala, who regarded him as 'most emphatically a good man, but one continually struggling with an uneven and sometimes objectionable temperament', describes how, when Thackeray appeared to be in a cantankerous humour, 'I gave him the widest of wide berths' rather than risk an encounter (below, II, 226).

Thackeray himself was well aware of the animosities, as well as affection, which he aroused, and of the unfavourable reputation which he bore. He was in many ways a self-aware, self-critical, and self-accusatory man. This is another point reiterated by people who knew him: Sir John Skelton, for instance, writes of his 'almost infantile openness of nature. . . . He is willing that his whole life should be laid bare and looked through'; and Anthony Trollope, noting that 'Other men keep their little troubles to themselves', remarks how exceptional Thackeray was in confessing his reverses and shortcomings – 'who else would have told such a story of himself to the first acquaintance he chanced to meet?' (below, II, 327, 334). As John Forster commented in an obituary, he had an 'inconveniently large window in his breast' (*Wisdom*, p. 420). In letters to his mother and other intimates he is notably candid about his unpopularity in various quarters, and about those faults of character which perhaps half-justified it. 'My heart . . . is very generous I think but dreadful unforgiving', he wrote, after an experience which was still rankling in him. Lord Ashburton, he continued, 'told a friend of mine that "I was as tender as a woman but as cruel as Robespierre." I wonder whether it's true?' (*LPP*, III, 608). After another reverse – his being blackballed, and not for the first time, at a club election – he wrote to his friend Whitwell Elwin,

All people don't like me as you do. I think sometimes I am deservedly unpopular, and in some cases I rather like it.

> Why should I want to be liked by Jack and Tom? ... I know
> the Thackeray that those fellows have imagined to
> themselves – a very selfish, heartless, artful, morose, and
> designing man.... Ah if I dared but put all those fellows
> into a book! And suppose they put me into another – giving
> their views of your humble servant? Those books would be
> queer reading. (*LPP*, IV, 238).

'Those fellows' were, in this letter of 1861, Charles Dickens
and his associates Wilkie Collins and John Forster. Some of
the same demonology appears in a letter to his mother,
fourteen years earlier, when he was at last achieving a large
reputation, with *Vanity Fair*:

> Jerrold hates me, Ainsworth hates me, Dickens mistrusts
> me, Forster says I am false as hell, and Bulwer curses
> me – he is the only one who has any reason – yes the others
> have a good one too as times go. I was the most popular man
> in the craft until within abt 12 months – and behold I've
> begun to succeed. It makes me very sad at heart though, this
> envy and meanness – in the great sages & teachers of the
> world.

And then, characteristically, he wonders whether he should
accuse himself as well: 'Am I envious and mean too I wonder?
These fellows think so I know. Amen. God knows only' (*LPP*,
II, 308).

The recurrence of Dickens's name in so many statements by
and about Thackeray was inevitable. 'Thackeray and Dickens,
Dickens and Thackeray – the two names now almost necessarily go together', David Masson began an important critical
essay in the *North British Review* (May 1851).[5] In the opinion of
John Cordy Jeaffreson, Thackeray 'suffered from Dickens-
on-the-brain', and he is reported as saying that Dickens
'doesn't like me: he knows that my books are a protest against
his – that if the one set are true, the other must be false'
(below, II, 290; I, 179). Dickens, as I think, 'knew' no such thing,
and certainly he was much less interested in this comparison
than was Thackeray; as the reigning king of novelists he could
take a more relaxed view of the competition than did his
envious challenger. Anyone, however, who reads the critical
reviews, or the memoirs, of mid-Victorian England will
endorse Masson's comment, and I, happening to come to the

present task soon after compiling the Dickens volumes in this series, have just as 'necessarily' found the comparison intriguing. As I have remarked elsewhere, critical comparisons between Dickens and Thackeray became as frequent a set-piece for mid-Victorian commentators as Shakespeare/Ben Jonson ones had been in the mid-seventeenth century, and with many of the same implications: Dickens, like Shakespeare, had the greater 'genius' but Thackeray, like Jonson, was the more learned and 'correct' writer.[6] But in terms of personality, origins and life-style – which, more than critical assessment, are the subject of the present volumes – the contrast was equally striking and compelling. Thackeray was of 'good', Dickens of 'no', family. Thackeray received the education of a gentleman, at Charterhouse and Cambridge; Dickens's schooling was nondescript. Dickens was much more active and successful in public appearances, a splendid orator, a brilliant platform performer, relishing and thoroughly believing in all these public occasions; Thackeray, to his chagrin, was uncomfortable and ineffective as a speaker, and when he became a paid lecturer he disliked the whole business, despising it as 'quackery'. Dickens was exhaustingly energetic, Thackeray a prey to indolence; Dickens almost always super-efficient, Thackeray not so. Both were, over much the same decades, prolific authors by trade, and both became magazine editors, but Thackeray was not always sufficiently the professional for Dickens's taste. Both inspired affection and loyalty in bands of followers and associates, who sometimes approximated – in cricketing terms – to Gentlemen and Players: and some unseemly matches, verging upon gang-warfare, occurred, not always by the desire or at the instigation of the captains of these teams. The Garrick Club row of 1858, in which both the principals were involved (see below, II, 313), was only the most open and bitter, and the last, of these displays of antagonism. Many items below develop such comparisons between these two great contemporaries, contrasting their social and working habits, their manners and standing, and much else.

Not that it is wholly a matter of contrast. There were similarities: and, over a century later, they may well appear to us, like the seventeenth-century antagonists in T. S. Eliot's 'Little Gidding', as

United in the strife which divided them . . .
Those men, and those who opposed them
And those whom they opposed

are now 'folded in a single party'. To some overseas observers
at the time, they seemed so then. 'Dickens . . . writes London
tracts' and Thackeray observes 'the like municipal limits',
remarked Emerson in his *English Traits* (1856, ch. 14). Marx in
1854 saw them as co-workers in that 'present splendid
brotherhood of fiction-writers in England', who had delivered
'more political and social truths than have been uttered by
all the professional politicians, publicists and moralists put
together' ('The English Middle Class', *New York Daily Tribune*,
1 Aug 1854). Both were, indeed, metropolitan by residence as
well as imaginatively, and were public figures, members of the
Establishment as much as critics of their society, diners-out,
men widely recognised in the street – unlike George Eliot,
whom we more than many of their contemporaries would see
as a novelist of comparable or greater stature. Her sex and
temperament, however, and her dubious marital status,
debarred her from establishing this kind of ubiquitous social
presence, or generating affection and respect on a comparable scale.

Living such a social life, mainly in the metropolis and in
circles handy with the pen and much given to gossip,
Thackeray – who, as Trollope remarks, 'was one so well
known in society as to have created many anecdotes'[7] – is
amply documented, particularly in the second half of his
career, when literary fame, together with his genteel birth and
his taste for good living, much enlarged his social circle: and
then his visits to America and his sociability brought him into
contact with a further band of admirers who proved eager to
record their impressions of 'dear old Thack'. He is indeed,
conveniently for such a compilation as this, well documented
from the start. His forebears, though not illustrious, had
enjoyed sufficient professional distinction for a substantial
volume, *Memorials of the Thackeray Family*, to be compiled by
two of its members in 1879; it is not until p. 325 that the
novelist appears, as an observant three-year-old. At Charterhouse and Trinity College, Cambridge, Thackeray's contemporaries included many lads who later became eminent and

articulate, and they recorded in letters or diaries at the time or in subsequent reminiscences a fair amount about his boyhood and youth. The diligence of Gordon Ray and other of my predecessors has discovered similar records of the continental Thackeray of the 1830s. From 1837 onwards he was mainly resident in London, slowly making his way as a literary journalist and miscellaneous author. Authors tended then to lead a communal life, often centred on the magazines to which they particularly contributed, and Thackeray was a regular attender at 'Fraserian' dinners, the *Punch* Table, and other such gatherings through to the monthly *Cornhill* feasts over which he presided. Moreover, he belonged to many of the clubs, temporary or permanent, in which the artistic fraternity forgathered, joined in some of them (such as the Garrick) by lawyers and others with no professional involvement in the arts or journalism. Even during the few years of his married life, before his wife lost her wits and became a chronic patient living under others' care, he still felt and gave way to the constant need to hobnob over a bottle with his cronies; 'without my favourite talk about pictures or books I am good for nothing', he confessed in 1840, irked by the constraint of having to nurse Isabella (*LPP*, I, 467). To quote a few other phrases from letters in the early 1840s: 'Solitude creates a muzziness and incoherency in me'; 'scribble scribble in the morning, hob and nob in the evening – that has been my life during the Season'; 'I am very hard at it indeed now . . . but I could not go on with this unless I had the fun in the evening, and the quantum of wine: – it is very brutal and unworthy but so it is'; 'The dinner-parties pour in rather too plentifully. I had 5 invitations for last Saturday; and a dinner every day in the week, the same this week' (*LPP*, II, 84, 209, 101, 97). His resumption of a more domestic establishment, when his daughters came to live with him in 1846, did not end this habit of dining out, or having nightly recourse to the club or theatre or supper-room. Two little girls could not provide that necessary 'talk about pictures or books', nor feed his imagination with more glimpses of or news from 'Vanity Fair', nor give him the relaxation among male companions – including some bouts of raucous bawdiness – which was by now the habitual need of his bachelor clubman existence. Even abroad, he still needed his nightly dining-out, to the detriment of his health and peace of mind, as Elizabeth Barrett Browning was to remark in Rome in 1853 (below, I, 104): she was censorious about his declaration that he 'can't write in the morning without his good dinner and two parties over-night'.

His elder daughter Anny was later to write much, and valuably, about her father's methods of composition and way of life. (Other useful intimate accounts of Thackeray at work came from the amanuenses or henchmen whom he employed from time to time – James Hannay, Eyre Crowe and George Hodder, excerpted below.[8]) But, as Cordy Jeaffreson remarked in 1894 when – as Thackeray had wished – no biography had yet appeared but suggestions had been made that Anny should repair this deficiency, she was, despite other advantages, hardly the person to produce an adequate account of a man 'who was very much of a Bohemian to the last' (below, II, 286). Much of his existence was exclusively masculine, to some extent from inclination, but perforce in the many years when his wife was 'dead or worse' (*LPP*, II, 429) – the 'worse' for him because he could not hope to remarry while she lived, and she long outlived him. His friends and acquaintances, whether or not 'Bohemian', left ample record of this large area of his life about which, as Jeaffreson said, Anny would be under-informed, aware though she was that 'My father's club was so much a part of his daily life, that it seemed at last to be a part of his home' (*Biog. Intros*, XII, xxi). Obituaries remarked on how sorely missed a man so clubbable would be (*Illustrated London News*, 2 January 1864). 'To London literary men', wrote John Blackwood, 'Thackeray's death is a very serious loss. He was a central figure' (below, II, 381). The literary and social memoirs of the period are full of his presence, whether in Grub Street, Clubland or Belgravia, as will be evident in this compilation.

Bereft of a wife, and inured to the substitution of bachelor pleasures for the joys of domesticity, he continued however to yearn for female companionship. 'Very likely it's *a* woman I want more than any particular one . . .' he wrote to his mother in 1851, hinting at his sexual frustration as much as his emotional needs (*LPP*, II, 813). To Mrs Brookfield, the object of his most enduring and deepest affection of this kind, he wrote two years later, 'I can't live without the tenderness of some woman; and expect when I am sixty I shall be marrying a girl of eleven or twelve, innocent, barley-sugar-loving, in a pinafore' (*LPP*, III, 183) – a typical wry confession, this, of one of his weaknesses, as he recognised the indignity of his antics as an 'elderly Cupid', or, in 1856, proclaimed that his love-life must at last be coming to an end (*LPP*, III, 220, 586). Some of the young women who thus knew him familiarly are represented below. So is another group upon whom he conferred his affection and generosity – those who were children when they first, or best, knew him. He was an enchanting and kindly avuncular figure to many boys and girls, a number of whom recorded endearing memories of him in this role.

Another of the inevitable comparisons with Dickens can advert us to a usefulness which this compilation may have for readers of his novels. 'No one', wrote Sir Frederick Pollock, 'could be more free from egotism than Dickens was. He never talked about himself or his books, and was thus in great contrast with Thackeray, who, after he became famous, liked no subject so well.'[9] Macaulay also thought him too forthcoming on this topic: 'Talks too much about his *Vanity Fair*', he wrote in his diary after an encounter. 'I suspect that success, coming late, has turned his head. . . . At all events, I am sure that I never, except to a friend of many years' standing, introduced the subject of my own works' (*Wisdom*, p. 48). Ill-mannered, maybe: but there is much of interest and benefit for his readers in what he is thus reported as saying about the intentions and processes of his creative work. Dickens was, indeed, less forthcoming and less articulate and intelligent about his art, whether in conversation or on paper. Moreover Thackeray was a more autobiographical novelist than Dickens, continually using in his fiction scenes and people from his life, and dramatising aspects of himself in various characters from Pendennis onwards, besides being very present in his fiction as a narrator much given to addressing his readers. So, as James Hannay remarks, his life and his writings illuminate one another, and 'the more fully his life is made known to the world, the more clearly will the harmony of his works with it appear' (below, I, 97). It is not only when he is talking about his art that one will be reminded of it in the selections below.

Thackeray of course, shortly before his death, emphatically forbade the writing of any biography of himself (see below, II,

372). It was an unfortunate decision, loyally accepted by his daughters for many years, and it ran counter to many earlier pronouncements by him on such matters. 'All that I can remember out of books generally is the impression I get of the Author', he remarked (*LPP*, III, 19), and like most readers he was curious about what could be discovered about authors from outside their works. As he wrote in a *Roundabout* essay, 'We all want to know details regarding men who have achieved famous feats, whether of war, or wit, or eloquence, or endurance, or knowledge' ('On a Joke I once Heard from the Late Thomas Hood'). His *English Humourists* lectures notoriously do not confine their attention to 'the words on the printed pages' of the authors discussed. Thackeray's proclaimed object was indeed more biographical than critical, as he remarks in the section on Gay: it was 'rather to describe the men than their works; or to deal with the latter only in so far as they seem to illustrate the character of their writers'. Nor was he specially defensive about his own privacies. He was, as we have been reminded above, a decidedly candid letter-writer, and was content for posterity to see him, warts and all. Why, he wrote, should he 'care to appear to future ages . . . as other than I really am?' (*LPP*, III, 616). Who had the gall to pretend to be faultless? – 'Which of us has not idle words to recall, flippant jokes to regret? Have you never committed an imprudence? Have you never had a dispute, and found out that you were in the wrong? . . . As I write [this], I think about one or two little affairs of my own . . .' (*Roundabout Papers*, 'On Screens in Dining Rooms').

As I have insisted, the present book's purposes are distinct from those of a biography. It excludes, apart from annotatory citations, Thackeray's own letters and diaries, let alone his published writings. It is only incidentally concerned with his reception, in reviews and critiques. Interpretation and assessment are not my primary intentions, though inevitably both my selection of materials and some of my editorial attempts to clarify their circumstances and significance imply an understanding, whether adequate or otherwise, of the man. Here is presented a selection, from a large amount of relevant reminiscence, of some of the first-hand accounts which constitute one important ingredient in a biography. 'It seems to me', wrote Thackeray's daughter Anny, in 1891, 'it is

the short, natural, by-the-way things that are most vivid.' She
had been trying to write a magazine article about her father,
and the editor had asked her 'to say what I thought of my
father's Biographies, and I began to think that three words of
Mr FitzGerald's put him more vividly before me than pages of
disquisition. "There the door opened and Thackeray came in,
grand, gay and white-headed." I know that phase of him so
well.'[10] Readers will, I hope, light from time to time in the
following pages upon the specially illuminating 'three words'
which capture, for them, the 'real' Thackeray.

The arrangement of this collection is broadly chrono-
logical – only broadly so, because many items span more
than one period of Thackeray's life and career. The
chronology observed is of course that of his life, not of the date
of the items' publication. Normally items are dated by their
authors' first meeting with Thackeray, but some items are
grouped together in ways that may prove helpful to the
reader. Thus a number of items about Thackeray's relations
with Dickens and his circle are placed together. There are
some composite items, gathering the reports by various
observers on some phase of his life – his schooldays at
Charterhouse, for instance, or his career as a lecturer. For
readers unfamiliar with the detail of Thackeray's career, a
chronology is provided, and 'Suggestions for Further Reading' on his biography are offered at the end of volume II.
    Typographical errors in the extracts reprinted, and such
minor slips as wrong dates, have been silently corrected; the
editorial fussiness of '*sic*' or the paraphernalia of emendatory
footnotes hardly seem warranted. (Who, for instance, would
benefit much from the information that, in my first item
below, a French journalist in 1846 spelt Edward Sterling's
name incorrectly?) The convention for indicating book-titles,
etc., has usually been regularised as italic; spelling and
punctuation have likewise generally (except in extracts from
letters, diaries and the like) been made consistent.

Leicester
October 1980   PHILIP COLLINS

NOTES

1. References to frequently cited texts are given thus, bracketed, in the editorial matter. See the 'List of Abbreviations' on p. xii.

2. These Thackeray volumes contain, however, no 'interviews': this was a journalistic form only then being developed in America, whence it was imported into Britain. In his 'Glimpses of Thackeray', an American, Richard Henry Stoddard (1825–1903), remarks of his *Humourists* tour (1852–3) that 'That terror of the public man, the interview, was not as yet....' In 1870, however, seven years after Thackeray's death, a crusty Englishman, William Archer Shee, deploring the 'flagrant Yankeeisms' now rapidly ruining the English language, gave this instance: 'When... our newspaper correspondents daily "interview" all the great men of the day... it becomes serious.' See Richard Henry Stoddard, *Recollections, Personal and Literary* (New York, 1903) p. 215; William Archer Shee, *My Contemporaries 1830–1870* (1893) p. 322, diary, Jan 1870. Cf. II, 259, below.

3. Walter Jerrold, *Douglas Jerrold and 'Punch'* (1910) p. 27. Cf. a reported conversation of Jerrold's in 1846–7: 'He chatted of Dickens, Thackeray [*et al*]. Of all he spoke frankly, but discriminatively, and without a trace of malice or ill-nature. In answer to the enquiry, "What like was Thackeray?" he said: "He's just a big fellow with a broken nose, and, though I meet him weekly at the *Punch* dinner, I don't know him as well as I know you." Dickens he mentioned with the greatest affection...' (ibid., p. 26). Ten years later, Jerrold was up for election at the Reform Club, and wrote to his proposer rejecting the idea of soliciting Thackeray's vote: 'Thackeray and I are very good friends, but our friend T. is a man so full of crotchets, that, as a favour, I would hardly ask him to pass me the salt. Therefore, don't write to him' – Walter Jerrold, *Douglas Jerrold: Dramatist and Wit* (1918) II, 645–6. Thackeray, however, went out of his way to promote Jerrold's election (*Wisdom*, pp. 329, 485): evidently Jerrold still 'didn't know' him, and had underestimated his good will.

4. George Henry Baker to Bayard Taylor (on whom see below, II, 264), 24 Jan 1857, in Edward Sculley Bradley, *George Henry Baker: Poet and Patriot* (Philadelphia, 1927) p. 173. The affectionate adjective 'old' in both Cooke's and Baker's phrases about Thackeray, and in many other invocations, does credit to its subject: and, to anticipate a comparison made in the next two paragraphs, nobody (I think) spoke of 'good old Dickens'.

5. Reprinted, selectively, in *Dickens: The Critical Heritage*, ed. Philip Collins (1971) pp. 249–59, and in *TCH*, pp. 111–26.

6. *Dickens: The Critical Heritage*, p. 3. For examples of such comparisons, see the indexes of that book, p. 640, and of *TCH*, p. 386, and Dudley Flamm, *Thackeray's Critics: An Annotated Bibliography of British and American Criticism 1836–1901* (Chapel Hill, N. C., 1967) p. 177.

7. Anthony Trollope, *Thackeray* (1879) p. 1.

8. The topic is well discussed, more from manuscript and documentary evidence than from anecdotes, by J. A. Sutherland, in his *Thackeray at Work* (1974).

9. *Personal Remembrances of Sir Frederick Pollock* (1887) I, 289. Pollock

(1815–88), 2nd Baronet, lawyer and author, held the office of Queen's Remembrancer.

10. *Letters of Anne Thackeray Ritchie*, ed. Hester Ritchie (1924) p. 218. Anny is quoting, from memory, incorrectly: gray, grand and good-humoured' were FitzGerald's adjectives (see below, I, 30).

A Thackeray Chronology

1811   Born in Calcutta, only child of Richmond Thackeray (of the East India Company) who died in 1815.

1817   Arrives, by himself, in England. Schooling at Southampton, Chiswick, and (1822–8) Charterhouse. His mother marries Captain – later Major – Henry Carmichael-Smyth, later in 1817, and they return to England, 1818, living at Larkbeare, Devon, 1825–35.

1829–30   At Trinity College, Cambridge. Heavy gambling losses. Leaves without graduating, and spends seven months in Germany, chiefly in Weimar.

1831–2   Law student at the Middle Temple, inconclusively.

1833–4   Paris correspondent of the short-lived *National Standard*.

1833–5   Studying art in Paris. Loses most of his patrimony in a bank failure, 1833.

1836   Marries Isabella Shawe, of an Anglo-Irish family, in Paris. Living in London, from 1837. Three daughters: Anne Isabella ('Anny', later Lady Ritchie, 1837–1919), Jane (1838–9), Harriet ('Minny', later Mrs Leslie Stephen, 1840–75). Wife goes mad, 1840, and spends most of her remaining life in sanatoria and asylums, dying in 1893.

1836   *Flore et Zéphyr* (satirical lithographs) published. Applies, in vain, to become *Pickwick Papers* illustrator. Career as graphic artist fizzles out. Instead, sundry posts and engagements over the next decade as newspaper correspondent, staff member and miscellaneous journalist, reviewer, story-writer, etc., for numerous journals, notably

Fraser's Magazine from 1837 (e.g. Yellowplush Papers, 1837–8) and Punch from 1842 (e.g. The Book of Snobs, 1846–7). Living sometimes in Paris but mostly in London lodgings.

1840   The Paris Sketch Book. Other travel books: The Irish Sketch Book (1843) and Notes of a Journey from Cornhill to Grand Cairo (1846).

1844   Barry Lyndon serialised in Fraser's.

1846   Settles at 13 Young Street, Kensington, and is joined by his two surviving daughters, who had been living with grandparents.

1847–8   Vanity Fair, serialised in monthly numbers, establishes him as a major novelist.

1848   His attachment to Jane Brookfield, wife of his old friend the Revd W. H. Brookfield, increases in intensity. After various altercations with Brookfield, the friendship virtually ends in 1851.

1848–50   Pendennis serialised. Its animadversions on literary men provoke the 'Dignity of Literature' controversy, which rumbles on over the next decade, involving sharp exchanges with Dickens, John Forster, and their associates.

1851   The English Humourists lectures given in London, and subsequently in the provinces. Series repeated in an extensive American tour, winter 1852–3, with the addition of the 'Charity and Humour' lecture.

1852   The History of Henry Esmond published by George Smith; not serialised.

1853–5   The Newcomes serialised. Many continental trips, holidays and periods of residence throughout these years, alone or with his daughters. Falls ill in Rome, winter 1853–4; beginning of the breakdown of his health.

1854   Moves to 36 Onslow Square, Brompton. The Rose and the Ring, last and most successful of the series of Christmas books published since 1846.

1855–6   Winter, The Four Georges lectures given in America, and subsequently in Britain.

1857   Liberal parliamentary candidate at Oxford (unsuccessful).

1857–9	*The Virginians* serialised.
1858	The 'Garrick Club affair', provoked by Edmund Yates's article in *Town Talk*, 13 June; end of friendship with Dickens.
1859	George Smith engages him to write serials for the forthcoming *Cornhill Magazine*; later, Thackeray agrees to edit it.
1860	January, first issue of the *Cornhill*, remarkably successful. It includes the first instalment of *Lovel the Widower* and the first of the *Roundabout Papers*.
1861–2	*Philip* serialised in the *Cornhill*. Thackeray resigns the editorship, March 1862.
1862	Moves to 2 Palace Green, Kensington, a very superior residence, with an enlarged establishment.
1863	Begins *Denis Duval* (unfinished; serialised posthumously in the *Cornhill*, 1864). Squabble with the National Shakespeare Committee, partly occasioned by one of its organisers' being suspected of having published a severe review of Anne Thackeray's *Story of Elizabeth*. Thackeray, in poor health, dies suddenly (24 December) and is buried in Kensal Green Cemetery.

An Account of Thackeray, by Himself

PHILARÈTE CHASLES

From 'Le Roman de moeurs en Angleterre. – *La Foire aux vanites*', *Revue des deux Mondes*, Feb 1849, pp. 538–40. Several years later, Thackeray wrote to another Frenchman interested in contemporary English literature, Amedee Pichot: 'In an article about Vanity Fair years ago Chasles applied to me for and used a biography – wh I wrote and he "arranged" for French readers' (*LPP*, III, 411; cf. his letter to Chasles, 6 Feb 1849, *LPP*, II, 503n). The extract here translated indicates, therefore, how Thackeray was willing to present himself to the public at this time, when fame had lately come to him. My collection *Dickens: Interviews and Recollections* similarly begins (I, 1–2) with a letter in which Dickens was briefing a French journalist about his early life. Thackeray is more informative, and very much more candid about his misfortunes and mistakes.

Thackeray has the advantage over some of his predecessors [in English fiction] of having seen and observed many things, men and countries. His horizons are much wider than Walter Scott's. Cast here and there, like Aeneas, by the accidents of his life, he has talked with dressing-gowned German students and with our felt-hatted art students; he is as familiar with the musical restaurants along the shores of the Rhine as with the clubs of London or Paris. He has mixed as much with the marvellously stupid nabobs who have returned from India to England as with the *habitués* of Tortoni.[1] He is, then, a man of experience and of *savoir-vivre*, not a mere scribbler filling up his pages – a man who has felt much and suffered much: a precondition for all original talents. His books are but experience dramatised.

Born in Calcutta in 1811, son of a high-ranking civil servant (and we know how well rewarded and highly regarded these British civil servants are), he lost his father while very young, and was sent to England. Like most radicals and liberals, he was well-born and was educated in the style of his class, first in a school kept by 'a horrible tyrant' (as he describes it) and then at Charterhouse and Cambridge, where his contemporaries included Warburton, Kinglake and Monckton Milnes.[2] Corporal punishment, fagging . . . and bullying . . . seem to have left a deep and bitter impression on him; these early miseries and sufferings often recur in his writings. So does the image of his mother, a woman of rare quality and great beauty.

She had married again. With a fortune of 20,000 francs [£800] and the expectation of inheriting more from his stepfather, who was very fond of him, our young man, thoroughly lazy, given to smoking and idling and to reading novels and books of all kinds, happily devoted himself to a branch of art unlikely to earn him much money, caricature. After spending a year in a small German town, he settled in London and made some pretence of studying for the Bar. But in fact he was ruining himself, or allowing himself to be ruined; with a small patrimony, and being high-spirited, careless, good-humoured and pleasure-loving, this was not difficult. By the age of twenty-three, William Makepeace Thackeray had hardly anything left, and his family's financial position was compromised, too. Recalling his youthful fondness for sketching, he fondly dreamed he might become a painter, and came to Paris, where he dashed off some water-colours of mediocre quality. Meanwhile, his stepfather had lost most of his capital, having invested it in an unsuccessful journalistic venture in London, the *Constitutional*, a newspaper which he had founded. The son, who had lately married in Paris an Irishwoman of good family, had naturally become the Paris correspondent of his stepfather's newspaper. This was indeed a very modest début in a literary career, but he had found his true vein.

This was truthfulness in expression and in thinking – fine, frank, satirical and unpretentious observation – the dash and verve of a man of the world rather than the conventional ways of authorship. To *Fraser's Magazine*, a Tory miscellany which made a point of seeking out originality, he sent a comic series, which was very successful, *The Yellowplush Papers*. . . . Undeniably he was a wit, but his literary status remained uncertain. A *protégé* of some of the most notable judges in British journalism – the brilliant and profound Carlyle, and Mr

Sterling and Mr Barnes[3] – he wrote critical articles for *The Times*: and for *Fraser's Magazine* he wrote a satirical story aimed against the ultra-philanthropic novels, then very fashionable in England and since then imported into France, novels populated by amiable convicts and philosophical hang-men.[4] The public, resentful of such a sharp attack upon its taste, did not receive *Catherine* well. Soon after this, Mr Thackeray was afflicted by a great domestic calamity: his wife went mad during a voyage they were making to Ireland. At this crisis of his fortunes various friends came to his aid, and, in these painful circumstances, the editor Mr Fraser, with whom he had quarrelled, generously opened his purse to Thackeray. A delightful story, *The Great Hoggarty Diamond*, the *Irish Sketch Book*, the *Snobs* and other sharply amusing series in *Punch* widened his reputation [as did further publications of these years]. Mr Thackeray did not set himself up as a great philosopher but as a sensible fellow with no affectation about him, and one took him for that and no more. . . . It was not until the later numbers of *Vanity Fair*, which appeared in serial form, that one realised that a new novelist had emerged, not only a satirist and a philosopher but also a formidable assailant of some of the vices of the English. . . . The publication of *Vanity Fair* caused a sensation, almost a scandal . . . .

NOTES

1. Tortoni's was a well-known Paris restaurant.
2. Eliot Warburton (1810–52), Irish barrister, novelist, and miscel-laneous writer; A. W. Kinglake (1809–91), author of *Eothen* (1844) and later of *The Invasion of the Crimea*; Richard Monckton Milnes, first Baron Houghton (1809–85), politician, poet, and famous host and man of society.
3. See below. I, 33, for Thomas Carlyle's remarks on Thackeray. Edward Sterling (1773–1847) was on the Staff of *The Times*, which was edited from 1817 until his death by Thomas Barnes (1785–1841).
4. *Catherine: A Story*, serialised in *Fraser's Magazine*, May 1839 to Feb 1840: an attack upon *Oliver Twist* and other such 'Newgate Novels'.

An Observant Boy with a Large Head

ALICIA BAYNE AND ANNE CARMICHAEL-SMYTH

(1) from Jane Towneley Pryme and Alicia Bayne, *Memorials of the Thackeray Family* (privately printed, 1879) pp. 325–7; (2) from *Biog. Intros*, I, xvi, VIII, xviii, and *Adversity*, pp. 75–6. Mrs Pryme (1788–1871), a distant relative of Thackeray's, and her daughter Mrs Bayne wrote this family history, the latter compiling the chapter on the novelist. Her account of the adult Thackeray appears below (I, 85); in this childhood section, she is relying upon family tradition. Thackeray arrived in England from India shortly before his sixth birthday. His mother followed him two years later, having meanwhile married Captain (later Major) Henry Carmichael-Smyth.

(1) ... his habit of observation began very early. His mother told me that once, when only three or four years old, and while sitting on her knee at the evening hour, she observed him gazing upwards and lost in admiration. 'Ecco!' he exclaimed, pointing to the evening star which was shining, like a diamond, over the crescent moon. This struck her the more as she had herself noticed the same beautiful combination on the night of his birth. . . .

When still quite a little boy he was taken into the City, and, as they passed by the great cathedral, he exclaimed, 'That is St Paul's!' He had recognised it from a picture, and his aunt was much impressed by this. At another time she noticed that his uncle's hat, which he put on in childish play, quite fitted him. Alarmed at this proof of the unusual size of his head she took him to Sir Charles Clark, the great physician of the day. He examined him and said, 'Don't be afraid, he *has* a large head, but there's a great deal in it, and one day you will find it out.'

Soon after he arrived in England he began to write to his mother in India. [His earliest surviving letter, 12 Feb 1818, is printed; see *LPP*, I, 3–4, where the drawing mentioned is reproduced.] Beneath the signature is a small pencil drawing of an officer on horseback. The horse is very weak upon its legs, but the figure of the officer is well done, and he sits quite firmly. It was intended to represent his future stepfather, Major Carmichael Smyth, of whose engagement to marry his mother he had probably just been informed. There is a ... P.S. ... from his Great-grandmother Becher ... 'William got so tired of his pen he could not write longer with it so he hopes you will be able to read his pencil. The little one lives half the day with us, and calls, "Grandmama and Aunt Becher win you give me a penny *win* you?" He drew me your house in Calcutta, not omitting his monkey looking out of the window, and Black Betty at the top drying her towels, and told us of the numbers you collected on his birthday in that large room he pointed out to us!'

(2) He had a perfect recollection of me [wrote his mother, about their reunion in 1819]; he could not speak, but kissed me, and looked at me again and again, and I could almost have said, 'Lord, now lettest Thou thy servant depart in peace.' He is the living image of his father, ... tall, stout, and sturdy. His eyes are become darker, but there is the same dear expression. His drawings are wonderful.[1]

Nothing is like my William's affection [she wrote later], he takes my hand & kisses it and looks at me as if he never could look long enough, the other day he said to me 'Mama its a long time since I have seen a Play and I should like to have a treat.' 'Very well dear I said if there's a Theatre at Gosport you shall go, but I can't go with you.'[2] 'Then I'm sure I shan't what's the use of going without you I had rather see you than the play.' ... Dr Turner [his headmaster at Chiswick] says he is one of the cleverest boys in the School that he sees things in a minute which others plod over for hours, but his idleness is almost unconquerable.

My Billy-man is quite well [his mother writes in August 1821]. I must trespass and give him a day or two of the holidays. You would laugh to hear what a grammarian he is. We were talking about odd characters; some one was mentioned. Billy said, 'Undoubtedly he is a Noun-Substantive.' 'Why, my dear?' 'Because he stands by himself.'

NOTES

1. His daughter Anny reports that 'He liked to draw not so much the things he saw, as the things he thought about – knights with heraldic shields, soldiers, brigands, dragons, demons; his schoolbooks were ornamented with funny, fanciful designs, his papers were covered with them. When he was still quite a little fellow he used to manufacture small postilions out of wafers, with the topboots in ink, and the red wafer coats nearly stuck on. As he grew older he took to a flourishing style, sketching gentlemen with magnificent wreaths of hair and flaps to their coats, ladies with wonderful eyes and lips, in a curly and flourishing style' (*Biog. Intros*, VIII, xviii–xix). His cousin Maria (later Mrs Brotherton) recalled that his bedroom drawers at the family home Larkbeare, a few years later, were crammed with delightful 'pen and ink caricatures. . . . Backs of letters, both sides of bills, visiting cards, all available odds and ends, were covered with these pen and inkings. Sometimes there were words in little writing under the figures – Downstairs, in the drawing-room, the drawers of the old fashioned piano were stuffed in the same way' (*Adversity*, p. 103).

2. As an earnest Evangelical, Mrs Carmichael-Smyth would eschew theatre-going.

Charterhouse or Slaughter House or Grey Friars

VARIOUS

Sources given in the notes. Thackeray attended Charterhouse from January 1822 to May 1828, as a dayboy from mid-1824, and often reverted to it in his fiction (where it appears first as 'Slaughter House' and later as 'Grey Friars') and in his essays. Though historic and illustrious, the Charterhouse of his day was in many ways a disagreeable school, partly because its headmaster, Dr John Russell, was a fierce and narrow Classic and a dedicated flogger, but also because the school was enduring a brief and disastrous experiment with the 'Bell' monitorial system, under which much of the teaching devolved upon the senior boys, the 'praepositi'. Thackeray's *cris de coeur* at the time go beyond routine schoolboy's grumbles: 'Every day [Russell] begins at me: Thackeray, Thackeray, you are an idle profligate shuffling boy, (because) your friends are going to take you away in May, &c. . . . Doctor Russell is treating me every day with such manifest unkindness and injustice, that I really can scarcely bear it. . . . He has lost a hundred boys within two years, and is of course very angry about [it] – There are but 370 in the school, I wish there were only 369' (*LPP*, I, 23–5). Looking back, in 1830, he defended his lack of 'Academical honours', which grieved his mother: 'Do not lay it all to my wilful idleness – Mother, mother would it not have been better to have consulted my inclinations & have fostered them . . .? For ten years of my life at school, it was thought that this discipline of misery was necessary to improve & instruct me; with all the power I had I struggled against it – the system was persevered in – & the benefit of ten years schooling was a little Latin & a very little Greek' (*LPP*, I, 138). Later, however, he softened towards Charterhouse, and expressed very orthodox Old Boy sentiments: Founder's Day (12 Dec) was 'sacred to all old Charterhouse men' (*LPP*, II, 465) – he attended the celebrations often, including the one eleven days before his death – and, though they had trembled under Russell, all Old Carthusians 'have the honor of the old place at heart' (*LPP*, III, 435). His Charterhouse years are well documented in reminiscences, several of his contemporaries having become writers or eminent enough to be the subject of biographies, etc.

[John Frederick Boyes (1811–79) attended the nearby Merchant Taylors' School, but his parents kept a boarding house for Charterhouse boys, to which Thackeray belonged.] It was when he was between the ages of thirteen and fifteen and a half or sixteen that I knew Thackeray best. He was then a rosy-faced boy with dark curling hair, and a quick, intelligent eye, ever twinkling with humour, and *good* humour. He was stout and broad-set, and gave no promise of the stature which he afterwards reached. It was during a short but severe illness, just before he left school, that he grew rapidly, leaving his sick-bed certainly a good many inches taller than he was when he entered it, and heading at once nearly all his contemporaries. No man ever owed more of his mental growth to time and exercise, and less of his bodily stature.

For the usual schoolboy sports and games Thackeray had no taste or passion whatever, any more than in after-life for those field-sports which seem to have been the delight of his schoolfellow and fellow humorist, Leech. Such amusements would have come probably next to Euclid and algebra in his list of dislikes. But he was by no means what a good many men of genius are said to have been in their youth – disposed to isolation or solitary musing. For a non-playing boy he was wonderfully social, full of vivacity and enjoyment of life. His happy *insouciance* was constant. Never was any lad at once so jovial, so healthy, and so sedentary. Good spirits and merriment seemed to enable him to dispense with the glow of cricket or football; and if in his still earlier days he ever 'fagged out', it must have been most bitterly against his will. We were now and then, indeed, out together in small fishing parties, but it was for the talking, and the change, and the green fields, and the tea abroad instead of at home – cakes, etc. accompanying (for he was always rather gustative, never greedy) – that Thackeray liked these expeditions. I question whether he knew the difference between a roach and a gudgeon – except when fried – whether he ever caught either the one or the other I am much disposed to doubt; or whether he cared about doing so. . . .

I have just now lying on the table beside me, in Thackeray's handwriting of some forty years ago – his writing was always beautiful – a little programme of *Bombastes Furioso*, enacted by himself and some three or four of his schoolfellows, in which he took the part of Fusbos, and to the best of my recollection, did it very well; but the thing dropped through, and there were no repetitions; the rest had very little dramatic zeal. This was almost the only common amusement in which I ever knew him join, *con amore*. He had a passion for theatricals, of course kept under restraint at school, but now and then gratified when he visited friends in London, on the half-holidays.

There was also a little speaking club in which he would sometimes take part merely out of good nature, for he hated speaking then, and I do not believe he liked it much better afterwards.

He was eminently good-tempered to all, especially the younger boys, and nothing of a tyrant or bully. Instead of a blow or a threat, I can just hear him saying to one of them, 'Hooky' (a sobriquet of a son of the late Bishop Carr, of Bombay), 'go up and fetch me a volume of *Ivanhoe* out of my drawer, that's a good fellow; in the same drawer you will, perhaps, find a penny, which you may take for yourself.' The penny was, indeed, rather problematical, but still realised sufficiently often to produce excitement in the mind of the youth thus addressed, and to make the service a willing one. When disappointed, it was more than probable that the victim would call Thackeray a 'great snob' for misleading him, a title for which the only vengeance would be a humorous and benignant smile. In the two or three years that I am recording, I scarcely ever saw Thackeray seriously angry, or even his brow wrinkled with a frown. He has been called a cynic; it is

doubtful whether a real cynic could ever be manufactured out
of a boy who had such powers as he had of sarcasm, and who
used them so little unkindly. Nor is it to be believed, by those
who knew him well, that, though in after-life he had his
eruptions of wrath, and moments of severity, after he had
undergone the tremendously searching hot and cold ordeal of
great trials and great triumphs, his nature was radically
changed.

Thackeray had nearly all the materials that usually go to the
making of a first-rate classical scholar. He had wonderful
memory, an absolute faculty of imitation, which might have
been employed in following the great classic models of verse
and prose; he had the power of acquiring language; and, it is
needless to say, an intense admiration of the beautiful. He got
to love his Horace, and was, no doubt, *actually* a better scholar
than many of our first-rate writers of English; but he was not,
and never pretended to be, a high classical scholar. . . .

Though keenly ambitious, and very sensitive of failure,
Thackeray was wonderfully free from anything like vanity or
conceit. He had small confidence in his own powers, and was
naturally inclined to rate himself below his mark. The better
scholarship of many of his contemporaries may have had
something to do with this. However, this want of confidence
showed itself in many ways afterwards, and even at a time
when his genius and his fame were at their full growth. For
example, he was, even to the last, sensitive of blame to a degree
scarcely ever found in men satisfied of their own powers. Like
other great but inwardly modest men, his first impulse was to
overrate rather than underrate the ability of others, and he
readily accorded the 'clever fellow', uttered in perfect sincerity, though, when he came to a thorough examination of their
performances, he was keen critic enough. Not many years
ago, he complained to me, with most earnest sincerity, of the
poorness of his memory, when every book that he wrote was
giving fresh proof of its retentiveness, and the readiness with
which it recalled everything that he had read or seen – a
faculty that gave him a power of varied allusion *without cram*, in
which he seems to have only one rival among the writers of
fiction of the present day. To his friends he talked freely of the
difficulties he experienced in writing. His own final great and
deserved success, he never anticipated. Some years before the

publication of *Vanity Fair*, he told me, whilst passing a day with me in the country, that he had a novel in his desk which, if published, would sell, he thought, to about 700 copies. Could this have been *Vanity Fair*? I rather think it must have been.

I dwell the more upon this point, because it appears to me to be a key to a certain characteristic of his writing, the constant introduction of the *non tanti est*[1] both as regards things in general, and his own lucubrations upon them. His first sobriquet of 'Michael Angelo Titmarsh' had a great deal of meaning for those who knew him well. His *beau-ideal* was serious and sublime; he was too familiar with, too much a master of, the humorous, to think as much about that mastery as his admirers did. I have heard him speak in terms of homage to the genius of Keats which he would not have vouchsafed to the whole tribe of humorists. But when he himself launched out of the playful into the serious, how often do we find him half 'mocking himself and scorning his spirit', not for 'smiling' but for the contrary. He seems to shrink from the idea of incurring the satire conveyed in these lines of Churchill:

> When humour was thy province, for some crime
> Pride struck thee with the frenzy of sublime.

And he descends quickly again to the humorous, where he fancied himself, though perhaps he was not, more at home.

Let me be pardoned for this excursion, if I have struck upon a key which has been missed in the general criticisms on Thackeray, by those who knew little or nothing of his early character. . . .

Men are reluctant enough – boys perhaps even more than men – to allow more than one forte to the same individual; all would have accorded two to Thackeray. First and foremost, his power of drawing, especially caricature; it was probably the high esteem in which this was held by his friends and schoolfellows, that led him afterwards to think of the pencil as a resource before the pen. Leech,[2] at Charterhouse, was too much his junior to cope with him, and so he was *facile princeps* in drawing of an amusing kind: indeed very much of his time was taken up with it. . . . It seems to me sometimes, as I look them over, that his power of drawing fell rather back as he advanced in authorship; at least, in his early drawings the types were much more varied, indeed they seemed scarcely to have any limit. . . .

Thackeray was decidedly musical as a boy, and had a capital ear; but just as he disliked formal speaking, so it was his nature to shrink from the small amount of personal display involved in singing a song – i.e. after the age of self-consciousness. In short, he was highly nervous in all such matters, and could never, I think, in his earlier years, be made anything of as a small 'show-child of genius'. . . .

He was not, I think, in those days an inventor of stories; certainly I never knew him try his hand at a plot; this power was gained afterwards, and gradually, as must be very evident to those who have followed his works in their series. He was an omnivorous reader, that is, of good English books; a trashy volume he would have thrown down in five minutes. His taste selected good books, and so his style was in a continual course of formation on good models. Memoirs, moralists like Addison and Goldsmith, and fiction and poetry from the best hands, were his favourites; but in those days he never worked in earnest at anything serious in the way of composition, or put his power to the stretch in any way.

We took in the Magazines – *Blackwood*, the *New Monthly*, the *London*, and the *Literary Gazette* – then in nearly their first glory, and full of excellent articles. I do not know who first suggested this, or whether it was a common thing for the senior boys at the public schools to club together for any such purpose; probably not, from the incuriosity about such reading that generally prevailed at one at least of the universities. I am sure there was very little indeed of any such leaven in the mingled mass of undergraduates of my own college. It was a positive intellectual descent from the school set to which Thackeray belonged to the ordinary college level, and a very considerable one. With the exception of a small group here and there, a knowledge of and interest in the better kinds of contemporary literature was very rare indeed at the colleges. . . . This was the real commencement of Thackeray's connection with the Magazines, which he used to read with the greatest eagerness, little interfered with by any school responsibilities. No doubt he often then thought what a pleasant thing it would be to be one of the guild, and first felt that 'indrawing into the sea' of letters, which he afterwards obeyed. This kind of reading, too, led to much youthful criticism of the topics and merits of the 'periodical' men of the day; the *Quarterly* and *Edinburgh* only being rather too high and dry for us. . . .

Stoddart,[3] who was, perhaps, Thackeray's greatest favourite of all [his school fellows], afterwards fellow and tutor of St John's College, Oxford, lies in the English cemetery at Genoa; one of the most noble-hearted men I ever knew, and one of the faithfulest friends: as such he was cherished to the last by Thackeray. He brought from home anecdotes of the men in whom we were interested – of Scott, Coleridge, Wordsworth, Lamb, and Hazlitt, with all of whom his father, Sir John Stoddart, was closely intimate. How well I remember his bringing in the first series of Hood's *Whims and Oddities*, then a new book, and how we all crowded round him! He was well read and quiet, and had an infinite relish for Thackeray's humour.[4]

[George Stovin Venables (1810–88) was the boy who broke Thackeray's nose (see below, I, 15), but they remained lifelong friends. He became a lawyer and literary journalist, and was a close friend of Tennyson. He wrote this account for Anthony Trollope's study of Thackeray, 1879.] My recollection of him, though fresh enough, does not furnish much material for biography. He came to school young – a pretty, gentle, and rather timid boy. I think his experience there was not generally pleasant. Though he had afterwards a scholarlike knowledge of Latin, he did not attain distinction in the school; and I should think that the character of the Headmaster, Dr Russell, which was vigorous, unsympathetic, and stern, though not severe, was uncongenial to his own. With the boys who knew him, Thackeray was popular; but he had no skill in games, and, I think, no taste for them. . . . He was already known by his faculty of making verses, chiefly parodies. I only remember one line of one parody on a poem of L. E. L.'s, about 'Violets, dark blue violets'; Thackeray's version was 'Cabbages, bright green cabbages', and we thought it very witty.[5] He took part in a scheme, which came to nothing, for a school magazine, and he wrote verses for it, of which I only remember that they were good of their kind. When I knew him better, in later years, I thought I could recognise the

sensitive nature which he had as a boy.... His change of
retrospective feeling about his school days was very characteristic. In his earlier books he always spoke of the Charterhouse as Slaughter House and Smithfield. As he became
famous and prosperous his memory softened, and Slaughter
House was changed into Grey Friars where Colonel Newcome
ended his life.[6]

[The Revd Thomas Mozley (1806–93), Tractarian divine and
journalist, recalls an assistant master, Edward Churton, whose
gentleness and encouragement contrasted with Dr Russell's
bullying.] I felt it invaluable. Nor was I alone in this.
Thackeray had the benefit of this personal instruction, and he
acknowledged the debt. Meeting him one day in the Strand, I
told him I had just had a talk with Churton. He exclaimed, 'O
tell me where he is, that I may fall down and kiss his toe. I do
love that man.'... Russell was rough with Thackeray, not
more so perhaps than with many others, but when he saw
Thackeray's spirit and humour rising with him, that made
matters worse.[7]

['D.D.', a Charterhouse master of later years, wrote in 1889 an
article based mainly on the recollections of Charles Rowland
Dicken (1801–73), a young master in Thackeray's time. With
elaborate facetiousness, he disguised most of the names. The
actual names are here given, where possible, in square
brackets, following the key given by Ray, *LPP*, I, 12n.] Among
my senior colleagues ... was the Revd Charles [Dicken], who
remembered Thackeray's coming to [Charterhouse] as a boy.
'Take that boy *and his box*' were the imperious directions
thundered out by Dr [Russell] in his big brassy voice to the
school janitor, as though sentencing a culprit for execution, 'to
Mrs Juno' (the matron of the boarding-house); 'and make my
compliments to Mr Smiler' (then junior master), 'and tell him
the boy knows nothing and will just do for the "lowest form".'
[Russell's] Rhadamanthine tones, and power of storming the
feeble wits out of dullard idlers by vociferous exaggeration of
their school peccadilloes, seem to have impressed Thackeray
even more than his heavy hand, which swung round on you
like the paddle of an ichthyosaurus with stunning effect.
Thackeray, thus, in the innocent, *tabula rasa* state of mind,

consigned to the mill of the prison-house, seems from [Dicken's] account to have shirked his share of the grinding all he could, read his story-books, about Scottish chiefs, Corinthian Tom, and Fielding's *Amelia* to more purpose than the more ponderous stuff to which the finger of authority – from Mr Smiler upwards – duly pointed him; and, taking his fights and floggings with a light heart, I should suppose, to have made his mark among his schoolmates by his ever ready fun of pen-and-ink sketches. [Dicken] remembered a series of these, labelled 'fine arts' by the author; 'Painting' was illustrated by a young ragamuffin, shoeless himself, laying blacking on a boot, the blacking bottle very big with label to match, 'Warren's Best'. The next was 'Carving', representing a pimple-faced man with strong Jewish features, going in with a huge knife and fork at a similarly exaggerated ham; while 'Music' showed an Italian of the stage-bandit type, slouch-hatted, gaitered, and monkeyed, grinding a hurdy-gurdy.

. . . when *The Newcomes* story was running towards its end, a buzz went round [Brook] Hall that Thackeray the Great was actually coming to refresh his recollections at the fountain-head of genuine tradition. . . . It was understood that he was studying for the closing scenes of *The Newcomes*, and had been introduced specially for that purpose to one of the lay brothers of the 'Orders Grey', a highly respected Captain L——, who, being in reduced circumstances, had accepted a vacancy in those privileged ranks. 'I'm told I'm to sit for Colonel Newcome', said the veteran (so the *on dit* went) with considerable glee.[8]

[Gerald S. Davies, a latter-day Carthusian, collected in the 1890s much useful information about Thackeray and Charterhouse, and called upon his memories of encounters with the novelist. He gives an account of how Venables broke Thackeray's nose.] The writer, as a Charterhouse boy, heard Thackeray speak of this fight to a select audience of three or four boys after one Founder's Day Dinner (about 1862). We remember vividly how he spoke of the 'scrunch' with which the fatal blow landed. But that detail was so satisfactory, we suppose, that it seems to have usurped the place of all others and driven them from the writer's mind. Since then we have come to know how Torrigiano said the same of the blow wherewith he crooked the nose of Michelangelo, and we have always treasured the historic parallel.

'Do you remember', we wrote, knowing that Mr Roupell was monitor in Penny's[9] in 1822, 'anything of the fight between Thackeray and Venables?' The answer delighted us beyond our hope. 'Oh! that unlucky fight. Yes! I remember it well. It was on a wet half-holiday, Wednesday, I think, when a boy named Gossip came and asked leave for Thackeray and Venables to fight. We wanted some amusement, so I let them fight it out in our (Penny's) long-room, with the important result to Thackeray's nasal organ.' To have hit on the very monitor who gave leave for that fight was beyond our wildest dream. We promptly returned to the charge: 'Do you remember what the fight was about, and who won?' 'No', Mr Roupell does not remember what it was about, but since news was brought to him later that Thackeray's nose was still bleeding, *that* probably stopped the fight, and Venables was doubtless considered to have won. Thackeray was indeed Roupell's fag, but there must have been five or six years' difference in age, and Mr Roupell remembers little more of him than this fight of his....

In the Charterhouse days of the present writer (1856–64) any feeling that Thackeray ever may have had, had given way to the strong affection for the place which sooner or later overmasters, in most men, any less happy memories. He came amongst us pretty often, sometimes on state occasions, Founder's Day and the like: sometimes unexpectedly, after a call at the 'Master's Lodge' or the 'Headmaster's House' perhaps; sometimes, no doubt, when he wanted 'another look at the model'. One visit in particular we remember well. It was the summer of 1858, when there had been a meeting of Carthusians in the Great Hall ('Codd's' Hall) to found a memorial to Havelock, who died in the November before. Thackeray came prepared to pay on the nail, but there was no collection that day. An hour or two later the news reached the Long-rooms that 'Thackeray had been on Green distributing sovereigns, but that he had got down to shillings now.' Now we were of the mature age of twelve-and-a-half: impecunious after the manner of small boys: unlettered too: of Thackeray we had read probably no one line unless the titles on the backs of his books, which as Library fags we dusted fortnightly (mark that, ye Library fags of today), may count as such. Yet Thackeray was to all of us a hero – held so with none the less enthusiasm as it was obviously quite unprejudiced, and we resolved (it was base of us, sordid, and the rest, but it is true) that we would have one of those shillings and bore a hole in it. So we went forth and placed ourselves in the great man's way. We found him on the edge of Green, just between Gownboy entrance to Cloisters and Middle Briars, surrounded by small boys. But the silver shower had ceased, and the hands were both thrust deep into empty pockets. We took nothing.

Of far more interest was a visit for which the Revd J. W. Irvine, whose Charterhouse days lay between 1846–55, is our authority. Irvine, by the way, was son of an old Charterhouse master, Andrew Irvine, of Thackeray's own day. Thackeray knew young Irvine at home, and used to come and see him and 'tip' him. 'Kindness itself to a boy', says Mr Irvine of him, and we think how Thackeray himself would like that verdict if he could hear it. One day when *The Newcomes*, which, of course, came out in numbers, had run pretty far into the second volume, came Thackeray to Charterhouse to see Irvine. With his hand on Irvine's shoulder, he told the great secret, 'Colonel Newcome is going to be a Codd.'[10] Here and there one of the pensioners would be known to us boys in those days, and nothing was said against our going to see them at times, though otherwise there was complete separation between us and the pensioners' quarters. Such a friend had Irvine, who therefore had nothing to do but to lead Thackeray from Gownboy's across Scholars' Court into Pensioners' Court, where he introduced Thackeray to a very dear old gentleman, Captain Light, known for his kindness to young Carthusians of that day, and whom we remember to have had pointed out to us among the Codds in our own early days at school. From this visit, and the chat in old Codd Light's room, grew the local colour of that sweet sketch – in the twenty-seventh chapter of vol. II of *The Newcomes* – of Colonel Newcome as a Codd at Greyfriars. Mr Irvine says of this interview, 'Thackeray was most courteous, kindly and genial in Captain Light's rooms. But every now and then he relapsed into deep thought, no doubt as Colonel Newcome grew in his mind.'[11]

Side by side with that picture there comes naturally to one's mind, from the same chapter, the description of a 'Founder's Day'. It was indeed at J. W. Irvine's 'Oration' on Founder's Day in 1855, that Thackeray said to a friend 'I am going to work this in.' Thackeray came very often on a Founder's Day – we cannot say how often, though we fancy a record is kept. . . . Thackeray was at Charterhouse for the last time on Founder's Day, 12 December 1863. He sat at dinner two places to the right (north) of Archdeacon Hale, with Leech very nearly opposite. Of course he was down for a speech and made it – we fancy he never was let off on a Founder's Day. We can see him very plainly now as he spoke,[12] one hand thrust into his breeches pocket and the other held slightly forward, the fingers moving expressively as he made some quaint point, his head thrown a little forward with the chin somewhat projecting, after the manner of short-sighted people. The shoulders were carried very square. Indeed the statuette [by Boehm] always strikes us as a very happy hit of Thackeray's general carriage, but very few of his portraits have seemed to us to quite give the man. The snow-white lion-like mane of hair, and the shrewd kindly look through the big round spectacles made strong points, of which the one (the whiteness of hair) could not be given in sculpture, and the other (the spectacles) is commonly omitted. And no likeness of Thackeray without the spectacles can have much chance. The little bust of him as a boy of eleven, by S. Devile, 'moulded from nature', just at the age when he went to Charterhouse, 'after the Christmas vacation of 182–' as he says in *The Newcomes*, is really strangely like him in full age.[13]

[Thackeray 'was very lazy in school work', Davies was told by Henry George Liddell (1811–98), the distinguished scholar, who became Headmaster of Westminster, Dean of Christ Church, and Vice-Chancellor of Oxford University. There was at this time an intermediate form between the Vth and the VIth, admission to which was gained by learning all of Horace's odes and epodes by heart.] Before I rose to a place in this curious form, it was my lot to sit next W. Makepeace Thackeray. *He* never attempted to learn the lesson, never exerted himself to grapple with the Horace.[14] We spent our time mostly in drawing, with such skill as we could command.

His handiwork was very superior to mine, and his taste for comic scenes at that time exhibited itself in burlesque representations of incidents in Shakespeare. I remember one – Macbeth as a butcher brandishing two bloodreeking knives, and Lady Macbeth as the butcher's wife clapping him on the shoulder to encourage him. Thackeray went to Cambridge, and I never met him after we left school till I went to Westminster as Headmaster in 1846. After that he often used to join Mrs Liddell and myself when riding in Rotten Row. On one occasion he turned to her and said, 'Your husband ruined all my prospects in life; he did all my Latin verses for me, and I lost all opportunities of self-improvement.' It is needless to add that this was a pure fiction – I had trouble enough to do my own verses. At this time *Vanity Fair* was coming out in monthly parts in its well-known yellow paper covers. He used to talk about it, and what he should do with the persons. Mrs Liddell one day said, 'Oh, Mr Thackeray, you must let Dobbin marry Amelia.' 'Well,' he replied, 'he shall; and when he has got her, he will not find her worth having.'[15]

['My father never spoke much of his time at Charterhouse', writes his daughter Anny; but he] once took us [girls] there, and showed us the old haunts, and the house where he lived – Penny's house, they called it – and the cloister, and the playground where he fought and played. . . . There were many things he liked to remember about Grey Friars, as well as those he wished to forget. He certainly liked to go back and be young again with his old friends on Founder's Day [and he] sent most of his characters to Charterhouse – Pendennis and Clive [Newcome] and Philip [Firmin] all went there in turn.[16]

NOTES

1. *Non tanti est*: it's not all that important.
2. John Leech (1817–64), cartoonist and illustrator, was later Thackeray's closest ally on *Punch*.
3. William Wellwood Stoddart (1809–56) lodged in Thackeray's house though, like Boyes, he attended the Merchant Taylors' School.

4. J. F. Boyes, 'A Memorial of Thackeray's School-days', *Cornhill Magazine*, XI (1865) 118–27.

5. Boyes, also remarking upon this fondness for parody, prints the 'L. E. L.' poem and quotes from memory Thackeray's lampoon (ibid., p. 125). Laetitia Elizabeth Landon (1802–38) was a popular poetess of the day.

6. Anthony Trollope, *Thackeray* (1879) pp. 4–5.

7. Thomas Mozley, *Reminiscences, Chiefly of Oriel College and the Oxford Movement*, 2nd edn (1882) I, 63–4. For further tributes to Churton, see *LPP*, I, 25–6.

8. 'D. D.', 'Some Few Thackerayana', *National Review*, XIII (1889) 795, 801.

9. The Revd Henry Penny was Thackeray's housemaster at this time; John Stuart Roupell was a monitor in this house, and Thackeray was his fag.

10. The Charterhouse foundation included provision for gentleman-pensioners, the 'Poor Brothers' nicknamed 'Codds', as well as for a school.

11. See Irvine's 'A Study for Colonel Newcome', *Nineteenth Century*, XXXIV (1893) 584–95.

12. Davies notes (*Greyfriar*, II, 67) that his voice 'had a slight metallic ring in it ... and we think also a slight lisp'.

13. G. S. D[avies], 'Thackeray as Carthusian', *Greyfriar*, II (1890–5) 65–7. Another essay in the same number of this Carthusian journal, pp. 75–9, presents a useful account of the school in Thackeray's day: H. W. Phillott, 'Some Charterhouse Reminiscences'.

14. Davies possessed Thackeray's school copy of Horace, and notes that it was suspiciously 'clean, beautifully clean, unthumbed, unsoiled' (*Greyfriar*, II, 63). Later Thackeray had a great feeling and affection for Horace.

15. Ibid., p. 62; Henry L. Thompson, *Henry George Liddell, D. D.: A Memoir* (1899) pp. 8–9.

16. *Biog. Intros*, II, xiv; XVIII, xix–xx. Thackeray's fictional presentations of Charterhouse are surveyed by E. C. S. Gibson, 'Thackeray and Charterhouse', *Cornhill Magazine*, n.s., LII (1922) 641–59, who aptly quotes *The Roundabout Papers*, 'On a Joke I Once Heard from the Late Thomas Hood': 'Men revisit the old school, though hateful to them, with ever so much kindness and affection ....'

The Cambridge Year or So

JOHN ALLEN AND W. H. THOMPSON

Sources given in the notes. Thackeray's period at Trinity College, Cambridge, was brief (Feb 1829 to June 1830) and inglorious: he left without graduating, and in financial difficulties mainly caused by gambling losses. He began with high hopes ('Men will say someday, that Newton &

Thackeray kept near one another!' i.e. his rooms were close to those which Newton had occupied – *LPP*, I, 35) but subsequently he had to confess to his mother that he had picked up 'expensive habits' and been 'idle & extravagant' (*LPP*, I, 137–8). Surprisingly few reminisćences of him at Cambridge survive – surprisingly, because a remarkable number of his Trinity contemporaries proceeded to distinguished careers and thus became the subjects or authors of memoirs, published letters and diaries, and so on: and Thackeray was a friend of many of these men, though in some cases the friendship began after their undergraduate years. *Pendennis* – where the university is fictionalised as 'Oxbridge', one of Thackeray's few contributions to the vocabulary of English – famously celebrates student friendships: 'Every man, however brief or inglorious may have been his academical career, must remember with kindness and tenderness the old university comrades and days.... What passions our friendships were in those old days . . . !' (chs 17, 18).[1] Whitwell Elwin capably discusses the relations of Pendennis and Oxbridge to their creator and his university, in 'Thackeray at Cambridge', *Monthly Review*, XVI (1904) 151–74; see also *Adversity*, ch. 5, and *Biog. Intros*, II, xix–xxxiii.[2] Edward FitzGerald (on whom see below, I, 27) and John Allen were lifelong friends from their student days; other Cambridge contemporaries whom he later knew well include Alfred and Frederick Tennyson, James Spedding, Richard Monckton Milnes, John Sterling, A. W. Kinglake, William Brookfield, and sundry others destined for episcopal or diaconal elevation.

[John Allen (1810–86), later to become Archdeacon of Salop, was even in his student years decidedly serious and devout. His son-in-law R. M. Grier notes that his diaries show how often his studies were interrupted by less diligent friends.] Of these Thackeray . . . was apparently the chief offender. He would go into Allen's room and sit there talking . . . by the hour, his pen and ink busy the while in producing all manner of humorous sketches. These sketches were seized and carefully preserved by his host in a large scrap-book.[3] . . . Thackeray who was warmly attached to Allen,[4] endeavoured to induce him to leave Cambridge before taking his degree, and accept the post of second master in a school at Pimlico. [Allen's father prevented this, but two years later Allen did obtain this post through Thackeray's intervention. They continued to meet in London.] Anyone who knew the subject of this memoir and has studied *Vanity Fair* will recognise his portrait, *mutatis mutandis*, in the simple-minded, chivalrous Major Dobbin.[5]

[Extracts from Allen's 1830–1 diary are printed in *LPP*, I, 493–8, from which the following are taken.]

[*3 Feb 1830*.] Thackeray came in, we had some serious conversation when I affected him to tears he went away with a determination tomorrow to lead a new life, Prayed for him FitzGerald & myself afterwards in tears.

[*5 Feb 1830*.] ... went with Thackeray & Young to Alford's rooms where the debate was Whether the Elizabethan age merited being called the golden age of English literature.

[*7 Feb 1830*.] Thackeray came up – expressed some doubts of X^t being = with God, read over St Matthew together & he was convinced thank God for it.

[*13 Feb 1830*.] ... at ½ past 5 went to dine with Sansum where I met Thackeray Evans Broking Matthew & Heaviside – Thackeray got a little elated.[6]

[*9 Mar 1830*.] ... read ... some of Bolingbroke's letter on Abp Tillotson's Sermon,[7] in order that I might convince Thackeray ....

[*18 Mar 1830*.] Heathcote called on me also Thackeray walked out with the latter in Trinity Walks & had a long and interesting conversation with him about Bolingbroke &c – Poor dear fellow!

[William Hepworth Thompson (1810–86), another Cambridge contemporary, became Regius Professor of Greek, a canon of Ely, Master of Trinity College, and Vice-Chancellor of the University. Mrs Alicia Bayne, preparing the chapter on the novelist in *Memorials of the Thackeray Family* (1879), persuaded him to write down his memories of Thackeray. She writes:] I shall now refer to the reminiscences of Mr Thackeray sent me by Dr Thompson. In answer to a question as to whether he used to like to walk in the beautiful cloistered Court of Trinity? he writes, 'He did it is true "pace the studious cloister pale" – on a rainy day – more by token that it was in that place and under those circumstances that I was first made aware of the name of a tall thin, large-eyed, full and ruddy faced man with an eye glass fixed *en permanence* – the glass he has immortalised – or ought to have done so – for on consideration he supplied its place in his portrait of Titmarsh with a *pair*. I did not know him personally until his second year, when a small literary society was made up of him, John – now Archdeacon Allen, Henry – afterwards Dean Alford, Robert – now Archdeacon Groome, and Young of Caius [Mr Young was one of last year's friends in the Essay Club] with another of whom I am not sure, and myself. We were seven – I don't know that we ever agreed on a name. Alford proposed the "Covey" – because we "made a noise when we got up" – to speak that is, but it was left for further consideration. I think Thackeray's subject was "Duelling" – on which there was then much diversity of opinion. We did not see in him even the germ of those literary powers which under the stern influence of necessity he afterwards developed. One does not see the wings in a chrysalis. He led a somewhat lazy' (?) 'but pleasant and "gentlemanlike" life in a set mixed of old schoolfellows and such men as the two archdeacons named above; with them and with my friend Edward FitzGerald he no doubt had much literary talk, but not on "University Subjects". He sat, I remember, opposite to me at the "May Examination";[8] he was put in the 4th Class' [it will be remembered that he said himself – 'If I get a fifth class I shall be lucky']. 'It was a class where clever "non-reading" men were put, as in a limbo. But though careless of University distinction, he had a vivid appreciation of English poetry, and chanted the praises of the old English novelists – especially his model, Fielding. He had always a flow of humour and pleasantry, and was made much of by his friends. At supper parties, though not talkative – rather observant – he enjoyed the humours of the hour, and sang one or two old songs with great applause. "Old King Cole" I well remember to have heard from him at the supper I gave to celebrate my election as Scholar. It made me laugh excessively – not from the novelty of the song – but from the humour with which it was given. Thackeray, as you know, left us at the end of his second year, and for some time I saw him no more. Our debating club fell to pieces when he went.'

NOTES

1. A coincidence with, or an echo of, Disraeli's remark 'At school, friendship is a passion'? Thackeray had read, because he reviewed, *Coningsby* (1844), where this sentence occurs (Bk I, ch. 9).

2. Thackeray, of course, referred to himself as 'Pendennis' but the fictional character by no means coincides wholly with the novelist himself. Anny Thackeray remarks that 'my father's relations to Edward FitzGerald had perhaps some resemblance to those of Pendennis and Warrington; and yet my father was not Pendennis any more than the other was Warrington' (*Biog. Intros*, II, xxx). Other alleged (part-) originals include the young author Charles Lamb Kenny – 'we were told', writes Anny Thackeray (ibid., p. xxxiii), 'that he was to be the hero of the new book [*Pendennis*], or rather, that the hero was to look like Mr Kenny' – and one of the three Paget boys who accompanied Thackeray from Charterhouse to Cambridge: 'In his later years Charles Paget used to say that it was he who had advised Thackeray to "take to writing" when they were together at Cambridge; and that the character of Arthur Pendennis was drawn from Arthur Paget' – *Memoirs and Letters of Sir James Paget*, ed. Stephen Paget (1902) p. 16n. Thackeray said in 1856 that Warrington was drawn from his schoolfriend G. S. Venables (*LPP*, I, 207n), on whom see above, I, 12.

3. This scrap-book, like Allen's diary (quoted below), is now in the Library of Trinity College, Cambridge.

4. 'John Allen, I rejoice in you', he wrote in 1840 (Whitwell Elwin, *Monthly Review*, XVI, 165). In the same year he described Allen as 'just a perfect Saint nor more nor less' (*LPP*, I, 413).

5. R. M. Grier, *John Allen, Vicar of Prees and Archdeacon of Salop: A Memoir* (1889) pp. 26–9. See also Anna Otter Allen, *John Allen and His Friends* (n.d. [1922]) ch. 9, 'Thackeray'. Anny Thackeray accepts the Allen/Dobbin assertion, *Biog. Intros*, I, xxx.

6. See his later reflections on such episodes, in *The Book of Snobs*, ch. 15, 'On University Snobs': 'a parcel of lads . . . fuddle themselves with champagne and claret . . .'. .

7. 'A Letter Occasioned by One of Archbishop Tillotson's Sermons', first published in Bolingbroke's *Works* (1754) [Ray's footnote]. Bolingbroke (1678–1751) was a 'freethinker'.

8. The first-year examination, traditionally held in May.

That Excellent and Facetious Young Man

VARIOUS

Sources given in the notes. After leaving Cambridge, Thackeray spent some months in Germany, mainly in Weimar (some memories of which inspire the Pumpernickel of *Vanity Fair*). He attended the ducal Court, and met Goethe, then over eighty; his reminiscences appear in G. H. Lewes's *Life of Goethe* (1864). See *LPP*, III, 442–5, and Walter Vulpius, 'Thackeray in

Weimar', *Century Magazine*, n.s., XXI (1897) 920–8. A young member of the Goethe circle, and maid of honour at the Court, Jenny von Pappenheim (1811–90), later Frau von Gustedt, recalled the Thackeray of 1830–1.

Thackeray's *Vanity Fair* . . . reminded me vividly of its genial author, who was so dévoted a friend of our family. His ready wit and his kind heart permeate all his works. He was in Weimar principally to develop his remarkable talent for drawing. As we sat round the tea-table and talked, he would sketch the funniest scenes. He would draw himself in just one minute, always beginning with the feet and without taking the pen from the paper; alongside the figure he would put a little street-urchin mocking him because of his boxer's crooked nose. Otherwise his appearance was good. He had beautiful eyes and thick curly hair, and he was quite tall. There were plenty of English visitors who made a lengthy stay in Weimar, and he was one of the most popular of them.[1]

[Thackeray returned to London in March 1831, and became, briefly, a law student. Among the young men he met then, through an old Cambridge friend, was Henry Reeve (1813–95), journalist and man of letters, now best remembered as editor of *The Greville Memoirs* (1865), who became a lifelong acquaintance. In these letters Reeve records meetings with him in Paris, in 1835–6. By this time, Thackeray was studying art and embarking upon journalism.]

[*14 Jan 1835*.] Thackeray is flourishing, and after the opera we took tea, and had a long talk of the doings of French artists. He complains of the impurity of their ideas, and of the jargon of a corrupt life which they so unwisely admit into their painting-rooms. Thackeray's drawing – if I may judge by his note-book – is as pure and accurate as any I have seen. He is a man whom I would willingly set to copy a picture of Raphael's, as far at least as the drawing goes; but he does not seem likely to get into a system of massive colouring, if I may judge by what he said . . . .

[*16 Jan 1836*.] I have seen a good deal of Thackeray this last week. That excellent and facetious being is at the present moment editing an English paper here, in opposition to

Galignani's.[2] But what is more ominous, he has fallen in love, and talks of being married in less than twenty years. What is there so affecting as matrimony! I dined yesterday with his object, who is a nice, simple, girlish girl . . . .[3]

[Many years later, in 1897, 'la Comtesse Dash' (Gabrielle Anne Cisterne de Courtiras, Vicomtesse de Saint-Mars) recalled the young Thackeray, whom she met at the hospitable Paris *salon* of 'Roger de Beauvoir' (Edouard Roger de Bully), author and dandy (1809–66).] Among its frequenters at that time was a man later illustrious in modern literature, though this was then quite unforeseeable – Thackeray, the famous English novelist. He was then engaged on water-colours and sea-scapes, and trying hard to earn a livelihood with his pencil – he, who has since become so rich by the use of his pen.

He was then a rather whimsical young man, witty and full of 'humour'.[4] He was decidedly talented as a caricaturist, and exercised that talent to perfection. He talked by fits and starts, but when he was on good form he could make jokes in a thoroughly French fashion, and uttered them with his characteristic phlegm.

He had a long struggle against sorrow and misfortune, and when he left Paris he was in despair of ever making his way in the world. What he did become, we now know.

When I was in England in 1862, I sent Thackeray a note recalling our former acquaintance and asking him to call upon me. He did not fail to do so. I did not recognise him; he was not the same man. He had become sad, while becoming rich; his health had broken down. . . . I only saw him once . . . .[5]

[James Robertson Planche (1796–1880), dramatist and anti-quary, also met Thackeray in Paris at this period.] He was at that time a slim young man, rather taciturn, and not display-ing any particular love or talent for literature. Drawing appeared to be his favourite amusement; and he often sat by my side while I was reading or writing, covering any scrap of paper lying about with the most spirited sketches and amusing caricatures. I have one of Charles IX firing at the Huguenots out of the windows of the Louvre, which he dashed off in a few minutes beside me on the blank portion of the yellow paper cover of a French drama. A member of the Garrick, who was specially unpopular with the majority of the members, was literally *drawn* out of the Club by Thackeray. His figure, being very peculiar, was sketched in pen and ink by his implacable persecutor. On every pad on the writing tables, or whatever paper he could venture to appropriate, he represented him in the most ridiculous and derogatory situation that could be imagined, always with his back towards you, but unmistakable. His victim, it must be admitted, bore this desecration of his 'lively effigies' with great equanimity for a considerable period; but at length, one very strong – perhaps too strong – example of the artist's graphic and satirical abilities, combined with the conviction that he was generally objectionable, induced him to retire from the Club, and leave the pungent pen of Michael Angelo Titmarsh to punish more serious offenders than bores and toadies.[6]

NOTES

1. Lily Braun, *Im Schatten der Titanen* (Stuttgart, 1910) p. 115, quoted in *LPP*, I, 129n; translation by J. V. Gough. In later life, it may be noted, Thackeray 'was fond of airing his German', as the German-born artist Rudolph Lehmann (1819–1905), who first met him in 1850, recalls. He 'even went so far as to pun in quasi-German. "This is really *vortrüfflich*", I have heard him call out as he tasted a dish with truffles in it' – R. C. Lehmann, *Memories of Half a Century* (1908) p. 197.

2. *Galignani's Messenger* was an English-language newspaper published in Paris, to which Thackeray had contributed.

3. *Memoirs of the Life and Correspondence of Henry Reeve*, ed. John Knox Laughton (1898) pp. 35, 59.

4. The Comtesse here uses the English word 'humour'.

5. *Souvenirs anecdotiques sur le Second Empire* (Paris, n.d. [1897]) pp. 87–8 (*Memoirs des autres*, vol. V). The comtesse's memory was at fault in what she goes on to say – that a further meeting was prevented, to Thackeray's great regret, by his having to take his wife to Brighton for her health. (It was many years before 1862 since he had lived with, or been able to tend, his wife.) Or maybe Professor Sylvere Monod – who kindly supplied photocopies of these pages – is right in his unkind guess: 'I suspect that she must have been a hare-brained bore, and that this accounts for W. M. T.'s claim that he was taking his wife to Brighton in 1862, rather than face a second meeting with this unspeakable Frenchwoman.'

6. James Robertson Planché, *Recollections and Reflections*, rev. edn (1901) pp. 117–18.

Would Have Cogged Well with Scott and Johnson

EDWARD FITZGERALD

(2), (6), (7), (8), (9), (10), (13), (17), (18) and (21) from *Letters of Edward FitzGerald*, ed. William Aldis Wright (1901) I, 17, 193, 238, 250–1, 257, 272–3, 310–11; II, 50, 53, 198. (3) from Thomas Wright, *Life of Edward FitzGerald* (1904) I, 114–15. (4), (11), (14), (16) and (19) from *A FitzGerald Friendship: Being Hitherto Unpublished Letters from Edward FitzGerald to William Bodham Donne*, ed. Neilson Campbell Hannay (New York, 1932) pp. 6, 47, 56, 70, 72. (5) and (15) from *Letters and Literary Remains of Edward FitzGerald*, ed. William Aldis Wright (1902) I, 64; II, 137. (20) from *Letters of Edward FitzGerald to Fanny Kemble 1871–1883*, ed. William Aldis Wright (1902) p. 91. FitzGerald (1809–83), a poet best remembered for his translation *The Rubaiyat of Omar Khayyam* (1859), was a Cambridge contemporary and thenceforth lifelong friend of Thackeray – and of several other of their Cambridge generation, including Tennyson, who said on his death, 'Dear old Fitz – I had no truer friend.' He spent most of his life living in retirement in Woodbridge, Suffolk, seeing his old friends during visits to London, and corresponding amply and brilliantly with them, though apt to be cantankerously critical of their writings and censorious about hints of their becoming over-worldly. He was closest to Thackeray in his years of unsuccess. Anny Ritchie writes, of the early 1840s, that FitzGerald's 'faithful goodness seems to have been [her father's] constant resource in these days', and she recalls from her childhood how this 'dear and impressionable friend, so generous and helpful in time of trouble', used to cheer them by his occasional visits; he never stayed long, for, as he said, he 'preferred the fresh air and fields to the wilderness of monkeys in London' (*Biog. Intros*, XIII, xxiii; IX, xliii). He used to complain, Anny continues, 'that there were too many people in my father's life; that my father did not write to him; that he was carried away by London life: they were for many years apart from circumstance, but circumstance does not change such men as they are' (ibid., XIV, xliv). Shortly before his death, she asked her father which of his old friends he cared for most, and he replied, 'There was "Old Fitz", and I was very fond of Brookfield once', adding after a pause, 'We shall be very good friends again in hell together' (*LPP*, I, cxxxiii). Quotations are mostly from his letters.

(1) [*5–9 Oct 1831*, to Thackeray.] . . . the wind was blowing

hard at the windows & I somehow began to think of Will Thackeray: so the cockles of my heart were warmed, and up spouted the following: . . .

> I cared not for life: for true friend I had none
> I had heard 'twas a blessing not under the sun:
> Some figures called friends, hollow, proud, or
>   cold-hearted
> Came to me like shadows – like shadows departed:
> But a day came that turned all my sorrow to glee
> When first I saw Willy, and Willy saw me!
>
> The thought of my Willy is always a cheerer;
> My wine has new flavour – the fire burns clearer . . .

[and so on, for six stanzas]. (*LPP*, I, 167)

(2) [7 *Dec 1832*, to John Allen.] Thackeray has come to London . . . very opportunely to divert my Blue Devils. . . . He is as full of good humour and kindness as ever.

(3) It was about this time [1833, Thomas Wright records] that FitzGerald wrote a number of word pictures of his friends. . . . Of Thackeray, FitzGerald writes, 'A great deal of talent, but no perseverance or steadiness of purpose; very indifferent, almost cold in his feelings; a very despairing mind; quick in most things; impatient; exclusive in his attachments; very unaffected, and has great want of confidence in his own powers.'

(4) [*23 Oct 1836*, to W. B. Donne.[1]] Thackeray is married and happy as the day is long.

(5) [*20 July 1839*, to W. F. Pollock.] At your recommendation I shall read him [Gramont[2]] again. I have also heard Thackeray speak well of him: but he is naturally prejudiced in favour of the dirty and immoral.

(6) [*12 June 1845*, to Frederick Tennyson.[3]] If you want to know something of the [Royal Academy] Exhibition however, read *Fraser's Magazine* for this month; there Thackeray has a paper on the matter, full of fun. I met Stone in the street the other day; he took me by the button, and told me in perfect sincerity, and with increasing warmth, how, though he loved old Thackeray, yet these yearly out-speakings of his sorely

tried him; not on account of himself (Stone), but on account of some of his friends, Charles· Landseer, Maclise, etc. Stone worked himself up to such a pitch under the pressure of forced calmness that he at last said Thackeray would get himself horse-whipped one day by one of these infuriated Apelleses. . . . In the mean while old Thackeray laughs at all this; and goes on in his own way; writing hard for half a dozen Reviews and Newspapers all the morning; dining, drinking, and talking of a night; managing to preserve a fresh colour and perpetual flow of spirits under a wear-and-tear of thinking and feeding that would have knocked up any other man I know two years ago, at least.

(7) [*4 May 1848*, to the same.] Thackeray is progressing greatly in his line: he publishes a Novel in numbers – *Vanity Fair* – which began dull, I thought: but gets better every number, and has some very fine things indeed in it. He is become a great man I am told: goes to Holland House, and Devonshire House: and for some reason or other, will not write a word to me. But I am sure this is not because he is asked to Holland House.

(8) [*7 Dec 1849*, to the same.] I saw poor old Thackeray in London: getting very slowly better of a bilious fever that had almost killed him. . . . People in general thought *Pendennis* got dull as it went on; and I confess I thought so too: he would do well to take the opportunity of his illness to discontinue it altogether. He told me last June he himself was tired of it: must not his readers naturally tire too?

(9) [*17 Apr 1850*, to the same.] Thackeray is in such a great world that I am afraid of him; he gets tired of me: and we are content to regard each other at a distance. You, Alfred, Spedding and Allen,[4] are the only men I ever care to see again.

(10) [*Dec 1851*, to the same.] Thackeray says he is getting tired of being witty, and of the great world . . . .

(11) [*19 Apr 1852*, to W. B. Donne.] I found on my return from Ipswich today . . . a letter from Thackeray that wd puzzle the Critics of his Works – so full of the old Affection as it is. – He is 'dancing the slack wire'[5] at Glasgow, he says.

(12) [*15 Nov 1852*, to Thackeray.] My dearest old Thackeray I had your note – I dare scarce read it as it lies in my desk.[6] It affects me partly as those old foolscap letters did, of which I told you I burned so many this spring: & why: – I was really ashamed of their kindness! If ever we get to another world, you will perhaps know why all this is so – I must not talk anymore of what I have so often tried to explain to you – Meanwhile, I truly believe there is no Man alive loves you (in his own way of love) more than I do – Now you are gone out of England [to America], I can feel something of what I shd feel if you were dead: . . . were you back again, I should see no more of you than before. But this is not from want of love on my part: it is because we live in such different worlds: & it is almost painful to me to tease anybody with my seedy dullness, which is just bearable by myself – Life every day seems a more total failure & mess to me. . . .[7] But Goodbye, goodbye, my dear old Thackeray: & believe (for I can assert) that I am while I live yrs ever E. F. G. (*LPP*, III, 114–15).

(13) [*22 Jan 1857*, to E. B. Cowell.] I have now been five weeks alone in my old Lodgings in London. . . . I have seen scarce any Friends. . . . Oddly enough, as I finished the last sentence, Thackeray was announced; he came in looking gray, grand, and good-humoured; and I held up this Letter and told him whom it was written to and he sends his Love! He goes Lecturing all over England; has fifty pounds for each Lecture: and says he is ashamed of the Fortune he is making. But he deserves it.

(14) [*9 Apr 1861*, to W. B. Donne.] I had a kind Note from Thackeray some ten days ago:– but the *Author* is in his Letters now – He says he has often to write when only just able to do so after one of his Illnesses: and that his Age of Novel-writing is past. It is a pity he was not convinced of this before, I think.

(15) [*16 Jan 1862*, to W. F. Pollock.] So it isn't all Peace in one's Soul down here; we have our Grudges, as well as Thackeray his against Saturday Reviews, etc.[8] I think Thackeray must be much spoiled, judging by all that.

(16) [*3 Jan 1864*, to W. B. Donne.] *Now* I wish he were alive

that I might write & tell him how the *Newcomes* were illuminating my long Evenings. But, if he were alive, I don't think he'd care to be told so by me now; I think he had ceased to remember me; and I'm sure I can't wonder, nor (least of all) blame him.

(17) [7 *Jan 1864*, to Samuel Laurence.] Frederic Tennyson sent me a Photograph of W. M. T. old, white, massive, and melancholy, sitting in his Library. I am surprized almost to find how much I am thinking of him: so little as I had seen him for the last ten years; not once for the last five. I had been told – by you, for one – that he was spoiled.[9] I am glad therefore that I have scarce seen him since he was 'old Thackeray'. I keep reading his *Newcomes* of nights, and as it were hear him saying so much in it; and it seems to me as if he might be coming up my Stairs, and about to come (singing) into my Room, as in old Charlotte Street, etc., thirty years ago.

(18) [*31 Jan 1864*, to E. B. Cowell.] I had seen very little of him for these last ten years; nothing for the last five; he did not care to write; and people told me he was become a little spoiled: by London praise, and some consequent Egotism. But he was a very fine Fellow.

(19) [*29 Feb 1864*, to W. B. Donne: he has been re-reading Scott's novels and Boswell's *Johnson*.] I have also read Thackeray's *Pendennis* and *Newcomes* again – wonderful too – but not so comfortable – I think some of the Panegyrics in the Papers and Reviews throw some light on what I have been told of his later years; he must have got surrounded with a set of Praise-plasterers, so as scarce to be able to breathe without it. – Twenty years ago he used to let out against the Authors be-praising one another – But he remains something of a *Great Man* after all. I feel how he, Scott, & Johnson, would have cogged well together.

(20) [*29 Dec 1875*, to Fanny Kemble, regretting the recent publication of Anny Thackeray's *Orphans of Pimlico* collection of Thackeray's drawings.] I am convinced I can hear Thackeray saying, when such a Book as this was proposed to him – 'Oh, come – there has been enough of all this' – and

crumpling up the Proof in that little hand of his. For a curiously little hand he had, uncharacteristic of the grasp of his mind: I used to consider it half inherited from the Hindoo people among whom he was born.

(21) [*10 June 1876*, to C. E. Norton, discussing Charles Lamb.] . . . 'Saint Charles', as Thackeray once called him while looking at one of his half-mad Letters, and remembering his Devotion to that quite mad Sister.[10]

NOTES

1. The Revd William Bodham Donne (1807–82), cleric, scholar, literary journalist, and later Examiner of Plays in the Lord Chamberlain's office, was a former schoolfellow of FitzGerald's and acquainted with Thackeray. FitzGerald thought him 'a very delightful fellow' (*LPP*, I, 374).

2. *Memoirs of the Life of Count de Grammont: Containing in Particular the Amorous Intrigues of the Court of England in the Reign of King Charles II* (1714). Actually written by Anthony Hamilton. Thackeray refers to these *Memoirs* – now regarded as unreliable – when discussing Congreve in *The English Humourists*.

3. Frederick Tennyson (1807–98), eldest of the seven Tennyson boys, of whom the poet Alfred was the third; another friend from FitzGerald's Cambridge years.

4. James Spedding and John Allen, Cambridge friends of FitzGerald's and Thackeray's; see above, I, 20. 'Alfred' was of course the poet Tennyson.

5. That is, lecturing. Thackeray's loving letter does not survive, for reasons FitzGerald explains, writing to him that month: 'My dear old Thackeray, I have been looking over a heap of your letters – from the first in 1831 to the last of some months back – and what do you think I have done with the greater part? – why, burnt them! – with great remorse, I assure you; but I have two reasons – first I am rather *ashamed* (and nothing else) of your repeated, and magnanimously blind over-estimate of myself; and secondly I thought that if I were to die before setting my house in order those letters might fall into unwise hands, and perhaps (now you are become famous) get published according to the vile fashion of the day. But I have cut out and preserved many parts of these letters. . . . As I get older I don't get colder, I believe: which is lucky you will think . . . .' (*LPP*, III, 29–31).

6. Thackeray had written, 27 Oct 1852, just before embarking for America on his *Humourists* tour, asking FitzGerald to be his literary executor, if misadventure befell him: 'And I should like my daughters to remember that you are the best and oldest friend their Father ever had' (*LPP*, III, 98–9).

7. FitzGerald's success with *Omar Khayyam* lay, of course, some years in the future.

8. On Thackeray's public dispute with the acerbic and hard-hitting *Saturday Review*, see *Wisdom*, pp. 304–8, 372, 481.

9. '... which also some of his later writings hinted to me of themselves', he added, to another correspondent, a fortnight later (*Letters of FitzGerald*, II, 51–2).

10. In a later letter about this, Thackeray is described as reverently putting Lamb's letter to his forehead: and the editor specifies that it was Lamb's letter of 1 Dec 1824 to Bernard Barton (ibid., II, 243 and note).

Big, Fierce, Weeping, Hungry, but Not Strong

THOMAS CARLYLE

Sources given in the Notes, or after items. Carlyle (1795–1881) was acquainted with Thackeray from the early 1830s; soon they were both contributing to *Fraser's*, and they both appear in Maclise's 1835 drawing of the Fraserians. By 1840 they were on regular visiting terms. Thackeray, in that year, wrote of him and his wife Jane, 'pleasanter more high-minded people I don't know' (*LPP*, I, 413). In 1841 Carlyle, referring to Thackeray's wife's insanity, remarked, 'he is very clever, with pen and pencil; an honest man, in no inconsiderable distress! He seems as if he had no better place, of all the great places he once knew, than our poor house to take shelter in!' – Charles Richard Sanders, 'The Carlyles and Thackeray', in *Nineteenth-Century Literary Perspectives*, ed. Clyde de L. Ryals (Durham, N. C., 1974) p. 172. At this period Thackeray, like many of his generation, was considerably influenced by Carlyle. Later they grew more distant, socially and in outlook, and Thackeray was much annoyed by Carlyle's 'blind fiddler' charge (see below) in 1846. 'Gurlyle' – his hate-nickname for him – 'is immensely grand and savage now', he wrote in 1848, and a recent essay of his 'seems like insanity almost [in its] contempt for all mankind, and the way in wh he shirks from all argument when called upon to préciser his own remedies for the state of things' (*LPP*, II, 366). Carlyle became critical of the successful Thackeray's frequenting great houses; but Thackeray remarked (1858) that 'Carlyle hates everybody that has arrived – if they are on the road, he may perhaps treat them civilly' (*LPP*, IV, 82n). Anyway, as Francis Espinasse remarks, 'Carlyle's estimates of the British men of letters who were his contemporaries did not, as is well known, err on the side of over-appreciation' – *Literary Recollections and Sketches* (1893) p. 212. Some months after Thackeray's death, however, Anny met him in the street '& he suddenly began to cry. I shall always love him in future [she remarked], for I used to fancy he did not care about Papa' (*LPP*, IV, 304). The entries below consist first of letters, and then of accounts of Carlyle in conversation. Sanders's forty-page essay (above) provides the fullest account of this relationship; see also *LPP*, I, cvi–cix.

[*Summer 1837*, to his brother Alexander.] The author [of *The Times* review of *The French Revolution*] is one Thackeray, a half-monstrous Cornish giant, kind of painter, Cambridge man, a Paris newspaper correspondent, who is now writing for his life in London. I have seen him at the Bullers' and at Sterling's. His article is rather like him, and I suppose calculated to do the book good.[1]

[*11 Nov 1842*, to his brother John.] We have had Thackeray here . . . fresh from Ireland, and full of quizzical rather honest kind of talk; has a Book on Ireland with caricatures nearly ready: I cannot but wish poor Thackeray well. Nobody in this region has as much stuff to make a man of, – could he but *make* him.   (Sanders, in *Nineteenth-Century Literary Perspectives*, p. 173)

[*23 June 1847*, to Robert Browning.] Dickens writes a *Dombey and Son*, Thackeray a *Vanity Fair*; not *reapers* they, either of them! In fact the business of rope-dancing goes to a great height.[2]

[*3 Jan 1852*, to Dr Carlyle; he has just returned from Lady Ashburton's, with Thackeray.] I have never seen him so well before. There is a great deal of talent in him, a great deal of sensibility, – irritability, sensuality, vanity without limit; – and nothing, or little, but sentimentalism and play-actorism to guide it all with: not a good or well-found ship in such waters on such a voyage.[3]

[*25 Feb 1852*, Harriet Martineau to R. W. Emerson.] I saw the Carlyles a few months since; – just saw them, & O! dear! felt them too. They put me between them, at Thackeray's last [*Humourists*] lecture; & both got the fidgets. After the first half hour, C. looked at his watch, & held it across me, about once in two minutes; & he filled up the intervals with shaking himself, & drumming his elbow into my side.[4] [Carlyle himself describes the occasion, to his brother John:] The audience inferior to what I had heard; *item* the performance. Comic *acting* good in it; also a certain gentility of style notable: but of *insight* (worth calling by the name) none; nay, a good deal of *pretended* insight (morality &c with an ugly 'do' at the bottom of it) which was worse than none. The air grew bad; I had only one wish, to be out again, out, out! – Thackeray has not found his feet yet; but he may perhaps do so in that element, and get (as Darwin expresses it) into some kind of 'Thackeray at Home', in which he might excel all people for delighting an empty fashionable audience.[5]

[*23 Oct 1852*, to his mother; he is talking about visitors to the house.] Thackeray is coming, for whom I care nothing, tho' he is a clever and friendly man; he comes today with a nobleman and a Portrait-Painter; comes, but is soon to go: – 'Di tha naither ill na' guid!'[6]

[*9 Sep 1853*, to Emerson.] Thackeray has very rarely come athwart me since his return [from America]: he is a big fellow, soul and body; of many gifts and qualities (particularly in the Hogarth line, with a dash of Sterne superadded), of enormous appetite withal, and very uncertain and chaotic in all points, except his outer breeding, which is fixed enough, and perfect according to the modern English style. I rather dread explosions in his history. A *big*, fierce, weeping, hungry man; not a strong one. *Ay de mi*![7]

[*4 Nov 1854*, to Lady Ashburton.] Thackeray came over to see us one night; was very gentle and friendly-looking; ingenious too here and there; but extremely difficult to talk with, somehow – his talk lying all in flashes, little detached pools, you nowhere got upon a well or vein.[8]

[*30 Nov 1859*, to his brother John.] Thackeray *is* to do a new Magazine; has applied to me; one of my climbings upstairs was to say handsomely, 'No, can't at all.'[9]

[*29 Dec 1863*, to Richard Monckton Milnes.] Poor Thackeray! I saw him not ten days ago. I was riding in the dusk, heavy at heart, along by the Serpentine and Hyde Park, when some human brother from a chariot, with a young lady in it, threw me a shower of salutations. I looked up – it was Thackeray with his daughter: the last time I was to see him in this world. He had many fine qualities, no guile or malice against any mortal; a big mass of a soul, but not strong in proportion; a beautiful vein of genius lay struggling about in him. Nobody in our day wrote, I should say, with such perfection of style. I predict of his books very much as you do. Poor Thackeray! – adieu! adieu![10]

Carlyle, who had known Thackeray from his youth, told me [writes Moncure D. Conway] that at times he (Thackeray), having some urgent work on hand, escaped from invitations, callers, and letters, and went off from his house without leaving any address. One night a messenger came to him (Carlyle) from a public-house near by with a request from Thackeray for the loan of a Bible.[11]

Carlyle [writes George Venables] had naturally but little sympathy with Thackeray's instinctive dislike of greatness, as it is exemplified in his antipathy to Marlborough and to Swift. I think it was after a conversation between them on the character of Swift that I heard Carlyle say, 'I wish I could persuade Thackeray that the test of greatness in a man is not whether he (Thackeray) would like to meet him at a tea-party.' He liked Thackeray himself, and I think he never spoke of him with the contempt which, before he became comparatively intimate with Dickens, he expressed for 'the infinitesimally small Schnüspel, the distinguished novelist'.[12]

[Charles Gavan Duffy, the politician, in conversation with Carlyle in the late 1840s, suggested that the difference between Dickens's and Thackeray's fictional characters was like the difference between Sindbad the Sailor and Robinson Crusoe.] Yes, he said, Thackeray had more reality in him and would cut up into a dozen Dickenses. They were altogether different at bottom. Dickens was doing the best in him, and went on smiling in perennial good humour; but Thackeray despised himself for his work, and on that account could not always do it even moderately well. He was essentially a man of grim, silent, stern nature, but lately he had circulated among fashionable people, dining out every day, and he covered this native disposition with a varnish of smooth, smiling complacency, not at all pleasant to contemplate. The course he had got into since he had taken to cultivate dinner-eating in fashionable houses was not salutary discipline for work of any sort, one might surmise.[13]

I inquired if he saw much of Thackeray. No, he said, not latterly. Thackeray was much enraged with him because, after he made a book of travels for the P. & O. Company, who had invited him to go on a voyage to Africa in one of their steamers, he (Carlyle) had compared the transaction to the practice of a blind fiddler going to and fro on a penny ferry-boat in Scotland, and playing tunes to the passengers for halfpence. Charles Buller told Thackeray; and when he complained, it was necessary to inform him frankly that it was undoubtedly his opinion that, out of respect for himself and his profession, a man like Thackeray ought not to have gone fiddling for halfpence or otherwise, in any steamboat under the sky.[14]

[Duffy's diary for 1880.] Speaking of both after they were dead, Carlyle said of Dickens that his chief faculty was that of a comic actor. He would have made a successful one if he had taken to that sort of life.... Thackeray had far more literary ability, but one could not fail to perceive that he had no convictions, after all, except that a man ought to be a gentleman, and ought not to be a snob. This was about the sum of the belief that was in him. The chief skill he possessed was making wonderful likenesses with pen and ink, struck off without premeditation, and which it was found he could not afterwards improve.[15]

Of the novel, as a kind of attempt to delineate the real, or the possible, and at least written in prose [writes Francis Espinasse], Carlyle, though the translator of the two *Meisters* and of the *Specimens of German Romance*, was but slightly more tolerant than of the poem.... For Charles Dickens Carlyle had a personal liking, and thought it worth while to report to me that he had seen him give a 'little bob', when introduced to Lord Holland, of a kind intended to mean that he did not much plume himself on making his Lordship's acquaint-

ance.... Of Thackeray's earlier performances Carlyle said
that they showed 'something Hogarthian' to be in him, but
that his books were 'wretched'. Of course this was before the
appearance.of *Vanity Fair*, the immense talent displayed in
which Carlyle fully recognised, pronouncing Thackeray 'a
man of much more judgement than Dickens'. Yet, when
Vanity Fair in its yellow cover was being issued contempor-
aneously with *Dombey and Son* in its green ditto, Carlyle spoke
of the relief which he found on turning from Thackeray's
terrible cynicism to the cheerful geniality of Dickens. The
highest praise bestowed by him on Thackeray's lectures was
that they were 'ingenious'. Personally Carlyle preferred
Dickens, who always treated him with deference, to Thackeray, who often opposed to his inopportune denunciations
of men and things at miscellaneous dinner-parties some of
that persiflage which was more disconcerting to Carlyle than
direct contradiction.[16] It was a startling parallel between two
surely most dissimilar men which was drawn by Carlyle, when
he once said to me, 'Thackeray is like Wilson of Edinburgh'
(Christopher North), 'he has no convictions.' Possibly this was
said after Carlyle had been more than usually irritated by
Thackeray's persiflage.[17]

NOTES

1. *Letters of Thomas Carlyle to his Youngest Sister*, ed. Charles Townsend
Copeland (1899) p. 86. *The Times* review, 3 Aug 1837, reprinted in *Critical
Papers in Literature* (1904) and elsewhere, though critical of Carlyle's
eccentric style ('prose run mad'), was highly laudatory. Charles Buller, M. P.
(1806–48), a Cambridge friend of Thackeray's, had been tutored by
Carlyle, 1822–5, and it was probably through him that Thackeray met
Carlyle. John Sterling (1806–44) was another Cambridge man and friend
of Thackeray.
2. *Letters of Thomas Carlyle to John Stuart Mill, John Sterling and Robert
Browning*, ed. Alexander Carlyle (1923) p. 284. For Carlyle's comparative
estimate of these two novels, see Espinasse's account, below.
3. *New Letters of Thomas Carlyle*, ed. Alexander Carlyle (1904) II, 122. 'On
such a voyage': he has just been writing about problems facing Britain –
unemployment, a useless aristocracy, etc. Four days earlier Carlyle had
written to his brother John about the Ashburton house-party: 'Thackeray ... is not of great profit to talk with, but he is easy and agreeable, and

his presence, taking away the burden of talk from others, is so far very welcome' (Sanders, in *Nineteenth-Century Literary Perspectives*, p. 189).

4. *The Correspondence of Emerson and Carlyle*, ed. Joseph Slater (1964) p. 474n. After an earlier *Humourists* lecture, Jane Carlyle wrote, 'The Lectures between you and me are no great things – as *Lectures* – but it is the fashion to find them "so amusing"! and the *audience* is the most brilliant I ever saw in one room – unless in Bath House drawing-rooms' – *Jane Welsh Carlyle: Letters to her Family 1839–1863*, ed. Leonard Huxley (1924) pp. 350–1. Carlyle's impatience may have been caused by his realising that, as Ray points out (*Wisdom*, pp. 144–5), the *Humourists* lectures were pointedly anti-Carlylean, anti-'Heroes'.

5. Sanders, in *Nineteenth-Century Literary Perspectives*, pp. 185–6. The 'Thackeray at Home' jibe is a reference to the popular one-man-shows given by several actors and actresses under such titles as 'Mr Charles Matthews "At Home"'.

6. *New Letters*, II, 139. The painter was Samuel Laurence.

7. *Correspondence of Thomas Carlyle and Ralph Waldo Emerson*, ed. Charles Eliot Norton (1883) II, 230. The concluding phrase is Spanish for 'Alas, poor me.'

8. Sanders, in *Nineteenth-Century Literary Perspectives*, p. 192.

9. Ibid., p. 195. But he wished the *Cornhill* well: see *LPP*, IV, 188.

10. T. Wemyss Reid, *Richard Monckton Milnes* (1890) II, 113.

11. Moncure D. Conway, *Autobiography, Memories and Experiences* (1905) II, 4.

12. Review of J. A. Froude's *Carlyle's Life in London*, in *Fortnightly Review*, n.s., XXXVI (1884) 605. Dickens is referred to as 'Schnüspel' in *Past and Present* (1843) Bk II, ch. 3.

13. 'It is not true,' Thackeray told Edward FitzGerald in 1848, 'what Gurlyle has written to you about my having become a tremenjuous lion &c – too grand to &c – but what is true is that a feller who is writing all day for money gets sick of pens and paper when his work is over. . . . I cant eat more dinners than I used last year and dine at home with my dear little women three times a week: but 2 or 3 great people ask me to their houses: and Vanity Fair does everything but pay' (*LPP*, II, 365).

14. See *Adversity*, p. 301, for Thackeray's resentment over this 'blind fiddler' jibe, and his riposte in *Punch*, 14 Mar 1846. The P. & O. voyage had resulted in *Notes on a Journey from Cornhill to Grand Cairo* (1846).

15. Charles Gavan Duffy, *Conversations with Carlyle* (1892) pp. 76–7. Carlyle, it is piquant to notice, regarded both of these great novelists as having a chief 'faculty' or 'skill' for something other than literature.

16. Ray quotes Kate Perry's manuscript diary for 22 Jan 1850: 'Carlyle was discussed. . . . Thackeray said he was a bully – attack him with persiflage & he was silenced, in fact Carlyle is no longer the Prophet he used to be considered – I remember his palmy days when his words were manna to the Israelites' (*LPP*, I, cviii)

17. Francis Espinasse, *Literary Recollections and Sketches* (1893) pp. 215–16.

A Cynicism Not of the Heart

CHARLES MACKAY

From *Forty Years' Recollections of Life, Literature, and Public Affairs from 1830 to 1870* (1877) II, 294–301. Mackay (1814–89), journalist and popular poet, was assistant sub-editor on the *Morning Chronicle*, 1835–44, and later edited the *Illustrated London News* and other journals. He last met Thackeray a week or so before his death, dining at Evan's Supper Rooms with his old schoolfellow and *Punch* colleague John Leech: 'They both complained of illness, but neither of them looked ill enough to justify the belief that anything ailed them beyond a temporary indisposition, such as all of us are subject to.' Leech died the next year.

Mr Thackeray, from so early a period as 1839–40, was a frequent contributor to his favourite journal, the *Morning Chronicle*, though he never succeeded in establishing a permanent connection with it.[1] But he was always on excellent terms with the staff, and on the welcome Saturday evenings, when there was no paper to prepare for the morrow, he was a frequent guest at the chambers in the Temple, of one of the assistant editors, the late Mr Thomas Fraser, of Eskadale – the 'Laughing Tom', whom in after-years he celebrated in his ballad of 'Bouillabaisse'. . . . I constantly met Mr Thackeray at Mr Fraser's hospitable board, both in London and Paris, long before the world suspected how great a novelist was striving in vain to excite its attention. His fame – unlike that of Dickens – did not come to him early; and the tardiness of the public favour, which he had the abiding consciousness of deserving, possibly infused into his later writings that flavour of cynicism which did not exist in his heart.

When I first made his acquaintance, Mr Thackeray was known among his friends as the best *improvisatore* of his time, far superior to Mr Charles Sloman, once well known in the musical world – and who used to supplement a scanty income by improvising in public-houses, and 'free and easies', for the amusement of the company. Mr Thackeray's powers of impromptu rhyming were great and brilliant, and in congenial society he was never loth to exert them. On one occasion, when every one in the room was smoking but myself, and he had learned from my own lips that I never smoked, and that I detested tobacco, he singled me out for the exercise of his wit, and poured out a string of verses on the Pleasures of Smoking, ending each stanza with the lines, which include a common mispronunciation of my name,

> And alas, for poor Mackay,
> Who can't smoke his baccy!

No more of the composition remains in my memory, but the effort did not exhaust his powers for the evening, as he ran over the whole company – I think there were seven or eight of us – and hit off the peculiarities of each with much pungency, but without a taint of ill-nature.

... his lectures on the Four Georges ... were not quite so popular in the Old World as they had proved in the New. They ran counter to existing prejudices, as well as to some strong feelings of loyalty towards the House of Hanover. I remember at this time finding him alone in the library of his club, with a newspaper in his hand, which he had clutched tightly, as if about to destroy it, and with an expression of anger on his face which was seldom seen there. I asked him what was the matter, and he gave me the newspaper to look at. It appeared that he had recently delivered his lectures on the Four Georges at a certain fashionable town in the centre of England, of which the rector was a leading contributor to one of the local journals. The rectory was a valuable one, and had been conferred on the rector's father by the influence of George IV. The son had succeeded his father in the incumbency, and venerated the memory of the king who had been so good a friend to the family. Mr Thackeray's portraiture of George IV had excited the good gentleman's wrath, and he had penned an indignant article on the subject, which Mr Thackeray had just read as I entered the room. It began with the following words: 'An elderly, infidel buffoon of the name of Thackeray has been lecturing in town on the subject of the Four Georges.' I am afraid I laughed at this passage, but Mr Thackeray thought it no laughing matter, and threatened an action for libel with damages laid at a thousand pounds. I tried to pacify his wrath, and told him my opinion, that however offensive the words might be, no lawyer would hold them to be libellous. It is not a libel on a gentleman to call him elderly, though it possibly might be so considered if he applied the disagreeable epithet to a young woman of twenty-five. 'But it is libellous to call a man an infidel', he said. 'Unfaithful to what?' I replied. 'To some form of belief that somebody else holds. The most orthodox man in the world might be called an infidel, by some one whom he thought heterodox. And as for buffoon – it is a word which no gentleman would use to another – and which you may well treat with contempt.' 'Yes; all very well,' he replied, 'for you have not been attacked; but we all bear with perfect equanimity everybody's annoyances but our own.' The threatened action for libel was never commenced. . . .

Mr Thackeray, like Dr Johnson – and all the ancients – was singularly indifferent to the beauties of natural scenery – and took more pleasure in contemplating the restless tide of human life in the streets of London, than in looking at or wandering among the most glorious panoramic splendours of mountain and forest, or wide stretching river, lake, or sea. It was reported of him in America, that he was within an hour and a half's run of the magnificent Falls of Niagara, when he was strongly pressed by a friend and companion to visit that renowned wonder of America, and that he refused, with the contemptuous observation, 'All the snobs go to Niagara, I shall not make one of them.' When this story reached England, he was indignant at the reason which gossip had erroneously assigned, but admitted that he had not visited the Falls, and was sorry that he had not done so. . . .

Thackeray was not witty in the same sense or to the same degree as Douglas Jerrold, yet resembled him in the fact that the cynicism of many of his good sayings was that of the fancy, not that of the heart; and like Jerrold, was always ready to do a kind action if he could serve a literary brother. When poor Angus Reach died in early manhood of overwork, and left a widow in distress, Thackeray, who had known but little of his fellow-worker, came to the rescue simply because he was a fellow-worker. . . .

NOTE

1. For his connection with this newspaper, see *W. M. Thackeray: Contributions to the 'Morning Chronicle'*, ed. Gordon N. Ray (Urbana, Ill. 1955).

Thackeray Sells *Vanity Fair*: and Other Matters

HENRY VIZETELLY

From *Glimpses Back Through Seventy Years: Autobiographical and Other Reminiscences* (1893) I, 249–53, 283–95, 316–18; II, 14–15. Vizetelly (1820–94), of Italian ancestry, had printers' ink in his veins and was artist, engraver, illustrator, publisher, printer, author, translator and literary *entrepreneur*, with a lengthy career in the book and magazine world, culminating in his being imprisoned in 1889 for persisting in publishing Zola's 'obscene' novel *La Terre*. His firm had been among the pioneers in illustrated journalism with the *Pictorial Times* (1843–8), to which Thackeray contributed. Among other journals with which Vizetelly was associated were the *Illustrated Times*, *Welcome Guest* and *Illustrated London News*. At the beginning of this extract from his memoirs, he is describing his preparations for the new *Pictorial Times* during the winter of 1842–3. Having engaged Knight Hunt as sub-editor, Douglas Jerrold as leader-writer, and Mark Lemon as theatre critic, he next approached Thackeray, an introduction to whom he had obtained from George Nickisson of *Fraser's Magazine*.

On calling at the address given me – a shop in Jermyn Street,[1] eight or ten doors from Regent Street, and within a few doors of the present Museum of Geology – and knocking at the private entrance, a young lodging-house slavey in answer to my inquiries bade me follow her upstairs. I did so, to the very top of the house, and after my card had been handed in, I was asked to enter the front apartment, where a tall slim individual between thirty and thirty-five years of age, with a pleasant smiling countenance and a bridgeless nose, and clad in a dressing gown of decided Parisian cut, rose from a small table standing close to the near window to receive me. When he stood up, the low pitch of the room caused him to look even taller than he really was, and his actual height was well over six feet. . . . The apartment was an exceedingly plainly furnished bedroom, with common rush seated chairs and painted French bedstead, and with neither looking-glass nor prints on the bare, cold, cheerless-looking walls. On the table from which Mr Thackeray had risen, a white cloth was spread, on which was a frugal breakfast tray – a cup of chocolate and some dry toast – and huddled together at the other end were writing materials, two or three numbers of *Fraser's Magazine*, and a few slips of manuscript. I presented Mr Nickisson's letter and explained the object of my visit, when Mr Thackeray at once undertook to write upon art, to review such books as he might fancy, and to contribute an occasional article on the opera, more with reference to its frequenters, he remarked, than from a critical point of view. So satisfied was he with the three guineas offered him for a couple of columns weekly, that he jocularly expressed himself willing to sign an engagement for life upon these terms. I can only suppose from the eager way in which he closed with my proposal that the prospect of an additional £160 to his income, was at that moment anything but a matter of indifference. The humble quarters in which he was installed seemed at any rate to indicate that for some reason or other strict economy was just then the order of the day with him. . . .

Mr Thackeray was at this period painfully cognisant of his lack of technical skill as an etcher, and he asked me to find him some one who would etch the frontispiece to the *Cairo* volume from his water-colour sketch. I gave the job to a young fellow in our employment named Thwaites, who subsequently put a number of Thackeray's sketches for *Mrs Perkins's Ball* on the wood, and touched up the hands and other matters in those subjects drawn on the blocks by Thackeray himself. . . . From the little services in this way which I had been able to render Mr Thackeray, I had become rather intimate with him, and while the drawings for *Perkins's Ball*, and others of his Christmas books printed by us, were in progress, I saw a good deal of him, for he was almost as fastidious, as I afterwards found Mr Ruskin to be, in regard to the manner in which his sketches were transferred to the wood. One afternoon, when he called in Peterborough Court, he had a small brown paper parcel with him, and opened it to show me his two careful

drawings for the page plates to the first number of *Vanity Fair*.
Tied up with them was the manuscript of the earlier portion
of the work, of which he had several times spoken to me,
referring especially to the quaint character that Chiswick
Mall – within a stone's throw of which I was then living – still
retained. His present intention, he told me, was to see
Bradbury & Evans, and offer the work to them. Although
Thackeray never showed himself eager after praise – Serjeant
Ballantine's assertion to the contrary notwithstanding[2] – he
was always depressed by disparaging remarks, and I felt glad
at being able to praise his two drawings, respecting the merits
of which he professed to be in considerable doubt, and to
congratulate him on the capital title he had chosen for the
work, which he then mentioned to me for the first time.

In little more than half-an-hour Mr Thackeray again made
his appearance, and with a beaming face gleefully informed
me that he had settled the business. 'B. & E.', said he, 'accepted
so readily, that I am deuced sorry I didn't ask them another
tenner. I am certain they would have given it.' He then
explained to me that he had named fifty guineas per part,
including the two sheets of letterpress, a couple of etchings,
and the initials at the commencement of the chapters. He
reckoned the text, I remember, at no more than five-and-
twenty shillings a page, the two etchings at six guineas each,
while, as for the few initials at the beginning of the chapters,
he threw these in. Such was Mr Thackeray's own estimate of
his commercial value as an author and illustrator, A.D. 1846.[3]

The fable of *Vanity Fair* having gone the round of the
publishing trade before a purchaser could be found, has
appeared in print scores of times, and will, no doubt, continue
to be repeated, as a striking example of the dull-wittedness of
London bibliopoles of a past generation. And yet, there is not
a particle of truth in the story. If the records of the principal
publishing firms at that date were searched, I am confident
they would be found to contain nothing whatever relative to
the manuscript of *Vanity Fair* having been submitted for
consideration.[4] . . . The hawking about of *Vanity Fair* in the
way pretended, of course presupposes that the manuscript
was complete, and was submitted in this state to the half-score
fatuous fools who declined it with thanks, but I am positive
that, when arrangements were made with Messrs Bradbury &

Evans for the publication of the work, with no further knowledge on their part of its nature than could be gleaned from Mr Thackeray during a brief interview, nothing beyond No. 1 was written.

I have no doubt whatever that the publishers of *Vanity Fair* bought – like most works by known authors are purchased – solely on its writer's then reputation, which his *Snobs of England* in *Punch*, had greatly extended. I know perfectly well that, after the publication commenced, much of the remainder of the work was written under pressure from the printer, and not unfrequently the final instalment of 'copy', needed to fill the customary thirty-two pages, was penned while the printer's boy was waiting in the hall at Young Street. This was a common occurrence with much of Mr Thackeray's monthly work, and the strange thing is that, produced under such disadvantageous conditions as these, it should have been so uniformly and thoroughly good.[5] ...

I read with some surprise Dean Hole's statement that Thackeray, when he chose to talk, said so many good things that they trod down and suffocated each other.[6] Certainly this was not my own experience or that of many others who were in terms of intimacy with Mr Thackeray, and were a good deal in his society. During the seven or eight years that I saw much of Mr Thackeray, and knew him tolerably intimately, he never appeared to me to shine in conversation, and he most certainly made no kind of effort to do so – never in fact talked for effect, and indeed never usurped any large share of the conversation. Ordinarily he would interpose occasional quaint humorous comments, and would show himself far more tolerant that men of his capacity usually are of bores. Whenever the talk grew dull and wearying, he would content himself by filliping it up with some witty or shrewd satirical remark, and turn it into a new channel. None of the little aside sermons which he preached in his books by any chance fell from his lips. At this period of his career his placid temper and pleasant courtesy, in spite of the mild sarcasms in which he indulged, charmed all who came in contact with him.

On thinking over the many occasions on which I saw Mr Thackeray in his unreserved moments, I cannot call to mind a single instance of his showing himself at all ruffled when anything disagreeable had happened; and yet that he was unusually sensitive, there cannot be the smallest doubt, for more than a glimpse of this is had in his *Roundabout* paper 'Thorns in the Cushion'. To me he seemed to look at life in a light philosophic way, and to get all the harmless enjoyment he could out of it. And certainly at this time there was no trace of that reserve, or that austerity of manner, which in subsequent years, when 'Time had his flowing locks to silver turned', came to be attributed to him.

When I went to reside at Kensington again, I frequently had to see Mr Thackeray about the illustrations to his Christmas books, or the etchings to his novels, on which I still obtained him occasional assistance, finding him some new hand, perhaps, to do the mechanical biting in. At one period I generally called upon him on two mornings in the week. At these times, as he was a late riser, he was accustomed to have me shown up into his bedroom, when he would give me a cigar and chat whilst dressing in the most unreserved fashion on all manner of topics, talking to me in his habitual familiar way as though I was his equal. From his conversation I gathered that he was envious, but not ill-naturedly so, of the great influence which Dickens had acquired over his women readers, whom the misfortunes of his juvenile heroes and heroines were, he said, always moving to tears.

In spite of Thackeray's remark that he had never read the Nelly part of the *Old Curiosity Shop* more than once, whereas he had Dick Swiveller and the Marchioness by heart, there is no doubt of his having been genuinely impressed by Dickens's pathos.[7] ... Thackeray was on all occasions loud in his praise of Dickens as a writer, and yet no one could have been more conscious than he of the exaggerated amiability of those characters which evoked at the time such a prodigious amount of feminine sympathy.

We all remember Thackeray's observation, 'When I say I know women I mean that I know I don't know them' [*Mr Brown's Letters to his Nephew*, no. 11]. One thing is certain, however; he hungered after their admiration, for he openly confessed this on several occasions in my hearing, and he was, moreover, childishly vain when he succeeded in securing it. It may be bad taste to mention the circumstance, but more than once I received from him drawings on wood for his Christmas books, wrapped up in notes from his feminine correspondents, who at times allowed their admiration to wander somewhat indiscreetly beyond the range of his books. These communications could scarcely have been so numerous, I fancy, as to have been brought under my notice by mere accident on Mr Thackeray's part. He rather wished, I think, to publish abroad that he was overburthened with this sort of idolatry.

Today, with Douglas Jerrold's waning reputation, it seems strange to recall to mind that he was the one literary man, of whom Thackeray, when in his prime, seemed to be seriously jealous. I was several times present when the early number of *Punch* reached Young Street, and well remember how, as Thackeray nervously tore off the wrapper, he would exclaim, 'Now let's see what young Douglas has to say this week.' ... Thackeray was reticent in expressing his opinions upon people whom he did not like, and very rarely said ill-natured things about anyone. He took no pains, however, to disguise his contempt for Jerrold's democratic professions. I remember him mentioning to me his having noticed at the Earl of Carlisle's a presentation copy of one of Jerrold's books, the inscription in which ran: 'To the Right Honourable the Earl of Carlisle, K.G., K.C.B., &c., &c.' 'Ah!' said Thackeray, 'this is the sort of style in which your rigid, uncompromising radical always toadies the great.' 'There is', he remarked in one of his books, 'an odour in the English aristocracy that always intoxicates plebeians.' Unquestionably there was an utter want of sympathy between the two men. ...

Thackeray was especially good to young men, and personally I always met with the greatest kindness from him. He seemed to take especial pleasure in having young fellows at his house, in encouraging them, and putting them completely at their ease while drawing them out. I remember when several smart young writers – whose success had emboldened them to turn their backs on Bohemia and most of its free and easy ways, but who were still somewhat regardless of their personal appearance – were frequent guests at Thackeray's dinner-table where every courtesy was shown them by their distinguished host. After one of these entertainments I heard him remark, in the hope, no doubt, that the hint would be conveyed to those for whom it was intended, 'They are all capital fellows, but wouldn't be a whit the worse for cleaner shirts.' Before his daughters grew up, and while *Vanity Fair* was in progress, Thackeray had no home society, and he seemed thoroughly to enjoy these evenings, spent away from the club and Evans's late supper rooms of which he was at one time a rather constant frequenter. . . .

[Twice Vizetelly negotiated with Thackeray on behalf of publishers. The first time was in 1847 when the publisher David Bogue was elated by the success of a series of comic shilling booklets by Albert Smith.[8]] While their publication was in progress, at Mr Bogue's request I applied to Mr Thackeray (with whom I was then in close intercourse, and a single chapter of whose 'Snob papers' contained more wit than any half-dozen of Albert Smith's and Angus Reach's 'Physiologies') to write as many volumes as he chose to undertake at the price of one hundred guineas each. This being double the amount Thackeray was then receiving for a monthly part of *Vanity Fair* (including the etching of a couple of plates), he frankly admitted that the offer was a tempting one, but he eventually declined it, by reason of his strong disinclination to ally himself with anything that Albert Smith was connected with.

Thackeray, who had an abhorrence of things vulgar, found Smith's *mauvais goût* more than he could stand. When brought into contact with him he treated him with contemptuous toleration, showing him outward civility, but the occasional sarcastic observations which he permitted to escape him, disclosed his true sentiments respecting Albert's mountebank ways. Subsequently, when I offered Thackeray, on the part of Messrs Smith & Elder, a thousand pounds to write a novel for them, he at once accepted the commission, and the result was *Esmond*,[9] not published, I think, till two or three years afterwards. The publishers, who had expected that the work would relate to modern times, were in the first instance disappointed; but I subsequently learned from Mr Smith Williams, their literary adviser, that the immediate success of *Esmond* had so far exceeded their expectations, that a cheque for £250 beyond the sum agreed upon had been handed to Mr Thackeray. . . .

[Later Vizetelly refers to the Garrick Club affair of 1858.]

Thackeray, as everyone knows, showed himself absurdly sensitive, mounted the high horse, and scolded Yates as though he were a peccant schoolboy, whereupon the latter retorted with what was certainly a bumptious epistle to a man in Thackeray's position and so much Yates's senior. As we all know, the painfully susceptible author of *Vanity Fair* sent the correspondence to the committee of the Garrick Club, with the result that for a harmless bit of banter – altogether a mild production in comparison with similar flights of Thackeray's in his salad days – Yates was expelled the Club of which both he and Thackeray were members, and a lasting coolness ensued between Thackeray and Dickens, who had been Yates's adviser and principal supporter after the affair had grown to unpleasant proportions.

I have alluded to this literary squabble because the dissension, instead of being put an end to by the autocratic action of the Garrick Club committee, was kept alive on Thackeray's part by semi-veiled allusions, in *The Virginians*, to Yates as Young Grub Street, and on Yates's side by intermittent sarcastic references to the current writings of the author of *Vanity Fair*, in the 'Lounger' column of the *Illustrated Times* [which Vizetelly edited]. Several of Thackeray's youthful admirers on the staff of the paper conceived themselves to be in some way identified with whatever appeared in its columns, and, when Yates, among a batch of pretended Burns centenary prize poems, furnished a rather spiteful travesty of Thackeray's 'Bouillabaisse' ballad they urged me to curb the licence he was giving to his pen. The incriminated stanzas were, I fancy, these:

[*Thackeray loquitur.*]

. . . I show the vices which besmirch you,
   The slime with which you 're covered o'er,
Strip off each rag from female virtue,
   And drag to light each festering sore.

All men alive are rogues and villains,
   All women drabs, all children cursed;
I tell them this, and draw their shillin's;
   They highest pay when treated worst.

I sneer at every human feeling
  Which truth suggests, or good men praise;
Then, tongue within my cheek concealing,
  Write myself 'Cynic' – for it pays![10]

There is no denying the animus here. With all Thackeray's cynicism, no one who knew him intimately would for a moment deny that he was one of the most liberal-minded and kindest of men. As, however, he peevishly continued his uncomplimentary allusions to Yates, I declined to interfere – though Thackeray had himself sent me a message on the subject by Hannay – on the ground that it would be unfair to Yates to close the only channel open to him through which he could respond to these uncalled-for attacks. This brought about a crisis in our own little set, and some half-dozen valued members of my staff threatened to resign in a body unless the offending versifier were peremptorily dismissed. Their demand, however, was not acceded to; and, on reflection, they refrained from giving effect to their injudicious threat.[11]

NOTES

1. As Ray points out (*LPP*, II, 132n), while this description of the Jermyn Street lodgings may well be accurate, Vizetelly cannot have called upon him there in the winter of 1842–3, when the *Pictorial Times* was being planned. Thackeray did not move from Coram Street to Jermyn Street until May 1843.

2. For Ballantine, see below, II, 294, 298.

3. Thackeray received £60 a number for *Vanity Fair* – *LPP*, II, 225; and see Peter L. Shillingsburg, 'Thackeray and the Firm of Bradbury & Evans', *Victorian Studies Association* [*of Ontario*] *Newsletter*, no. 11 (Mar 1973) pp. 11–14. On the disputed date of this novel's writing, see John Sutherland, 'A Date for the Early Composition of *Vanity Fair*', *English Studies*, LIII (1972) 47–52, and his 'A *Vanity Fair* Mystery: the Delay in Publication', *Costerus*, n.s. II (1974) 185–92.

4. The publisher Colburn certainly had 'the commencement of a novel wh. I gave into your hands' (almost certainly *Vanity Fair*), the return of which Thackeray requested on 8 May 1845 (*LPP*, II, 198n). In an undated letter, Thackeray said that he had 'tried 3 or 4 publishers' with his manuscript, but they were not interested (*Adversity*, p. 384).

5. In the following paragraphs, here omitted, Vizetelly records the pleasant detail that, on the strength of the success of *Vanity Fair*, Thackeray 'now sported a young footman . . . a lackey out of livery'.

6. For Hole's statement, see below, II, 252.

7. Here Vizetelly cites the anecdote that 'Mark Lemon used to tell' about Thackeray's being much impressed by the death of Paul Dombey: see Hodder, below, II, 237–8. Thackeray's comments on *The Old Curiosity Shop* occur in 'Jerome Paturot', *Fraser's Magazine*, XXVIII (1843) 351.

8. See Raymund Fitzsimons's biography of Smith, *The Baron of Piccadilly* (1967) pp. 63–4. Albert Smith (1816–60), author, journalist, lecturer and showman, was a brash vulgarian. Vizetelly continues with descriptions of his 'imbecile canons of taste in literature and art . . . huge self-conceit . . . noisy self-assertion and boisterous behaviour', which 'few of [his] associates could stand' (*Glimpses*, I, 319). Earlier he had quoted Smith's famous 'praise' of Thackeray, in 1848: 'Last night I met Thackeray at the Cyder Cellars, and we stayed there until three in the morning. He is a very jolly fellow, and no High Art about him' (ibid., I, 171). Angus Reach (1821–56), mentioned below, was another Bohemian journalist, associated with *Punch*.

9. 'Although Mr Thackeray was undoubtedly a generous-minded man, he was not in the habit, after the success he had achieved with *Vanity Fair*, of setting less than a publisher's value upon his literary labours. And certainly when I proposed to him the by no means exorbitant sum of a thousand pounds, he never for one moment suggested that the amount was excessive' [Vizetelly's footnote].

10. *Illustrated Times*, 29 Jan 1859. On Yates and the Garrick Club affair, see below, II, 313.

11. Later Vizetelly offers an account of another literary squabble, which embittered the closing months of Thackeray's life: the coolness between him and the National Shakespeare Committee. Vizetelly, supporting Thackeray in this dispute and the subsequent recriminations, published a pamphlet impugning his alleged enemies: *The National Shakespeare Committee and the Late Mr Thackeray* (1864). See *LPP*, IV, 416–17, Appendix XXV.

With the Artist Banditti in Rome

SAMUEL BEVAN

(1) from Samuel Bevan, *Sand and Canvas: Narrative of Adventures in Egypt, with a Sojourn among the Artists in Rome* (1849) pp. 336–42; (2) from Eyre Crowe, *Thackeray's Haunts and Homes* (1897) pp. 41–2. Thackeray, stopping off in Rome from November 1844 to February 1845 on his way home from Egypt, wrote in his diary, 9 Dec 1844: 'In these days I've been . . . spending the night smoking with the Artist banditti' (*LPP*, II, 157). One of these was Samuel Bevan (who later indeed wrote a book on the art of smoking). Here he recalls 'Titmarsh' as a welcome addition to this Bohemian fraternity.

(1) Of the great men who visited Rome during this winter, M. A. Titmarsh was among the most popular. Himself an artist, he dropped down among us on his way from Cairo, no one knowing when he came or how he went away. Installed in a quiet bedroom at Franz's, in the Condotti, he appeared to amuse himself, like Asmodeus, with peering into the studios of his countrymen, and while he rummaged over their dusty portfolios, or critically scanned the pictures on the wall, would unconsciously read their secret thoughts, and penetrate, as it were, the arcana of their pockets, without allowing them for a moment to imagine that he intended aught save a mere friendly visit. Many, however, were the poor devils who managed to push through the winter on the strength of the timely fillip administered by Titmarsh,[1] who was moreover one of those pleasant paymasters who get a bad character because they make their settlements beforehand. . . .

I met Titmarsh at many of the evening parties which were held at this season by the artists. Perhaps the greatest display of this sort was made on a certain holiday, when the whole of us dined together at Bertini's, and he was voted into the chair. It happened unfortunately, that the dinner provided on the occasion was of a most indifferent character, and very ill-calculated to impress the F. C.[2] with any great idea of Roman advancement in gastronomy. Our motive, however, for thus meeting in a social way, was not that of mere feasting: a great amount of elocution had to be got through, in addition to the usual round of song and sentiment. It happened just at this time, that there was a schism among the members of the English Academy in Rome respecting a proposition originating with Mack – that an Italian Professor of drawing should be appointed to the Academy! This proposal had met with the most vigorous and animated opposition from the other faction, headed by O'Neil, who had proved himself a most able champion, having set forth in an eloquent and elaborate speech, the consequences of such a measure. . . .

With this important question fresh upon the tapis, it was no wonder that a considerable portion of the evening was consumed in long-winded speeches, and had it not been for a deeply guttural proposal on the part of our friend Beardman, 'to take the basso part in a glee', a harmonious feeling would scarcely have been arrived at. His instigation was succeeded by

a call for a song from the chair, amid a vociferous shout of
'Viva Titmarsh!' and a deafening clatter of dessert furniture.
Our great friend assured us he was unable to sing, but would
endavour to make amends by getting up a recitation, if
someone in the mean time would make a beginning. Whilst a
few, therefore, on the right of the chair, were tantalising the
company by a tortured version of one of Calcott's glees, the
F. C., busy with his tablets under the table, produced the
following affecting narrative, of which he soon after delivered
himself in a fittingly lugubrious tone of voice [Bevan gives the
text of Thackeray's ballad 'The Three Sailors']. It is needless
to say that the recital of M. A. Titmarsh was received with all
the applause it merited.

(2) [How Bevan was able to quote Thackeray's eighteen
stanzas is explained by Eyre Crowe, on whom see below, I,
133.] Mr Samuel Bevan . . . sent Thackeray a rough copy of
these verses, asking permission to publish them in his book.
With his astonishing *bonhomie* and anxiety to humour a
friend's wish, Titmarsh consented, repairing the vocabulary
where faulty, and making a present of what is the gem of that
work.[3] This was not done without a feeling of compunction, as
may be gathered from an exclamation of his, blurted out to me
to this effect: 'He might just as well have let me publish the
verses myself, when I should have pocketed the fiver, to which
I felt entitled.' The generosity was genuine; the lament
whispered in mock gravity.

NOTES

1. 'That artists are sometimes grievously *hard up*, there can be little
doubt . . .' [Bevan's footnote, which continues with an instance].
2. ' The Fat Contributor' was one of Thackeray's *Punch* pseudonyms.
3. For Thackeray's letter to Bevan, passing the proofs of these pages of
Sand and Canvas, see *LPP*, II, 483, where Ray notes that 'The Three Sailors'
was based upon an old Breton song.

Twopenny Tarts and Cigars

WILLIAM AND JANE BROOKFIELD

A Collection of Letters of W. M. Thackeray 1847–1855, ed. Jane O. Brookfield (1887) p. 176, for the 'twopenny tart' story; other items from Charles and Frances Brookfield, *Mrs Brookfield and her Circle* (1905) I, 7, 242–4, 247–8; II, 300–2, 354, 504–5. Charles Brookfield (1809–74) met Thackeray at Cambridge, where he was a witty, debonair and admired figure, and their friendship became very close after Brookfield, who had been ordained in 1834, became a curate in London in 1840. In 1841 Brookfield married Jane Octavia Elton (1821–96), daughter of Charles Elton, scholar and later 6th Baronet. Their household became, especially in the later 1840s, central to Thackeray's social and emotional life. He breakfasted with them every Saturday and often met or called upon them on other days. 'William', said Mrs Brookfield at this time, 'is always either dining with Mr Thackeray at some chop-house, or sitting late smoking cigars with the great author, or else to be found on his way to Kensington to visit him' – Frances M. Brookfield, 'W. M. Thackeray and his Friends', *Munsey's Magazine*, XLVI (1911) 367. In 1847 he could claim to have been more intimate 'than anybody else probably' with Brookfield over the past three years, and Brookfield was 'offering to go halves in housekeeping with me, Mrs B. managing the children – loving her as I do – mong Dieu what a temptation it was! but you see the upshot. That *would* be dangerous, and so I keep off!' (*LPP*, II, 280, 322). As this implies, Jane Brookfield had became more than the admired wife of his old friend. The intricate and painful story of Thackeray's growing, thwarted and disillusioned passion for Jane Brookfield – which considerably affected his fictional presentations of love – may be followed in *Wisdom*, chs 3 and 5. The Brookfields' marriage having deteriorated, Thackeray and Jane became declared lovers and mutual comforters in 1848; their love remained chastely sentimental, though Thackeray was explicit, to others, about his sensual attraction to her. In 1851 William Brookfield, who had more reasons than marital possessiveness to be an unhappy man, quarrelled violently with Thackeray, whose relationship with the Brookfields never regained its intimacy. Unfortunately, their published accounts of or references to Thackeray are by no means as revealing as the length and intensity of their knowledge of him might justify; Brookfield was emotionally very reticent, and sharply discouraged his wife from expressions of 'sentiment', and their children's memoirs and editing were appropriately discreet. In 1887, Mrs Brookfield shocked many people by publishing a collection – albeit highly selective – of Thackeray's letters to her.

[*17 May 1834*, Brookfield to his brother Charles.] Thackeray . . . may or may not call [upon you] – but in any case is a man utterly incapable of entertaining a moment's feeling towards any being on earth, which should give pain.

When, soon after our marriage [in 1841, writes Jane Brookfield], Mr Brookfield introduced his early college friend, Mr Thackeray, to me, he brought him one day unexpectedly to dine with us. There was, fortunately, a good plain dinner, but I was young and shy enough to feel embarrassed because we had no sweets, and I privately sent my maid to the nearest confectioner's to buy a dish of tartlets, which I thought would give a finish to our simple meal. When they were placed before me, I timidly offered our guest a small one, saying, 'Will you have a tartlet, Mr Thackeray?' 'I will, but I'll have a twopenny one, if you please', he answered so beamingly, that we all laughed, and my shyness disappeared.[1]

[*26 Aug 1847*, Brookfield to his wife.] [Thackeray] sits beside me – brewing *Vanity* – in a dreadful fright lest the month of Sept. should arrive before No. next.[2] . . . [Brookfield told her on the following day:] At eight last night I proceeded to the Garrick Club where Mr Thackeray had been writing, dinner consisted of oysters following stewed sammon, beef fillets with olives ensued, a grouse and cheese concluded, while champagne and claret accompanied. We then adjourned to another house in company with an old medical gentleman who had been at Waterloo. Thackeray wished to get some hints for his forthcoming No. We smoked a little and parted friends at about twelve.

[*2 Oct 1847*, Mrs Brookfield to Henry Hallam.] There is a new *Vanity* not good – except the wicked ones – Mr Thackeray has now got a 2nd Amelia, Lady Jane Sheepshanks. I wish he had made Amelia more exciting especially as the remark is he has thought of me in her character.[3] . . . You know he told William that though Amelia was not a copy of me he shd not have conceived the character if he had not known me – and though she has the right amount of antiphlegm and affectionateness she is really an uncommonly dull and selfish character. . . .

[27 Sep 1849, Mrs Brookfield to Harry Hallam.] I only wish Mr Thackeray had anything to fall back upon when he recovers from this illness, instead of that constant writing which wears him so much, and which he can never have any rest from, unless he could get some settled employment, which would not be such a strain upon him as this fagging composition is. . . .

[3 Oct 1849, Mrs Brookfield to her husband.] . . . still more uneasy about Mr Thackeray. . . . The doctors are there three or four times a day. . . . I feel sorry that you are not able to be with him, as he can see no one to whom he can talk at all seriously, or who can really be of comfort. The day I was there he talked of the end, as possibly near at hand, and said he could look forward without dread to it, that he felt a great love and charity for all mankind, and tho' there were many things he would wish undone in his life, he yet felt a great trust and hope in God's love and mercy, and if it was His will, he would go to-morrow, and only feel about leaving the children unprotected. I did not think then that he was likely again to be in danger, and felt afraid of his exciting himself by talking in that strain, but I am now sorry I did not encourage him to say more, as it seemed a comfort to him to speak of it, and he said he felt quite happy and peaceful, that it had done him good to speak to me, and that you were the only other person he could do so to, and he spoke of you with much affection.[4] Now I reproach myself for having rather turned off his thoughts from his own state, and tried to amuse him by talking of indifferent things, when perhaps it may have been the last opportunity he would have to talk to anyone of his feelings in dying, if that is really near at hand, which I cannot help fearing. . . .

[On Thackeray's death, Kate Perry (on whom see below, 1, 88) wrote to Mrs Brookfield that he had told her that the women he had loved were six – his mother and his daughters, herself and her sister Jane Elliott, and Mrs Brookfield: and she continued] Ah! you knew him better than anybody else. And he was always so delightful in your presence; I think you have a magic effect upon every one. You, Jane Brookfield, Jane Elliott, and I, were Thackeray's real friends, and, oh, the comfort he was to us all.

NOTES

1. This episode evidently became a well-remembered joke between them. Five years later, Thackeray, writing to reassure Brookfield that his feelings about Jane were 'not the least dangerous', stated that he was not ashamed of any of his thoughts about her 'since the days of the dear old twopenny tart dinner till now' (*LPP*, II, 272).

2. This September instalment (no. IX, chs 30–2) was the famous 'Waterloo' number.

3. Thackeray made various inconsistent remarks to her and to others, about how far Amelia's character derived from hers. Mrs Brookfield remained unflattered by 'appearing' thus in *Vanity Fair*.

4. Much of this letter, to here, is cited from the manuscript in *Wisdom*, p. 88, and continues with a sentence omitted in the 1905 text: 'If he ever has talked too much of "sentiment" – it was all forgotten then.' This alludes to Brookfield's strong dislike of emotional expressiveness, and his wariness about Thackeray's having overstepped the bounds of decorum in his affection for Mrs Brookfield.

Our Beloved Giant, Our King of Men

HENRIETTE CORKRAN

Celebrities and I (1902) pp. 18–30, 106–9. 'Among Thackeray's closest friends in Paris [1844] were John Frazer Corkran (d. 1884), his wife, and their five children. . . . Corkran, a miscellaneous writer and Paris correspondent of the *Morning Herald*, was a genial, impractical, and eccentric Irishman' (Ray, *LPP*, II, 140n). Thackeray continued to see him and his family when they moved to London in the late 1850s and, Corkran having fallen on bad times, he helped him financially (see *LPP*, IV, 8, 129, 156). He much liked Corkran, whose daughter records (*Celebrities and I*, p. 110) his saying that 'When Corkran dies he will go straight to heaven, and all the angels will turn out and present arms to him.' Henriette (d. 1911), Corkran's second daughter, wrote a few novels and other miscellaneous books. Another version of her early memories of Thackeray appeared in *Temple Bar*, LXXXI (1887) 238–41.

My earliest recollection of a celebrity is William Thackeray. I was then about seven years of age, and we were living in Paris. . . . My mother's . . . *salons* were the rendezvous of artistic and literary people, who met there to converse. No one made such a vivid impression on my childish imagination as Mr Thackeray. He is the central figure which stands out in strong relief from the blurred surroundings. He had a formidable appearance, being over six feet, and broad in proportion. I distinctly recall the big head with the silvery hair, the rosy face, the spectacles, and the sunny, sweet smile which illumined his face and made it beautiful. I even admired the broken nose, and wondered how a boy could ever have been so wicked and audacious as to punch this great man's nose. I had heard of the famous *Vanity Fair*, and wondered why so celebrated a man should care to talk to us little children, and even play with us in such a simple, kindly way. He certainly was not too great or too tall to take an interest in our games. He would inquire after my dolls (I had six), remembering their names, and he even made a genealogical tree, so that every *poupée* had a distinct history of her own. We five children clustered round his knees like Lilliputians round Brobdingnag. No wonder Mr Thackeray was our beloved giant.

One afternoon, as I was returning from the Tuileries with my father, we passed the famous English pastrycook's shop, Colombain, in La Rue du Luxembourg. I gave a longing look at the cakes so temptingly displayed in the window. Suddenly I heard a voice, which seemed something like an angel's from Heaven, saying, 'Oh, give her a tart.'

My father, who was a great dreamer (he was then in Dreamland), shook himself like a big dog and exclaimed, 'Hallo, Thackeray! Did not know you were in Paris.'

'Arrived last night', was the answer; then, taking me by the hand, 'Come with me, and choose what cakes you like best to eat. I see a grand display of open fruit tarts on that big table.' Mr Thackeray conducted me solemnly to the spot. 'Now, eat as many as you can devour, while I have a talk with your father outside.'

I suppose I was a greedy little girl, for I remarked, 'How nice to be always hungry, and always to have as many tarts as one can eat!'

Mr Thackeray's spectacles twinkled with fun. He left me, and while I devoured the cakes I saw Mr Thackeray go towards a very poor, delicate woman, holding in her arms a wretched baby. She was leaning for support against a tree, evidently in great destitution. He walked up to the woman, talked to her, and I saw him slip a five-franc in her hand.

He re-entered the shop with my father. 'Dear old plum-cakes!' exclaimed Mr Thackeray, 'how they remind me of my schooldays.' He took off his hat and bowed comically to them. When going out of the shop he presented me with a big one wrapped up in paper. . . .

[One summer day, Thackeray called. The children's parents were away, the cook had a day off, and Reine – the somewhat terrifying *bonne d'enfants* – was trying to make them drink some disgustingly greasy soup. Henriette had rebelled, throwing her soup away, and was expecting punishment. Thackeray's arrival was a godsend.] His gold-rimmed spectacles gleamed with suppressed fun. He took the spoon and . . . tasted the soup. I shall never forget the funny grimace he made.

He got up, smiled at us little ones (how delightful his smile was!), beckoned to Reine, whispered something into her ear, then they both went into the house. After a few minutes Mr Thackeray returned.

'It is all right now,' said our dear giant, 'I have pacified Reine, and you', putting his hand on my shoulder, 'will no longer be fed like a baby.' And to be sure, when Reine reappeared she looked crestfallen and almost meek.

'Put on your hats and *pelisses*, children, and I will take you out in a *voiture* and give you a treat.' Oh, how happy he made us that day! He told us a story of a giant who had a bed made of chocolate, which he licked continually; pillows of sponge-cakes; blankets made of jellies; chairs made of delicious *bonbons* – how we envied this personage. The *fiacre* stopped in front of a *patisserie*, and we all had cakes and *bonbons*. I remember Mr Thackeray pulled a large red silk pocket-handkerchief out of one of his pockets and wiped our faces. Small wonder that he was our king of men.

Most of my Thackeray incidents seem more or less to relate to food. . . . One late afternoon, after having told us many thrilling stories, Mr Thackeray looked at his watch, exclaiming, 'It is time for me to go and get some dinner. I am so hungry.' We coaxed him to remain, and asked him what he would like to eat. 'There is nothing, my little dear, you can give me', he answered with a funny little sigh. 'I have queer tastes, and could only eat the chop of a rhinoceros or a slice from an elephant.'

'I can give it you', exclaimed my youngest sister, disappearing into a cupboard. She emerged with a look of triumph on her face, holding in her hand a wooden rhinoceros, and an elephant from her Noah's ark, and, putting the two animals on a plate, she handed them with great gravity to Mr Thackeray. Oh, what a look of delight on the great man's face! How he chuckled and rubbed his hands! Then, taking my sister up in his arms, he kissed her, remarking, 'Ah, little rogue, you already know the value of a kiss.' Then he asked for a knife and fork, smacked his lips, and pretended to devour the elephant and rhinoceros.

One evening I had gone to bed, Mr Thackeray, peeping into the room, spied my crinoline, which was on a chair. He examined it, and to my horror put his big head through the aperture, and walked into the drawing-room with it round his neck, looking like Michael Angelo's statue of Moses.

A few months later Mr Thackeray and I had a quarrel. I was an impulsive child, unlike my sister Alice, who always had a loving manner and charming ways with almost everyone she knew. I used to envy her caressing, flattering manners, which seemed to express more than she could possibly feel for so many. I was brusque, and even to those I cared for most deeply, my manner was reserved and cold, almost rude.

One afternoon, about a year after the soup episode, as I was taking my usual promenade with my father, we met a friend, who casually remarked that Mr Thackeray would be in Paris on the following day.

'I am so glad, for I love Mr Thackeray, he is so kind; he always gives us each a new five-franc piece', I blurted out. The moment I heard my voice muttering this I could have torn my tongue out of my mouth. It would probably be repeated to Mr Thackeray, and he would think I cared for him because he gave me a five-franc piece every time he came to see us.

Nobody can know what I suffered. My affection for Mr Thackeray was entirely disinterested. He was my hero, who took such a tender interest in our little lives, and he would now imagine that I only cared for what he gave me. I was miserable. What could I say or do to obliterate this most unfortunate remark about his giving me a five-franc piece? How could I show him that I cared for him and not for any little present he made me? How could I prove that it was his sweet, kindly, delightful self alone that I loved?

The next night, when I and my two sisters were in our three respective beds, they soon fell fast asleep, but I could not close my eyes; I was too tormented. My unfortunate speech, 'He always gives us a new five-franc piece', resounded in my ears, making me feel miserable. I now heard his pleasant voice talking to my father and mother in the adjoining *salon*. Our bedroom door was cautiously opened, and in marched Mr Thackeray, my mother preceding him, holding a lighted candle.

Our three little iron beds were in a row; I closed my eyes, pretending to be asleep, but I could just see that he was smiling at us. Then, putting his hand in his pocket, he murmured, 'Now for the distribution of medals', and chuckling, he deposited on each of our pillows a five-franc piece, remarking, 'They will think the fairies have been here.' But the moment the coin was on my pillow I opened my eyes and hissed out impetuously, 'I won't have any money; no more five-franc pieces for me. I like you for *yourself*, not for what you give me.' Sitting up in bed I hurled the silver piece, and heard it rolling down the parquet floor.

'Oh, what can this burst of passion mean?' I heard my mother exclaim; 'oh, you naughty girl!'

'I suppose she thinks she is getting too big to have money given to her', remarked Mr Thackeray, with a shade of disappointment in his voice.

When they left the room I burst into an agony of tears, and sobbed and sobbed till I thought my heart would break. . . .

Though I was fond of Mr Thackeray, his old mother, Mrs Carmichael-Smyth terrified me. I can just recollect a very tal , handsome, stately, stern woman, arrayed in black velvet. . . . When Mrs Carmichael-Smyth talked about God to me she always made me think that He was an angry, harsh, old gentleman, who saw every little act of mine, and would eventually punish me. Her description of hell was terrible [and, after one such talk about damnation, Henriette fled from the apartment in terror]. I never would go again to see Mrs Carmichael-Smyth – wild horses could not have driven me there – the atmosphere stifled me. She sent me a message that she earnestly prayed God to make me a good, obedient child. I often wondered how the charming, humorous, kindly William Thackeray could be the son of such an austere old lady. I never solved that riddle. . . .

My sister fell dangerously ill [when the family was living in London], and Mr Thackeray, who was then living in Onslow Square, called nearly every day at our house in Thistle Grove, bringing delicacies of every sort to tempt the appetite of the young invalid.

His cook, who was a *cordon bleu*, had received orders to exert her culinary powers to their utmost, and she made the most exquisite dishes and jellies. I remember a note from Thackeray to my mother, with the words 'A Last Appeal' written in capital letters, begging that the jellies should in the future be made with old sherry or the best Madeira. The doctor had ordered claret. One day Mr Thackeray walked up to our house carrying a rug of very bright, pleasant colours under his arm, which he himself laid down on the floor of my sister's room, thinking it would tend to raise her spirits. With children he was always delightful; with older or unsympathetic people he could be satirical, cold and cynical. He one day remarked to an acquaintance, in my mother's hearing, that he only liked 'second-rate books, second-rate women, but first-rate wines'. I often wondered if he was sincere when he uttered this remark. . . .

Mr Thackeray suffered at times from mental depression, I heard my father say so more than once. He had a soft, low voice, and the most delightful smile. To ordinary acquaintances he was cold, dignified, impassible, but with a friend he was grave and sincere, and, my father often remarked, unrestrainedly expansive. He would then unveil his inmost thoughts, his secret and sacred feelings, but in his most attractive mood, he should be seen with little children.

'My [*Cornhill*] number is nearly due, and I cannot make it come', he once said to my father, tapping his forehead. 'Yes. I would like to rest my head in some quiet corner. I had a nice scene this morning, but it is all gone, and I cannot call to mind a bit of it now.' . . .

My father, who knew a little of him before the success of *Vanity Fair*, told me that when in Paris he often saw Thackeray writing in an old-fashioned *cabinet de lecture*. Then it dawned upon him that as literature was to be his profession he ought to settle in London. One day he remarked to my father, 'I think there is room for a light-comedy man. I think I am a good second, good for some seven hundred copies!' At this period he took a very modest estimate of himself; but of course such self-depreciation of his literary powers, as he so frequently expressed to my father, was before the publication of *Vanity Fair*. The enormous success of this novel at once ranked him with his favourite, Fielding.

Yet the same disposition to measure fairly his own strength was shown when speaking of his own illustrations. Though he had great artistic ambition he used to confess that it was his want of knowledge of the technique of art which prevented his completing his own conception. . . .

In my father's time of trouble Mr Thackeray was much more than a brother to him. I am sure that he fully appreciated my father's nature – a proud, over-sensitive man, full of intellect, but shy and unobtrusive. My mother told me that when he heard for the first time of my parents' pecuniary loss he was most agitated, and turning to my mother he asked her what she was going to do.

'I mean to trust to the ravens', she answered.

An expression of pain flitted over the great man's face, but after a few seconds of silence he put his large hand over hers, and in a husky voice said, 'And so you may; the ravens are kind friends.'

The Cockney in Ireland, 1842

HARRY INNES AND FRANK DWYER

From W. J. Fitzpatrick, *Life of Charles Lever* (1879) II, 396–7, 405–20. In the summer and autumn of 1842, Thackeray was in Ireland to work on his *Irish Sketch Book*, published the following year, and he visited the popular Irish novelist Charles Lever (1806–72), then also Editor of the *Dublin University Magazine*, at his country house outside Dublin. He 'made himself very agreeable during his stay', writes Fitzpatrick (*Life of Lever*, I, 337), 'and was a favourite with the children'. The *Sketch Book* was dedicated to Lever – 'who, I fear, must disapprove of a great deal which it contains' – and indeed Lever suffered from this association with a book which offended Irish susceptibilities. He reviewed it favourably, however, and was thus the more incensed when Thackeray a few years later reviewed him coolly and lampooned his work; Lever riposted by accusing Thackeray, with some justice, of viewing Ireland or any other country through complacently Cockney eyes (see next item). Thackeray's certainty that England and London were best appears in an account of their conversations which Lever soon afterwards gave to his cousin Harry Innes, in whose opinion Lever's moving to London in 1845 was much influenced by Thackeray's arguments.

He told me [writes Innes] that Thackeray arrived in Dublin under the impression that he (Lever) was under a cloud from some disagreement with London publishers, that otherwise he was unable to see a reason why he should settle in Dublin and not in London. And assuming this to be so, Thackeray offered assistance pecuniary or otherwise, to smooth matters, so as to open or reopen the way to literary headquarters. Lever's reply was, that he was an Irishman, body, soul and spirit; that his good name and fame, such as they were, were also Irish, and that he thought his duties lay in Ireland, and that he expected to make them both pleasant and profitable. Thackeray asked him to look around him. He was, he told him, surrounded by a lot of third-class men. Able Irish writers, he said, were numerous, but they had gone to London, where alone their talents would be rewarded. None remained at home except a few that looked for advancement in the professions or patronage from the sham court; that in Ireland there was no public opinion; that Dublin was split up into factions, coteries, and classes, jealous of each other, and engaged in miserable squabbles. That the *Magazine*, if carried across the water, would be more Irish than it was; for many Irishmen of real genius could be had in London, and none could be had in Ireland. Thackeray added that, though Lever was just then popular, he would some day, perhaps, inadvertently tread on some Irishman's corns, and Irishmen's feet are all corns (he remarked), and then his worshippers would treat him, as the Chinese do their gods when they disappoint them, chop off their heads. . . .

Lever concluded by telling me his determination was to stick to the ship, but I thought afterwards of the fact, that he put

Thackeray's arguments for the movement, in a strong and convincing way, and his own for remaining where he was, in the weakest possible manner. In this conversation Lever pronounced Thackeray to be the most good-natured man alive, but, that help from him would be worse than no help at all. 'He is like', he said, 'a man struggling to keep his head over water, and who offers to teach his friend to swim.' Thackeray, he said, would write for anything, and about anything; and had so lost himself that his status in London was not good. I know Lever's opinion of Thackeray underwent a complete change later on, but in 1842 with *Vanity Fair* unpublished, and *Esmond* unwritten, would the public verdict be very different from Lever's?

[Major Frank Dwyer, a lifelong intimate of Lever's, wrote a long account of the two authors' conversations. He and Captain William Siborne, author of *A History of the War in France and Belgium in 1815*, were invited to dine with Thackeray 'whose name was quite unknown' to them, though Lever had told them that he was a humorist writing under the name of Titmarsh.] His manner was at first reserved, earnest and quiet; rather a disappointment, perhaps, to those who may have expected some external manifestation of his supposed humoristic proclivities; what was most observable seemed to be, that he was, himself, carefully observing and desirous of not being drawn out, at least, not prematurely. . . .

Both Thackeray and Lever were political partisans, politicians they could scarcely be considered; the former adopted the liberal ideas of that period to their fullest extent, and the immediate object of his visit to Ireland was to write up something in the interests of his party – the coming question of the day was the repeal of the Corn Laws; there was also something to be ascertained about Maynooth, and a faint shadowing forth of what has, since then, been known as 'Upas-tree felling'.[1] Lever's politics at this time were of a very different character.

The *Magazine*, of which he had just been appointed Editor, was, to a certain extent at least, an organ of the Castle, and Lever himself hoped in that way to obtain some suitable official position in Ireland. In most of this he was doomed to be disappointed. . . . Thackeray was more successful as a political partisan, the line of policy he followed became every day more and more triumphant; he subsequently acquired some influence with persons of high position, including Lord Palmerston; and although he never aspired to official employment for himself, he must have been in a position to further the ambition of others in that line, for I well remember his saying to me in 1846, 'I am going to dine with Lord Palmerston today, shall I mention your name to him?' Thackeray was much too truthful and straightforward a man to have made an offer of the kind without knowing that he could act upon it. He abhorred boasting and exaggeration to such an extent as to be very frequently tempted to disbelieve the naked truth and to substitute for it something which, although not exactly fictitious, was but a clipped and shorn distortion of reality; this was one of his weaknesses in so far as it constantly jarred with the great kindliness of his heart; on the other hand it incontestably strengthened the poignancy of his satire, and rendered it perhaps more acceptable to the general public. This tendency to doubt, disbelieve or attenuate every positive statement of fact, was particularly conspicuous in his judgement of Irish people and Irish affairs; he distrusted everything he heard, and a great deal of what he saw in Ireland.[2]

It was for this reason most amusing to remark how dislike of Protestant ascendancy and Saxon supremacy in Ireland flourished in his mind, or, perhaps I should say feelings, side by side, in the same hot-bed as it were, with other distrust of the Celt; vindicating too for the Roman Catholic Church in Ireland, theoretically at least, a high position, whilst he was unable to conceal his contempt for the Irish themselves. . . . Of both Lever and Thackeray, it may be truly said, that they remained faithful to their political convictions to the end. . . . Lever really liked, if not the aristocracy, at least a great many men of high birth; he had had the good fortune to have been kindly and delicately treated by more than one peer. . . . Whether Thackeray's earlier experiences had been of a different character I know not, but at the period in question, there seemed to be a tinge of resentment, indicating something of the sort in his expressed estimate of the aristocracies of his own and other countries; the impression thus conveyed was an unpleasant one, being out of harmony with his real nature, perhaps it was merely a reflection of the anti-aristocratic spirit of the moment specially evoked by the struggle for the repeal of the Corn Laws, although something of the same feeling is apparent in all his later works.

As dinner proceeded, and after the ladies had retired, the two protagonists began to skirmish, endeavouring to draw each other out. Neither knew much of the other, beyond what could be gleaned from their published works. . . . The conversation had been led by Lever to the subject of the battle of Waterloo; he wished to afford Captain Siborne an opportunity of saying a word, perhaps too, he wanted to show that he himself knew something of the matter; he had in fact picked up during his *séjour* at Brussels a certain amount of anecdote and detail that did very well for after-dinner conversation. Thackeray soon joined in; he did not pretend to know anything about the great battle, but he evidently wished to spur on Lever to identify himself with Charles O'Malley[3]. . . . I have already alluded to Thackeray's ideas, imputing want of truthfulness to the Irish; he seemed always to wish to betray every Irishman he met into boasting in some shape or on some subject. . . . Irishmen are perhaps too frequently prone to undergo, with some self-complacency, this trotting-out process, and have therefore only themselves to blame for the results. With Lever this was not the case, on that occasion at least, and, quickly perceiving his antagonist's game, he met his feints with very quiet, but perfectly efficacious parries. It was highly interesting, and not a little amusing to observe how these two men played each a part, seemingly belonging to the other; Thackeray assuming what he judged to be a style of conversation suitable for Lever, whilst the latter responded in the same sarcastic and sceptical tone, proper to an English tourist in Ireland.

French and German literature next came on the *tapis*. Thackeray seemed to value the last named more highly than the other. . . . [He] paid Lever the very handsome compliment of saying, that he would rather have written Lorrequer's English version of the Student song, 'The Pope he leads a happy life', etc., than anything he had himself hitherto done in literature. Lever could scarcely give credence to this strong piece of flattery from the mouth of the future author of *Vanity Fair*; he had made the translation for the especial benefit of the Burschen Club of which he had been founder and President in early days, and never thought very much of this piece; now it was quite evident, however, that he was very much pleased, and also finally convinced that Thackeray really meant what he said. . . . Passing on to French authors, full justice was done to the celebrities of the day: Dumas, Alphonse Karr, Balzac, George Sand, etc. Thackeray criticised the French theatre very sharply, and came out with a strong bit of humorous representation, which convulsed us with laughter. . . .

[In a later conversation with Dwyer,] Thackeray remarked that a great amount of interest still attached to everything connected with Waterloo, the British public seeming never to tire of it; he had been thinking since we met at dinner of writing something on the subject himself, but he did not see his way clearly. Lever's treatment of it in *O'Malley* seemed to him much too imaginative and high-flown, in fact audacious and regardless of all probability. . . . Thackeray thought that the amount of interest shown was a proof of the existence of a very deep-seated national feeling, and having survived so long, 'how intense', said he, 'must it have been at the time, and how widely spread amongst all classes of society'. From what Captain Siborne had mentioned at Lever's house, added to what he had himself seen [at a military review], he seemed to have arrived at the conclusion that it would be useless for him to attempt anything in the way of military scene-painting that could lay the slightest claim to correctness, and he scarcely disguised his ridicule of Lever's method of treating such matters, which by the way, he caricatured so drolly in his imitations of 'Our Novelists', shortly afterwards. On the whole, too, he seemed much inclined to 'laugh at martial might', although he still held to the idea that 'something might be made of Waterloo', even without the smoke and din of the action being introduced. I have an indistinct recollection, too, of his having said as much subsequently at Lever's house. Years afterwards, on reading *Vanity Fair*, the whole conversation and the circumstances under which it took place, came back to me, and I became aware of the great thoughtfulness and foresight with which Thackeray planned out his work, and how careful he was to attempt nothing doubtful or beyond his power.

When Thackeray, in 1842, visited Ulster, he became a great favourite with the officers of a regiment, then stationed at Newry, and was a frequent and welcome guest at their mess. Here, too, he got useful materials, and found 'sitters' for some of the events and characters introduced in the Brussels scenes of *Vanity Fair*, and on his return to Dublin from the North, I found that he had got up a considerable stock of military characteristic and anecdote. . . .

[Dwyer describes Thackeray's excursions to a military review, where the novelist's extreme nervousness seemed strange in 'such a great powerful man', and to the Catholic College at Maynooth which, as Dwyer acknowledged, was housed in dirty, dismal and mean buildings] that looked very like a sadly neglected military barrack. This was previous to the erection of the new College. Thackeray was, as I saw, busily engaged in noting down all the 'features' of the place, a sardonic smile of utter derision and contempt overspreading his own. I confess to have felt dismayed at the withering expression, part of which was very like satisfaction at having found out something very positive to fasten on. [After a brief inspection of the College and a quick getaway] Thackeray expressed great disgust at the filth and discomfort he had seen.[4] I could not help saying that Maynooth certainly was most desolate-looking; but Thackeray shut me up, by replying that Trinity College [Dublin] was not a whit better in respect of cleanliness; he was evidently in a censorious and perhaps combative humour; I felt pained and disappointed; he had shown himself in a new, and, to me, unexpected light: he had hitherto seemed so genial and amicable that I began to doubt his identity; but I saw more of the same kind of thing subsequently, and can now, on looking back, estimate, at its real value, Charlotte Bronte's notice of *Esmond* ['But what bitter Satire, what relentless dissection of diseased subjects!']. If Thackeray did not wish all the world to be good, he certainly was only too happy, when he did meet what he thought good, to recognise and admire it. His affection for Lever to the last was in itself a proof of it. . . . He was not willingly blind to whatever good came in his way. Perhaps there was more plausibility in Miss Brontë's charge as regards his attitude towards women. . . . My own experience of him leads me to believe that he only understood one side of female character and nature, and was unable to do justice to the whole. . . .

I know that Lever sincerely rejoiced at Thackeray's great success, and was a warm admirer of his writings, and perhaps no man was ever so much improved by success as Thackeray, as was perhaps most apparent to those who came in contact with him only at intervals. I remember dining at his house near Kensington in 1846, and being much struck with the great change that had taken place in him since I had seen him in Ireland in 1842. Amongst his guests on that day were two Irishmen whose names are well known, or at least were so at that time, namely, Morgan John O'Connell, M.P., and Father Prout.[5] On my chaffing about finding him in contact with Irishmen, knowing, as I did, the estimate he had frequently expressed to me of their character, he said laughingly, 'one must have sitters'.

NOTES

1. The Catholic College at Maynooth, for the training of priests, occasioned much political controversy at this time, because of strong Protestant opposition to the proposal that the small Parliamentary grant paid to it be increased. Thackeray visited Maynooth: see below.

'Upas-tree felling': the upas tree is a reputedly poisonous tree, native to South America, which spreads itself wide; the phrase quoted became current as an expression of the need to eradicate the many interrelated ills of Ireland.

2. After a later anecdote, Dwyer remarks, 'It was very evident that he smelt imposture in everything that came under his notice, in Ireland at least, and perhaps elsewhere too.'

3. Lever specialised in military swashbuckling fiction, and his *Charles O'Malley* (1840) had included the Waterloo campaign.

4. In the *Irish Sketch Book*, ch. 32, Thackeray writes that he will speak only briefly about Maynooth, because 'an accurate description of that establishment would be of necessity so disagreeable. . . . An Irish union-house is a palace to it. Ruin so needless, filth so disgusting, such a look of lazy squalor, no Englishman who has not seen can conceive.' One of the reasons he gave, in 1857, for being unable to stand for a (very Protestant) Scottish parliamentary constituency was that he supported Government grants to Maynooth (*LPP*, IV, 31).

5. On 'Father Prout', wit and author, see below, II, 284.

The Biter Bit: Thackeray as a Fictional Character

VARIOUS

Thackeray often introduced acquaintances, and public figures, into his novels in a recognisable and generally an unflattering form; but he was unamused and resentful, and could be vindictive, when the like was done to him. An early example – not from a novel but a magazine essay – appears in *Fraser's Magazine*, Apr 1843, pp. 399–400, where, in an account of bill-discounting, one of the inglorious episodes of his earlier life is recalled. In 1833 he had briefly worked in this shady occupation, and 'In later life any reference to this venture, which had been both usurious and unsuccessful, touched Thackeray on the raw' (*Adversity*, p. 159). As a leading contributor to *Fraser's*, Thackeray immediately wrote to its editor strongly protesting against being 'grossly insulted [and] abused in the Magazine' by this 'shameful and unprovoked attack' and demanding that the offending author, Deady Keane, no longer be allowed 'to execute his office as satirist' in its pages: otherwise, he would withdraw his own services (*LPP*, II, 104–5).

The first person we met in the coffee-room [of the 'Grubwell'] was Bill Crackaway, one whom we have always looked upon as a bird of ill omen. His long ungainly person is crowned with a face which Dame Nature must have fashioned just after making a bad debt, and, therefore, in the worst of tempers. A countenance of preternatural longitude is imperfectly relieved by a nose on which the partial hand of Nature has lavished every bounty – length, breadth, thickness, all but a – bridge; a mouth that seemed suddenly arrested in the act of whistling, and, from its conformation, could only eliminate a sinister sneer, but was physically incapable of the candour of an honest laugh, which, with a most inhuman squint, gave a rare finish to the *os frontis* of this Corinthian capital of our club.

The first question this worthy lispingly asked of us was, 'Have you heard the news?' To which, answering in the negative, he proceeded to inform us that Lord Edward Softhead had, to use our informant's expression, 'cut his stick and bolted'.

'On what account?'

'Oh! the bums are making some kind inquiries after him.'

'And how much does he owe?' we asked.

'Only £300,000,' was the answer; 'but, then, it is to the discounters, and I suppose, as he is rather green, he will not have touched more than £30 or 40,000.'

Now, as Crackaway added to the occupation of editor of a pseudophilosophical magazine the business of a bill-broker in the City, we take it for granted he knew something about these matters, and that, therefore, the fact of a young nobleman obtaining £30,000 at the cost of £270,000 might be considered to be true, or very nearly true.

[Thackeray had enjoyed cordial relations with the Irish novelist Charles Lever (see above, I, 64–5), but Lever was much incensed by the lampoon of his fiction in the 'Novels by Eminent Hands' series – *'Phil Fogarty: A Tale of the Fighting Onety-Oneth*, by Harry Rollicker' (*Punch*, 7–21 Aug 1847), the surname of which refers to his best-known novel, *Harry Lorrequer* (1837). He had earlier, in 1844, been outraged by what he saw as 'Thackeray's rascality' and 'blackguardism' in an unfavourable review. He now riposted with a characterisation of Thackeray as 'Elias Howle' in the seventh instalment of his serial *Roland Cashel*, ch. 22 (published Nov 1848). 'He is very savage and evidently hurt', Thackeray noted (*LPP*, II, 452). To a French correspondent· he described the character as 'un portrait assez fidèle' (*LPP*, II, 460), but in a letter to Lever's publisher, while acknowledging that the offended author had the right to attack his art, he protested against the 'sheer personality' of this attack: 'Fancy a literary war in wh a man descends to describing odious personal peculiarities in his rival! . . . Make fun of my books, my style, my public works – but of me as a gentleman – O for shame' (*LPP*, II, 456). He responded in *Punch* (2 Dec 1848) with an 'Author's Misery' item referring to Lever.]

Mr Elias Howle was one of a peculiar class, which this age, so fertile in inventions, has engendered – a publisher's man-of-all-work, ready for everything, from statistics to satire, and equally prepared to expound prophecy or write squibs for *Punch*.

Not that lodgings were not inhabited in Grub Street before our day, but it has remained for the glory of this century to see that numerous horde of tourist authors held in leash by fashionable booksellers, and every now and then let slip over some country to which plague, pestilence, or famine had given a newer and more terrible interest. In this novel walk of literature Mr Howle was one of the chief proficients; he was the creator of that new school of travel which, writing expressly for London readers, refers everything to the standard of 'town'; and whether it be a trait of Icelandic life, or some remnant of old-world existence in the far East, all must be brought for trial to the bar of 'Seven Dials', or stand to plead in the dock of Pall Mall or Piccadilly. Whatever errors or misconceptions he might fall into respecting his subjects, he made none regarding his readers. He knew them by heart – their leanings, their weakness, and their prejudices; and how pleasantly could he flatter their town-bred self-sufficiency – how slyly insinuate their vast superiority over all other citizens, insidiously assuring them that the Thames at Richmond was infinitely finer than the Rhine or the Danube, and that a trip to Margate was richer in repayal than a visit to the Bosphorus! Ireland was, just at the time we speak of, a splendid field for his peculiar talents. The misery-mongers had had their day. The world was somewhat weary of Landlordism, Pauperism, and Protestantism, and all the other 'isms' of that unhappy country. . . . [People] voted Ireland a 'bore'. It was just then that 'this inspired Cockney' determined to try a new phase of the subject; and this was not to counsel nor console, not to lament over nor bewail our varied mass of errors and misfortunes, but to laugh at us. . . . His mission was to make 'Punch' out of Ireland, and no one was more capable for the office.

A word of Mr Howle in the flesh, and we have done. He was large and heavily built, but neither muscular nor athletic; his frame and all his gestures indicated weakness and uncertainty. His head was capacious, but not remarkable for what phrenologists call moral development, while the sinister expression of his eyes – half submissive, half satirical – suggested doubts of his sincerity. There was nothing honest about him but his mouth; this was large, full, thick-lipped, and sensual – the mouth of one who loved to dine well, and yet feel that his agreeability was an ample receipt in full for the best entertainment that ever graced Blackwall or the 'Frères'. . . .

Mr Howle made his round of salutations, and although by

his awkwardness tacitly acknowledging that [the people he met] were palpably more habituated to the world's ways than himself, yet inwardly consoled by remarking certain little traits of manner and accent sufficiently provincial to be treasured up, and became very droll in print or a copper etching.

[Benjamin Disraeli (1804–81) was another author much offended by his appearance in 'Novels by Eminent Hands' – 'Codlingsby, by D. Shrewsberry, Esq.' (Punch, 24 Apr, 15–29 May 1847). He never again spoke to Thackeray (LPP, II, 149n). After 1847 he wrote no more fiction until Lothair (1870) and Endymion (1880), in the latter of which he took a belated revenge. His biographer Robert Blake writes, 'Most of the portraits in Endymion are drawn with a kindly pen. There is one exception, Thackeray who is caricatured as St Barbe. . . . Thackeray had been dead for seventeen years and . . . it was felt by many people that there was something undignified in Disraeli's belated riposte. As a picture of Thackeray, St Barbe is grotesque' – Disraeli (1966) p. 737. It is indeed: but it is excerpted here as an instance of what could seem a recognisable if obviously jaundiced sketch of Thackeray. Unluckily, short excerpts convey an inadequate sense of the character – and lengthy excerpts would be unjustified. St Barbe is an episodic character, seen briefly at various states of his career. Disraeli refers to (or imputes) Thackeray's long struggle for success, his writing for Scaramouch (Punch), his reputation as a wit, his sardonic or cynical outlook, his reiterated jealousy of his rival 'Gushy' (Dickens) – but 'he was indeed jealous of everybody and everything' (ch. 82), 'St Barbe hated Jawett, as indeed he did all his brethren' (ch. 95) – his pride in his own birth and consciousness of others' inferior social origins, his uneasy relationship (now critical, now toadying) with the aristocracy, his chagrin over being black-balled at the Athenaeum, and what Dickens called his 'pretence of undervaluing his art' (' "I hate the craft", said St Barbe, with an expression of genuine detestation' – ch. 31). Endymion, running into him again after two years, reflects, 'Unchanged: the vainest, the most envious, and the most amusing of men! I wonder what he will do in life' (ch. 51). Their previous meeting had been at a 'rather grand party' at the mansion of the Neuchatels (sc. Rothschilds). St Barbe is just off to Paris, on an honorific journalistic venture: and 'as usual he began to talk about himself' (ch. 51).]

After dinner, St Barbe pounced upon Endymion. 'Only think of our meeting here!' he said. 'I wonder why they asked you. You are not going to Paris, and you are not a wit. What a family this is!' he said; 'I had no idea of wealth before! Did you observe the silver plates? . . . But they deserve their wealth', he added; 'nobody grudges it to them. I declare when I was eating that truffle, I felt a glow about my heart that, if it were not indigestion, I think must have been gratitude; though that is an article I had not believed in. He is a wonderful man, that Neuchatel. If I had only known him a year ago! I would have dedicated my novel to him. He is a sort of man who would have given you a cheque immediately. He would not have read it, to be sure, but what of that? . . . There are some topsawyers here today, Ferrars! . . . Now I daresay that ambassador has been blundering all his life, and yet there is something in that star and ribbon; I do not know how you feel, but I could almost go down on my knees to him. And there is a cabinet minister; well, we know what he is; I have been squibbing him for these two years, and now that I meet him I feel like a snob. Oh! there is an immense deal of superstition left in the world. I am glad they are going to the ladies. I am to be honoured by some conversation with the mistress of the house. . . . I should not be surprised if Mr Neuchatel were to present me to some of the grandees. I believe them to be all impostors, but still it is pleasant to talk to a man with a star. . . .'

St Barbe was not disappointed in his hopes. It was an evening of glorious success for him. He had even the honour of sitting for a time by the side of Mrs Neuchatel, and being full of good claret, he, as he phrased it, showed his paces; that is to say, delivered himself of some sarcastic paradoxes duly blended with fulsome flattery. Later in the evening, he contrived to be presented both to the ambassador and the cabinet minister, and treated them as if they were demigods. . . . (Chs 33–4)

[Success comes for St Barbe with his novel *Topsy Turvy* – 'the tone was so divertingly cynical!' Endymion congratulates him: 'I hear of nothing but of your book; I suppose one of the most successful that have appeared for a long time.'] 'Its success is not owing to your friends', said Mr St Barbe tartly. . . . 'They need not have dissolved Parliament. . . . It was nearly fatal to me; it would have been to anybody else. I was selling 40,000 a month; I believe more than Gushy ever reached; and so they dissolved Parliament. The sale went down half at once – and now you expect me to support your party!'

'Well, it was unfortunate, but the dissolution could hardly have done you any permanent injury, and you could scarcely expect that such an event could be postponed even for the advantage of an individual so distinguished as yourself.'

'Perhaps not,' said St Barbe, apparently a little mollified, 'but they might have done something to show their regret at it.'

'Something!' said Endymion, 'what sort of thing?'

'The Prime Minister might have called on me, or at least have written to me a letter. I want none of their honours; I have scores of letters every day, suggesting that some high distinction should be conferred on me. I believe the nation expects me to be made a baronet. . . .'

'I will dine with Lord Montfort [St Barbe responds, to an invitation]. There is no one who appreciates so completely and so highly the old nobility of England as myself. They are a real aristocracy. None of the pinchbeck pedigrees and ormolu titles of the continent. Lord Montfort is, I think, an earl. A splendid title, earl! an English earl; count goes for nothing. The Earl of Montfort! An enthusiastic admirer of mine! The aristocracy of England, especially the old aristocracy, are highly cultivated. Sympathy from such a class is to be valued. I care for no other – I have always despised the million of vulgar. They have come to me, not I to them, and I have always told them the truth about themselves, that they are a race of snobs, and they rather like being told so. . . .'   (Ch. 77)

We must not forget our old friend St Barbe [writes Disraeli, in his penultinate chapter]. Whether he had written himself out or had become lazy in the luxurious life in which he now indulged, he rarely appealed to the literary public, which still admired him. He was by way of intimating that he was engaged in a great work, which, though written in his taking prose, was to be really the *épopée* of social life in this country. Dining out every day, and ever arriving, however late, at those 'small and earlies', which he once despised; he gave to his friends frequent intimations that he was not there for pleasure, but rather following his profession; he was in his studio, observing and reflecting on all the passions and manners of mankind, and gathering materials for the great work which was eventually to enchant and instruct society, and immortalise his name.

'The fact is, I wrote too early', he would say. 'I blush when I read my own books, though compared with those of the brethren, they might still be looked on as classics. They say no artist can draw a camel, and I say no author ever drew a gentleman. How can they, with no opportunity of ever seeing one? . . . However, I shall put an end to all this. I have now got the materials, or am accumulating them daily. You hint that I give myself up too much to society. You are talking of things you do not understand. A dinner party is a chapter. I catch the Cynthia of the minute, sir, at a *soirée*. If I only served a grateful country, I should be in the proudest position of any of its sons; if I had been born in any country but this, I should have been decorated, and perhaps made Secretary of State like Addison, who did not write as well as I do, though his style somewhat resembles mine.'

Young Street and *Vanity Fair*

ANNE THACKERAY RITCHIE

Sources given in the Notes. Anne Isabella (1837–1919), usually called Anny or Annie, the eldest of Thackeray's three daughters, became a respected and prolific author, and wrote extensively about her father. Of her sisters, Jane (1838–9) died in infancy, and Minny – Harriet Marian (1840–75) – was not given to writing. Anny's earliest memory of her parents relates to the Great Coram Street days, c. 1839, with her mother 'with pretty shining hair' seated at her piano (*Biog. Intros*, IV, xiii–xiv); it was Isabella's singing that had first won Thackeray's heart, he later told Anny (ibid, III, xxxvi). Grimmer memories, long kept secret, were of her mother's half-attempt to drown her (*Adversity*, p. 254); and then 'After my mother's [mental] illness the little household in Coram Street was broken up, and we all went abroad. I can remember my father punishing me as we travelled to Paris all night in the creaking diligence. I wanted to get out and walk, and they wouldn't let me, and I cried on and on' (*Biog. Intros*, IV, xxix). The girls mainly spent the next few years in Paris with their great-grandmother Mrs Butler or their grandmother Mrs Carmichael-Smyth. A memorable trip to London took place in 1845:

> Our father was living in London in chambers opposite St James Palace & he came to meet us at the station & immediately gave us each 2 wax dolls, & at breakfast he gave us bigger helps of jam than we had ever had in our lives & after breakfast he took us to feed the ducks in St James Park, & then he bought us picture books, the Arabian Nights & Grimms Fairy Tales &

then he took us to a diorama & to the Colosseum. I thought he would
spend all the money he had in the world when I saw how much he had to
pay for us. One day he took us in our flapping straw hats to see Aunt Job
[Mrs Brookfield] who was quite a young lady with curls & who gave us a
book.   (MS. Recollections, *Adversity*, p. 305)

This reunion in London made him the more sharply aware of the emptiness
of his bachelor existence; he was 'child-sick' and 'getting weary of being
alone, and want some other companions besides those over the bottle' (ibid.,
p. 306). In 1846 he set up a modest establishment in Young Street, and
brought the girls to live with him, as Anny describes below.
  'He always loved children and peaceful home doings', Anny wrote –
S. M. Ellis, *William Harrison Ainsworth and His Friends* (1911) p. 44 – and he
'used to say that perhaps on the whole the most charming thing in the world
was a little girl of two years old' (*Biog. Intros*, IX, lvii). To his daughters he was
an affectionate if not always very resourceful father. 'Papa always liked
everything we did,' wrote Anny, '& we never liked anything much until we
knew he approved' (*Wisdom*, p. 15). He had been alarmed, however, in 1846,
by signs that Anny was 'going to be a man of genius: I would far sooner have
had her an amiable & affectionate woman' (*LPP*, II, 240). Anny remained
the brainier, happier and more positive sister; Minny was shier, quieter, but
of 'angelical . . . sweetness' (*LPP*, II, 288; III, 325). At fifteen, Anny had
written several novels and a tragedy, 'but then my father forbade me to
waste my time with any more scribbling, and desired me to read *other*
people's books. I never wrote any more except one short fairy-tale, until one
day my father said he had got a very nice subject for me, and that he thought
I might now begin to write again. That was *"Little Scholars"* which he
christened for me and of which he corrected the stops and the spelling' and
which he published in the *Cornhill* (1860).[1] He was inordinately proud of her
first novel, *The Story of Elizabeth* (1863), telling Dean Hole that she wrote 'ten
times more cleverly than I' (below, II, 252), and his *Punch* friends that her
fiction displayed 'all his better and none of his worse qualities' – G. S.
Layard, *A Great 'Punch' Editor: Shirley Brooks* (1907) p. 178. Back in 1848, Mrs
Brookfield had foreseen the ten-year-old Anny, '50 years hence', writing a
memoir of her father 'according to her discretion' (*LPP*, II, 478), and this in
effect occurred. Thackeray forbade the writing of any biography (see below,
II, 372), but the publication of his letters to Mrs Brookfield, and other
developments, persuaded Anny eventually both to authorise Herman
Merivale to write a biography and to publish a discreet selection of her own
memories (see *Adversity*, pp. 4–7). These appear in *Chapters from Some
Memoirs* (1894) and in substantial introductions to the Biographical Edition
of the *Works* (1898–9, amplified in the Centenary Biographical Edition,
1911). Some more unbuttoned reminiscences of Thackeray and his family,
written in 1864–5, 1878 and 1894, survive in manuscript, as does a
fragmentary journal, and they have been drawn upon by Gordon Ray, and
in her *Letters* (1924) and in *Thackeray's Daughter* (1951); there is a prospect
that these reminiscences will soon be published. In the present collection,
Anny's recollections appear in several instalments, and are used in the
annotation.

Thackeray's unwelcome labours as a public lecturer were undertaken mainly as the surest way of leaving a sufficiency to his wife and to the girls, neither of whom, to his consternation, had attracted many suitors. Minny married Leslie Stephen in 1867. Anny, in 1877, caused a stir by marrying her cousin Richmond Ritchie (later Sir Richmond), little more than half her age; George Eliot's marrying John Cross, twenty years her junior, in 1880 is said to have been encouraged by Anny's example.

When Papa was a tall young man with black hair and an eye glass, I can remember how we used to hold his forefinger when we walked out with him. He always talked to us very gravely as if we were grown women. Later on when we grew up he spoke to us, as if we were children and would say 'Come along my little dears.'

Papa used to talk to us a great deal, and tell us about the Bible and Religion. He would talk to us of a morning after breakfast in his study, and of an evening after dinner smoking his cigar, and we generally sat on the floor and listened to him. And then we would give him a chair for his legs and a little table for his candles and he would presently nod to us and go to sleep.

Papa could not bear the story of Abraham. He used to say that one day when I was a little girl he came in and found Mamma telling me in her sweet voice about Isaac, and that I burst into tears, and stamped and flew into a passion. I can remember it quite well too, and Papa taking me on his knee and Mamma looking a little shocked. . . .

We came to Young Street when I was nine and Minny was six. Papa was not at home when we arrived,[2] but early next morning when we were half dressed and the maid was tying our strings, he tapped at the door and came and took us in his arms.

Everything seemed so strangely delightful. The volumes of *Punch* on the drawing-room table, the delightful keepsake books in their red covers, the old school-room with the bookcase and the cupboards, and Papa's room with the vine round about the windows and the sun pouring in.

Papa called Minny Min and me Nan very often, and when we were little, he used to call Minny Finniken and me Buff and sometimes Frederica and Louisa. . . .

On Sunday mornings in Young Street we had no lessons and we used to sit with my father in his study and help him

with his wood blocks, also it was often our business to rub out
the failures and to wash the chalk off the blocks. I can still
remember a dreadful day when I washed away a finished
drawing for which the messenger from *Punch* was at that
moment waiting in the hall.

Upstairs in the schoolroom at the top of the house we used
to do our lessons of a week-day, and sometimes to our joy we
would be called downstairs by my father, and he would pose us
as models for his drawings to *Punch* or *Vanity Fair*.

Then when I was fourteen my father first began to make use
of me as his secretary and to dictate his books to me. That was
in 1851, the year of the great Exhibition, and one wonderful
and never-to-be-forgotten night my father took us to see some
great ladies in their dresses going to the Queen's fancy-dress
ball at Buckingham Palace.[3]

Ours was more or less a bachelor's establishment, and the
arrangements of the house varied between a certain fastidi-
ousness and the roughest simplicity. We had shabby table-
cloths, alternating with some of my grandmother's fine linen;
we had old Derby china for our dessert of dried figs and dry
biscuits, and a silver Flaxman teapot (which always poured
oblations of tea upon the cloth) for breakfast, also three
cracked cups and saucers of unequal patterns and sizes. . . .

Our London home was a happy but a very quiet home. One
day my father said that he had been surprised to hear from his
friend Sir Henry Davison how seriously our house struck
people, compared to other houses: 'But I think we are very
happy as we are', said he – and so indeed we were. We lived
chiefly with him and with quite little children, or with our
grandparents when they came over to visit us. There was
certainly a want of initiation: in our house there was no one to
suggest all sorts of delightful possibilities, which, as we grew
up, might have been made more of; but looking back, I chiefly
regret it in so far as I think he might have been happier if we
had brought a little more action and sunshine into daily life,
and taken a little more on our own responsibility, instead of
making ourselves into his shadows.

When my father had done his day's work, he liked a change
of scene and thought. I think he was always glad to leave the
ink-blots for his beloved dabs of paint. Sometimes he used to

drive into town on the top of an omnibus, sometimes in a
brougham; very often he used to take us with him in han-
soms (which we much preferred) on long expeditions to
Hampstead, to Richmond, to Greenwich, or to studios in
distant quarters of the town. There was Mr David Roberts's
studio [or Cattermole's or Edwin Landseer's].[4]

My grandmother, who had brought us over to England,
returned to her husband in Paris; but her mother, an old lady
wrapped in Indian shawls, presently came to live with us, and
divided her time between Kensington and the Champs
Elysées until 1847, when she died at Paris. We did not see very
much of our great-grandmother; she rarely spoke, and was
almost always in her room; but though my father was very
busy, and often away from home, we seemed to live with him,
and were indeed with him constantly – in the early mornings,
and when he was drawing, and on Sundays especially, and on
holidays when the work was finished. We often went for little
expeditions together, which he liked. He was well and strong,
and able both to work and to enjoy life to the full; though even
then he was not without anxiety for the future. Success was
slow; his great book [*Vanity Fair*] hung fire. One has heard of
the journeys which the manuscript made to various publishers' houses before it could find one ready to undertake the
venture, and how long its appearance was delayed by various
doubts and hesitations.[5] The book was at last brought out in its
yellow covers by Messrs Bradbury & Evans on 1 January 1847.
My great-grandmother did not speak much, as I have said, but
I think she put on her spectacles and read *Vanity Fair* in the
intervals of her books of devotion.

I still remember going along Kensington Gardens with my
sister and our nurse-maid carrying a parcel of yellow numbers, which she had given us to take to some friend who lived
across the Park; and as we walked along, somewhere near the
gates of the gardens we met my father, who asked us what we
were carrying. Then somehow he seemed vexed and troubled,
told us not to go on, and to take the parcel home. Then
he changed his mind, saying that if his grandmother wished it,
the books had best be conveyed; but we guessed, as children
do, that something was seriously amiss. Something *was*
seriously amiss. The sale of *Vanity Fair* was so small that it was

a question at that time whether its publication should not be discontinued altogether. . . .

I may as well also state here, that one morning a hansom drove up to the door, and out of it emerged a most charming, dazzling little lady dressed in black, who greeted my father with great affection and brilliancy, and who, departing presently, gave him a large bunch of fresh violets. This was the only time I ever saw the fascinating little person who was by many supposed to be the original of Becky; my father only laughed when people asked him, but he never quite owned to it. He always said that he never consciously *copied* anybody. It was, of course, impossible that suggestions should not come to him.

Concerning the originals of the characters in *Vanity Fair*, here is a quotation from *Yeast*, the accuracy of which I can vouch for from remembrance. Charles Kingsley writes, 'I heard a story the other day of our most earnest and genial humorist, who is just now proving himself also our most earnest and genial novelist. "I like your novel exceedingly", said a lady; "the characters are so natural, all but the baronet, and he surely is overdrawn: it is impossible to find such coarseness in his rank of life!" The artist laughed. "That character", said he, "is almost the only exact portrait in the whole book" ' (*Yeast*, ch. 2).

It must have been in the summer of 1847 that my father wrote to his mother saying everything had mended, and 'the book does everything but pay'. I can remember hearing him speak of that very time long after, and saying, '*Vanity Fair* is undoubtedly the best of my books. It has the best story, and for another thing,' he added, 'the title is such a good one, you couldn't have a better.'

Wood-blocks played a very important part in our lives in those days, and the house was full of them, and of drawings and note-books and scrap-books. Friends were constantly turned into models for wood-blocks and etchings. Once a month an engraver used to come to 'bite-in' the plates in the dining-room. One young friend of ours, called Eugénie [Crowe], used very often to sit to my father. She used to be Amelia and the Miss Osbornes, in turn, while my sister and I figured proudly as models for the children fighting on the floor. I also remember making one of a group composed of

the aforesaid Eugenie, representing Amelia after the battle of
Waterloo, with a sofa cushion for an infant; a tall chair stood in
the place of Dobbin who brings the litte horse for his godson to
play with. . . . (*Biog. Intros*, I, xxvii–xxxi)

[Just over a year after *Vanity Fair* was completed, Thackeray
suffered a near-fatal illness, while he was writing *Pendennis*.
Several years later, writes Gordon Ray, drawing upon Anny's
1878 manuscript reminiscences] Anny came to Thackeray in
his study and said, 'I am glad you did not die when you were so
ill [in 1849]. We should never have known you then or learnt
to care for you.' Thackeray replied, 'a little hurt and yet
touched too' – 'I have thought so myself but I do not think it
right ever to talk sentimentally about one's feelings.' (*Wisdom*, p. 233)

NOTES

1. *Thackeray's Daughter: Some Recollections of Anne Thackeray Ritchie*,
compiled by Hester Thackeray Fuller and Violet Hammersley (1951)
pp. 87–8. This book collects together a number of her published reminiscences, and gives an account of Anny's life after her father's death. A full
biography has lately appeared (too late to be drawn upon in the present
collection) – Winifred Gerin's *Anne Thackeray Ritchie* (1981).

2. '. . . he had not expected us so early', she explains elsewhere. 'We
saw . . . the empty study; there was the feeling of London – London smelt of
tobacco, we thought . . . and then climbing the stairs, we looked in at his
bedroom door, and came to our own rooms above it. There were pictures
ready hung on the walls of the schoolroom, and the adjoining fire-lit
nursery – the Thorwaldsen prints, Hunt's delightful sleepy boy yawning at
us over the chimney-piece, all of which he had caused to be put up; and the
picture of himself as a child he had hung up with his own hands . . .' (*Biog.
Intros*, I, xxvii).

3. 'Notes on Family History', 1894, *Letters of Anne Thackeray Ritchie*, ed.
Hesther Ritchie (1924) pp. 21, 22, 35–6.

4. *Chapters from Some Memoirs* (1894) pp. 81, 88–9.

5. The novel's composition, too, had been much delayed. Anny
elsewhere remarks that Thackeray's 'Chronicle of the Drum' was 'written in
Paris, about 1841. I can just remember the snow upon the ground, and a
room opening upon a garden in the Champs Elysees where he used to write.
He has since told me that he wrote a great part of *Vanity Fair* at that
time' – *The Orphan of Pimlico and other Sketches, Fragments and Drawings*, by
William Makepeace Thackeray with some Notes by Anne Isabella Thackeray (1876), unnumbered page facing 'Vanity Fair' sketch.

Living Always in the Almighty Presence

ALICIA BAYNE

From Jane Townley Pryme and Alicia Bayne, *Memorials of the Thackeray Family* (privately printed, 1879) pp. 368–9, 376–7, 384, 388–9. On Mrs Bayne, Thackeray's second cousin, see above, I, 4. She had met him when he was in his teens; seventeen years then passed before she met him again, when he set up house in Young Street, Kensington, in 1846.

[His] grand head ... was even then (at thirty-five) beginning to have a little snow upon its dark covering. He had the air of a thoroughbred polished gentleman, being at the same time perfectly simple and unaffected. He told us that he was delighted to be amongst his relations, that he hoped to be more stationary now, and to see more of us; and he was true to his word, always identifying himself with us, amid all his popularity and good fortune. Once when I spoke of the good old ladies at Harrow as '*your* aunts', he corrected me, saying, '*Our* aunts'; and such was the kindness of his heart, and the genial charm of his manner with those he cared for that they never were afraid of him. . . .

Mr Thackeray [later] twice visited America and lectured there, and his popularity was immense. He told me that on parting with his kind entertainers they expressed some fear that he might hereafter criticise them in his writings. 'No,' he said, 'it is not my way to repay hospitality *so*, but I should like to offer you, if I may, two pieces of advice.' One of them was, not to bring their children so early into society.

Mr Thackeray was now the brilliant, popular and successful man. He dined out a great deal during the season. He belonged to three clubs – the Athenaeum, Reform, and Garrick. He took a house in Onslow Square, where he was able to practise hospitality, which no man knew better how to do with dignity. I will give an amusing proof of this. A lady from whom he had received some kind civilities in the country came to Town one season. He called upon her and asked her to fix a day to dine with him. She, with well meant regard to the probable finances of an author, made some objections, but at last agreed *on condition* that Mr T. would give her only cold meat. The day arrived and the lady came. To her surprise she found a goodly company and a beautiful dinner, in the course of which the host took an opportunity of saying that he had not forgotten her ladyship's wish, and that there was cold roast beef on the side table. . . .

In the course of 1860 Mr Thackeray built for himself an ideal house in Kensington Palace Gardens in the Augustan style of the neighbouring palace.[1] When it was all but completed, I went by his invitation to look at it. He happened to be there himself, and as he asked me what I thought of it I suggested that it would be appropriate to put his arms over the front, in a little shield of stone, as a memorial, for all time, of *his* having lived there. 'What arms shall I put?' said he. 'Why not the *Cornhill* device,' I answered, 'for that gave you the money with which to build it.' But he replied, 'No, if I put any at all it shall be those of the good old men who went before me, and in whose footsteps I would humbly hope to tread', taking off his hat, as he spoke, to their memory. And thus he unconsciously verified the remark of the Edinburgh Reviewer that 'his originally fine and kind nature remained essentially free from worldliness and, in the highest pride of intellect, paid homage to the heart'. No arms of any kind were, however, placed over the house. . . .

When the house was furnished it was all that was most elegant and comfortable in a dwelling. It was described as 'worthy of one who really represented literature in the great world, and who yet sustained the character of his profession with all the dignity of a gentleman'. There was a library of sufficient length to enable its master, while composing, to walk up and down it and out of the open window into a garden. He was peculiarly susceptible of aesthetical influences, and once delighted me by saying of one of my rooms which opens to a garden 'It invites composition.' The house was full of treasures. Old English looking-glasses – cabinets filled with Sèvres, Dresden, and Chelsea china – quaint old high-backed chairs and settees – and many interesting pictures by Old

Masters. Among them were a charming specimen of Mytens signed and dated 1665. One represented a girl in a pink silk dress, plucking a rose; another a child in yellow, with a crimson hat and feather, carrying apricots – a dog at her side. A large picture of Queen Anne, seated on a throne attended by an allegorical female figure of Peace, painted by De Troye in commemoration of the Treaty of Utrecht. A *Conversation champêtre* by Watteau. Portrait of a lady in a ruff, white head-dress, rich crimson and gold dress and gold chain, by Pourbus, 1604. Cupids sporting by Boucher. Portrait of a lady, in a blue dress and pearl necklace. A landscape with peasants and cattle on a wooden bridge, Old Cuyp. A curious panoramic view in the Low Countries with a grand encampment of Spanish troops by E. Van de Velde.

And here the generous host lived and saw good company, and nowhere could you find a more refined and charming household. It was a treat only to make a morning call on his widowed mother and his two daughters; sometimes he would himself appear if he knew that a relative or intimate friend was there. I think I see him now – 'The spectacles and the wonderful up-looking face, the noble head crowned with its masses of grey hair.' *Here* he was in his element with those whom he loved to be with, and to think of, if absent. . . . [But the] shadow of Death was stealing onwards while the sunshine lay upon the house. But its master was one who lived always in the sense of an Almighty Presence. About this time he wrote as if sensible that the ebb-tide had begun. 'A few chapters more, and then the last, and then behold *Finis* itself coming to an end and the Infinite beginning.'[2]

Those who *only* saw Mr Thackeray in society – as the brilliant and successful man of letters – could have no idea of what was beneath the surface. Few had opportunities of knowing the awe and tenderness which thrilled his whole being when he contemplated God in his works.[3]

NOTES

1. The architecture of this house is well described, with new information and with architects' plans and other illustrations, in Patricia Metcalf,

'Postscript on Thackeray's House', *Journal of the Society of Architectural Historians*, XXVIII (1969) 115–23.

2. The closing words of his *Roundabout* essay 'De Finibus'.

3. She illustrates this by the pious ejaculations to which he was moved, in his writings and his talk, by sunsets. Dr John Brown's 'Calvary!' anecdote is cited: see below, I, 150.

Kind, Generous and Playful

KATE PERRY

From *A Collection of Letters of W. M. Thackeray 1847–1855*, 2nd edn (1887) pp. 177–83. Jane Brookfield, who compiled and introduced this collection, ended it with Kate Perry's 'charming recollection' of Thackeray reprinted from *Reminiscences of a London Drawing Room* (privately printed, n.d. [?1883]). As Kate Perry explains below, she met Thackeray in 1846, and became one of his most intimate friends. Though attractive and vivacious, she never married, and lived in London with her sister Jane, Mrs Frederick Elliot, at whose house (Chesham Place, Belgrave Square) Thackeray became a frequent visitor. He and Mrs Brookfield made these sisters their confidantes and messengers, during the crises in their relationship (see *Wisdom*, pp. 158–64). Half-joking to his mother in 1848 about being 'in love with my old flames... Mrs Brookfield... & no less than 3 others', Thackeray named Kate as one of them, the others at this time being Eugénie Crowe and the beautiful Virginia Pattle – though, he assured his mother, 'there's no danger with any of them' (*LPP*, II, 374). His correspondence contains many affectionate references and letters to Kate, and their friendship endured till his death. His gratitude for her friendship is also expressed in his poem 'The Pen and the Album', written in her autograph-book, 1852. A daughter of James Perry (d. 1821), Editor of the *Morning Chronicle*, she became a popular figure in London society.

My acquaintance with Mr Thackeray began at Brighton, where I was staying with my eldest brother, William Perry. In most cases there is a prelude to friendship – at first it is a delicate plant, with barely any root, gradually throwing out tender green leaves and buds, and then full-blown flowers – the root in the meanwhile taking firm hold of the earth – and cruel is the frost or cutting wind which destroys it. But Mr Thackeray and I went through no gradations of growth in our friendship; it was more like Jack's bean-stalk in a pantomime, which rushed up sky-high without culture, and, thank God, so remained till his most sad and sudden end.

In the earliest days of our friendship he brought his morning work to read to me in the evening; he had just commenced *Vanity Fair*, and was living at the Old Ship Inn, where he wrote some of the first numbers. He often then said to me, 'I wonder whether this will take, the publishers accept it, and the world read it?' I remember answering him that I had no reliance upon my own critical powers in literature; but that I had written to my sister, Mrs Frederick Elliot, and said, 'I have made a great friendship with one of the principal contributors of *Punch* – Mr Thackeray; he is now writing a novel, but cannot hit upon a name for it. I may be wrong, but it seems to me the cleverest thing I ever read. The first time he dined with us I was fearfully alarmed at him. The next day we walked in Chichester Park, when he told all about his little girls, and of his great friendship with the Brookfields, and I told him about you and Chesham Place.' When he heard this, and my opinion of his novel, he burst out laughing, and said, 'Ah! Mademoiselle (as he always called me), it is *not* small beer; but I do not know whether it will be palatable to the London folks.' He told me, some time afterward, that, after ransacking his brain for a name for his novel, it came upon him unawares, in the middle of the night, as if a voice had whispered, 'Vanity Fair'. He said, 'I jumped out of bed, and ran three times round my room, uttering as I went, "Vanity Fair, Vanity Fair, Vanity Fair."'

Afterward we frequently met at the Miss Berrys',[1] where night after night were assembled all the wit and beauty of that time.... My sister and I, with our great admiration and friendship for Mr Thackeray, used to think that the Miss Berrys at first did not thoroughly appreciate or understand him; but one evening, when he had left early, they said they had perceived, for the first time, 'what a very remarkable man he was'. He became a constant and most welcome visitor at their house; they read his works with delight, and, whenever they were making up a pleasant dinner, used to say, 'We *must* have Thackeray.' It was at one of these dinners that Miss Berry astonished us all by saying she had never read Jane Austen's novels, until lately someone had lent them to her. But she could not get on with them. . . . 'Thackeray and Balzac', she added (Thackeray being present), 'write with great minuteness, but do so with a brilliant pen.' Thackeray made two bows of gratitude (one, pointing to the ground, for Balzac). . . .

Thackeray's love of children was one of the strongest feelings of his heart. In a little poem, 'The Golden Pen', published in his *Miscellanies*, which is, perhaps, the truest portrait of him which has ever appeared, he writes,

> There's something, even in his bitterest mood,
> That melts him at the sight of infanthood;
> Thank God that he can love the pure and good.

This sympathy with the little ones was not only proved by his immense devotion to his own most gifted children, but extended to the little 'gutter child', as the trim board-school girl of today was called then. For this waif of society he felt the tenderest pity and interest. He used often to visit a school where my dear sister had collected nearly three hundred of these neglected children, feeding, teaching, and clothing them, and, with the help of other kind souls, preparing them in some degree to fight the battle of life, in which there are many crosses – but few Victoria ones. Turning his steps one day to this large, rough-looking schoolroom, he entered it just as these little Arabs were commencing, with more heartiness than melody [a hymn]. He turned to the lady superintending them, and said, 'I cannot stand this any longer – my spectacles are getting very dim.'[2]

One day, some few years later, I had been engaged in summing up the monthly expenses of the same school, and had left open on my writing-table, the much scored-over Soup Kitchen book. Mr Thackeray was shown into the room, and was for some minutes alone before I joined him. After he left, I resumed my labours, and found on the first page of the book a beautifully executed pen-and-ink sketch of little children crowding round the schoolmistress, who was ladling out, into mugs of various sizes and shapes, the daily meal of soup, above which was written, 'Suffer little children, and forbid them not.'

Another day, I found a sovereign under a paper containing

the names of some friends of the school who had joined in a subscription to give the children a day's holiday in the country. I said to my servant, 'Mr Thackeray has been here', and found from him this was the case. I knew my instinct was right, that it was his hand which had placed the money there. His charity was very wide, in the fullest sense of the word. He has been known to discover, in some remote corner, the hapless artist or dramatist who in his palmy days had not thought much of that night – old age – 'when no more work can be done'. Thackeray would mount the many steps leading to the desolate chamber – administer some little rebuke on the thoughtlessness of not laying by some of the easily gained gold of youth or manhood, and slipping, as in one instance, into an old blotting-book, a £100 note, would hurry away.

'I never saw him do it', said poor old P——. 'I was very angry because he said I had been a reckless old goose – and then a £100 falls out of my writing-book. God bless him!'

These good deeds would never have come to light but for the gratitude of those who, though they had the gentle rebuke, received also the more than liberal help. I know he has been accused of extreme sensitiveness to blame, either about himself or his writings, but the following story proves that he could forgive with magnanimity and grace when roughly and severely handled. This once occurred at my sister's dinner-table. Thackeray, who was almost a daily visitor at her house, for some time took it into his head, to be announced by the name of the most noted criminal of the day. Our butler did this with the greatest gravity.

On this occasion Thackeray had been asked to join some friends at dinner, but not arriving at the prescribed hour, the guests sat down without him. Among them was Mr H——, the author of some of the most charming books of the day.[3]

The conversation being more literary than otherwise, Thackeray (then at the very height of his fame) came under discussion, and, some of his greatest friends and admirers being present, he was spoken of with unqualified admiration. Mr H—— was the exception, and dissented from us, in very unmeasured terms, in our estimate of Thackeray's character. Judging, he said, 'from the tenor of his books, he could not believe how one who could dwell, as he did, on the weakness and absurdities and shortcomings of his fellow-creatures, could possess any kind or generous sympathies toward the human race'. He concluded his severe judgement by saying that he had never met him, and hoped he never should do so.

We were all so occupied by this fiery debate that we did not observe that, under the sobriquet of some jail-bird of the day, Thackeray had slipped into his chair, and heard much that was said, including the severe peroration. A gentle tap on Mr H———'s shoulder, and, in his pleasant, low voice, Thackeray said, 'I, on the contrary, have always longed for the occasion when I could express, personally, to Mr H———, the great admiration I have always felt for him, as an author and a man.' It is pleasant to think they became fast friends thereafter.

I find it difficult to check my pen from being garrulous as I remember the many instances of the kindness and generosity of his nature, though, at the same time, I feel how inadequate it is to do justice to all his noble and delightful qualities. His wit and humour and playfulness were most observable where he was happiest and most at ease – with his beloved daughters, or with his dear friends the Brookfields, who were the most intimate and valued of those he made in middle life. I am proud to say, also, that he was aware of the admiration in which he was held by every member of my sister's home, where his ever ready sympathy in all our troubles and pleasures was truly appreciated – and when he passed away, and the place knew him no more, a great shadow fell upon that house.

NOTES

1. This famous longlived pair of sisters, Mary Berry (1763–1852) and Agnes Berry (1764–1852), provided a social link between Georgian and Victorian London; see Ray's account, *Wisdom*, pp. 50–1. Thackeray, who frequented their salon and much liked both sisters, opened *The Four Georges* (1855) with a tribute to their linking him to the 'manners and life of the old world' described in those lectures: 'A very few years since, I knew familiarly a lady who had been asked in marriage by Horace Walpole, who had been patted on the head by George I. This lady had knocked at Johnson's door [etc.]. I often thought, as I took my kind old friend's hand, how with it I held on to the old society of wits and men of the world. I could travel back for sevenscore years of time. . . .'

2. A similar anecdote about Thackeray's sensibility over such 'ragged' children is told by the philanthropist and reformer Frederic Hill (1803–96). He was taken to see some Industrial Schools for the very poor, in Aberdeen, and remained very silent during the visit, explaining afterwards that, had he tried to speak, he would have wept – *Frederic Hill: An Autobiography of Fifty Years in Times of Reform*, ed. Constance Hill (1893) p. 227.

3. Arthur Helps (1813–75), knighted 1872; author and, from 1860, Clerk to the Privy Council. This dinner took place in January 1851; Mrs Brookfield, who was present, recalls Helps's asking whether Thackeray was 'an amiable man? . . . his books don't give me the impression that he is' – and his 'amusingly guilty' look when Thackeray appeared – C. and F. Brookfield, *Mrs Brookfield and her Circle* (1905) II, 343.

A Kensington Worthy

J. J. MERRIMAN

From 'Kensington Worthies. III', *St Mary Abbots* [*Kensington*] *Parish Magazine*, Sep 1889, pp. 225–6. John Jones Merriman (1800–81), surgeon, was Thackeray's neighbour in Young Street, Kensington, and his trusted physician. When Thackeray returned to live in Kensington, in 1862, Merriman saw more of him again, and was called in at his death.

I have been asked to give a few reminiscences of Thackeray in Kensington. On referring to my notes I find much that is too personal to repeat, yet there is enough to illustrate the kindness of his heart, the versatility of his nature, the innate horror that he had of snobbism, and the social qualities which accompanied his staunch friendship. Thackeray lived at No. 13 (now 16) Young Street, Kensington Square, from 1847 to 1853 – and I first knew him and his daughters here in 1848; his tall commanding figure, erect, with a fine stately tread, was familiar enough in the High Street, and also at the 9.30 a.m. service on Sunday mornings at the old parish church. His large candid face, serious, almost severe, was, on meeting a friend, instantly lit up with a glad smile, and his arm placed in yours, made you feel small in more senses than one. I remember meeting him outside Leech's house, 6, The Terrace; we walked through the town with arms hooked – at Colby House opposite the Palace Gate, a handsome carriage

full of people passed (I am glad I don't remember the number
of balls on the coronet), they did not notice him; a clutch was
the signal of something wrong! 'Did you see that? they'll want
to know me tonight, but they shan't!' It appeared that
Thackeray and these people were to meet at some great house
in London that evening, but I felt I would rather be what I was
than any of that party if they tried to know him only *when
convenient*! He had written years before, 'I have an eye for a
snob', and 'The jays with peacock's feathers are the snobs of
this world.'[1] On another occasion I was strolling with him
through the town, I made a pun, so bad that I apologised for
it. 'Oh! but a good one is not worth listening to', was the kindly
reply.

In 1848 it fell to my lot to watch him through his dangerous
illness in September, October, and November, with Dr
Elliotson, then one of the leading physicians in London. He
never forgot it, and was always 'Your grateful friend and
patient', even years after he left the old house in Young
Street. . . .

During the building of his house on Palace Green, I
frequently met him, and we chatted on the project, the return
to old Kensington, the investment, etc., and in 1862 he
entered his new home, our elder children being at one of the
'house-warmings'. Like most great men he was fond of
children; hear his lines about his own:

> I thought, as day was breaking,
> My little girls were waking,
> And smiling, and making
> A prayer at home for me.[2]

This man a cynic! Never! He could be and was satirical, but his
satire purified society, for it came from one of the most
high-minded and tender-hearted of human beings.

The last time I heard him in public at Kensington was on
1 December 1862. Archdeacon Sinclair, at the height of the
Cotton Famine, resolved to hold a public meeting at Kensington to raise contributions in aid of the Lancashire Fund.
In *Old Times and Distant Places*, p. 270, the Archdeacon gives an
interesting account of his interview with the great novelist,
who left his sick bed to attend the meeting, as *a duty*.[3] The

Vestry Hall was crowded. When W. M. Thackeray rose, to second the resolution which Mr Heywood had moved, 'great applause followed; as soon as silence was restored, he began with perfect self-possession, and delivered with much emphasis a few weighty and well considered sentences'. I never shall forget the almost electric effect of his 'few remarks'; £627 were subscribed in the room, Thackeray himself giving £50.

But great also were the social qualities which accompanied his staunch friendship. In 1863, on Thursday 17 December, Thackeray and his elder daughter dined with us at No. 45, The Square. As he entered I saw he was not well, and with his usual kindness he said, 'I would only have turned out to come to you as an old friend.' I remember saying, 'Oh! but you, like every Englishman, will be better for your dinner. Do you know Jean Ingelow?'[4] 'No, the woman in all London I am most anxious to know', was the reply. 'Do you know the quondam Miss Croker?' 'No, but she is not here', he replied. They were *both* present, and I had the great pleasure of introducing him to them. He soon revived under this mental pleasure. Ere we reached the dining-room he was himself again, and falling in with an old Carthusian, Sir George Barrow, all went as pleasantly as possible. His conversation was most amusing. . . . My notes conclude: My friend stayed late, his daughter going on to some other party, and I strolled up Young Street with him; we halted by No. 13, when he alluded to old times and happy days there; he told me *Vanity Fair* was his greatest work, and the 'Canebottomed Chair' his favourite ballad; and we parted at the top of 'Our Street', never to meet again alive in this world: for on that day week, 24 December, I was summoned about 8 a.m. to Palace Green, to find him lying dead in his bed! Life had been extinct for some hours: effusion had taken place into his powerful and great brain (it weighed 58½ oz), and he passed away in the night to the better country where there is no night.

NOTES

1. *The Book of Snobs* (1847) 'Prefatory Remarks' and ch. 20.
2. Final lines of 'The White Squall' (1844).

3. John Sinclair (1797–1875), Vicar of Kensington and Archdeacon of Middlesex, was in frequent touch with Thackeray: see *LPP*, III, 158 for another instance of Thackeray's helping the poor, through him, ten years earlier. In 1862 there was great distress among Lancashire cotton workers, the American Civil War having caused a shortage in raw materials. Archdeacon Sinclair, knowing that Thackeray's name 'would be a powerful attraction' at a public meeting in aid of these workers, called upon him to urge him to attend and speak. Thackeray rose from his sickbed to say that he was both too unwell to attend a meeting and 'had never in his lifetime spoken from a platform. "You forget," he added, "that my vocation is not to be a speaker, but a writer." In reply I explained that I did not wish for a long harangue, that I had abundance of orators ready to come forward, and that in Kensington the great difficulty was to collect an audience. "But," I added, "if you will only let me print your name in my handbills, I shall be sure of a large attendance, and I can depend upon my orators to call forth contributions." Thackeray was amused at this unexpected turn, and in the kindest manner said, "Though I am far from well, you may depend upon me. *If I am alive I shall be with you.*" I immediately issued handbills, announcing among other speakers that W. M. Thackeray would address the meeting. A crowd assembled. Great applause followed when he rose. As soon as silence was restored, he began with perfect self-possession, and delivered with much emphasis a few weighty and well-considered sentences. They were received with enthusiasm, and I was afterwards congratulated repeatedly on my success in calling forth for the first, and as unhappily it proved the last time, the rhetorical powers of the great novelist' – *Old Times and Distant Places* (1875) p. 270.

4. Jean Ingelow (1820–97), poetess. The other guests mentioned are Sir Giles Barrow (1806–76), 2nd Baronet, a distinguished civil servant, and his wife, who was an adopted daughter of the politician and essayist John Wilson Croker, a leading contributor to the *Quarterly Review*; he was the model for Wenham in *Vanity Fair*.

A Kind, Humane and Perfectly Honest Man

JAMES HANNAY

From *A Brief Memoir of the Late Mr Thackeray* (Edinburgh, 1864) pp. 17–31. This *Memoir*, a pamphlet reprinting Hannay's obituary of Thackeray in the *Edinburgh Courant*, of which he was Editor, was much admired and quoted at the time; Anthony Trollope for instance called it 'the only good attempt of its kind that I have seen'. It was further reprinted in Hannay's *Characters and Criticisms* (Edinburgh, 1865). Hannay (1827–73), a Scotsman, became a reporter, journalist and miscellaneous writer in 1845, after some unhappy years in the Navy. In 1848 he met Thackeray, whose works he had ardently admired and praised, and he greatly valued his friendship with the novelist, dedicating to him his own novel *King Dobbs* (1849). In 1852 he was engaged to annotate *The English Humourists* and see the book through the press; for Thackeray's cordial letter inviting him to do this (not in *LPP*) see George J. Worth, *James Hannay* (Lawrence, Kan., 1964) p. 96. Thackeray's patronage was valuable in other ways – he introduced him to the *Quarterly Review*, for instance – and Hannay reviewed Thackeray's novels in sundry periodicals warmly and intelligently though not uncritically. 'Quite better than the ordinary critics', said Thackeray of one notice (*LPP*, III, 469). His *Studies on Thackeray* (1869) is a valuable pioneer assessment. Carlyle was the other contemporary whom he greatly admired. He was a staunch Conservative. His *Memoir* aimed to make 'Mr Thackeray's Life and Writings illustrate each other. ... The more fully his life is made known to the world, the more clearly will the harmony of his works with it appear' (p. 3). Among the points he makes about Thackeray's earlier years is that 'If he had had his choice, he would rather have been famous as an artist than as a writer' (p. 9).

When Thackeray wrote *Vanity Fair*, in 1846, '7, '8, he was living in Young Street, Kensington – a street on your left hand, before you come to the church; and here, in 1848, the author of this sketch had first the pleasure of seeing him, of being received at his table, and of knowing how essentially a kind, humane, and perfectly honest man he was. *Vanity Fair* was then unfinished, but its success was made, and he spoke frankly and genially of his work and his career. *Vanity Fair* always, we think, ranked in his own mind as best in *story* of his greater books; and he once pointed out to us the very house in Russell Square where his imaginary Sedleys lived – a curious proof of the reality his creations had for his mind. The man and the books were equally real and true; and it was natural that he should speak without hesitation of his books, if you wished it; though as a man of the world and a polished gentleman who knew the world thoroughly, literature to him only took its turn among other topics. ... Thackeray was not bookish, and yet turned readily to the subject of books, if invited. His reading was undoubtedly large in memoirs, modern history, biography, poetry, essays, and fiction – and, taken in conjunction with his scholarship, probably placed him, as a man of letters, above any other novelist except Sir Bulwer Lytton. Here is a characteristic fragment from one of

his letters, written in August 1854, and now before us: 'I hate
Juvenal', he says; 'I mean I think him a truculent brute, and I
love Horace better than you do, and rate Churchill much
lower; and as for Swift, you haven't made me alter my opinion.
I admire, or rather admit, his power as much as you do; but I
don't admire that kind of power so much as I did fifteen years
ago, or twenty shall we say. Love is a higher intellectual
exercise than Hatred; and when you get one or two more of
those young ones you write so pleasantly about, you'll come
over to the side of the kind wags, I think, rather than the cruel
ones.' Passages like this – which men who knew him, will not
need to have quoted to them – have a double value for the
world at large. They not only show a familiar command of
writers whom it is by no means easy to know well – but they
show what the real philosophy was of a man whom the envious
represented to the ignorant as a cynic and a scoffer. Why, his
favourite authors were just those whose influence he thought
had been beneficial to the cause of virtue and charity. 'I take
off my hat to Joseph Addison', he would say, after an
energetic testimony to his good effect on English life. He was,
in fact, even greater as a moralist than as a mere *describer* of
manners; and his very hatred of quackery and meanness was
proved to be real by his simplicity, humanity, and kindliness of
character. In private, this great satirist, whose aspect in a
crowd was often one of austere politeness and reserve, unbent
into a familiar *naïveté* which somehow one seldom finds in the
demonstratively genial. And this was the more charming and
precious that it rested on a basis of severe and profound
reflection, before the glance of which all that was dark and
serious in man's life and prospects lay open. The gravity of
that white head, with its noble brow, and thoughtful face full
of feeling and meaning, enhanced the piquancy of his
playfulness, and of the little personal revelations which came
with such a grace from the depths of his kindly nature. When
we congratulated him, many years ago, on the touch in *Vanity
Fair* in which Becky *'admires'* her husband when he is giving
Lord Steyne the chastisement which ruins *her* for life, 'Well,'
he said, 'when I wrote the sentence, I slapped my fist on the
table, and said, "*That* is a touch of genius!" ' The incident is a
trifle, but it will reveal, we suspect, an element of fervour, as
well as heartiness of frankness in recording the fervour, both

equally at variance with the vulgar conception of him. This frankness and *bonhomie* made him delightful in a *tête-à-tete*, and gave a pleasant human flavour to talk full of sense, and wisdom, and experience, and lighted up by the gaiety of the true London man of the world. Though he said witty things, now and then, he was not a wit in the sense in which Jerrold was, and he complained, sometimes, that his best things occurred to him after the occasion had gone by! He shone most – as in his books – in little subtle remarks on life, and little descriptive sketches suggested by the talk. We remember in particular, one evening, after a dinner party at his house, a fancy picture he drew of Shakespeare during his last years at Stratford, sitting out in the summer afternoon watching the people, which all who heard it, brief as it was, thought equal to the best things in his lectures.[1] But it was not for this sort of talent – rarely exerted by him – that people admired his conversation. They admired, above all, the broad sagacity, sharp insight, large and tolerant liberality, which marked him as one who was a sage as well as a story-teller, and whose stories were valuable because he was a sage. . . . He never overvalued story-telling, or forgot that there were nobler things in literature than the purest creations of which the object was amusement. . . . 'Now is the time', wrote Thackeray, to a young friend in 1849, 'to lay in stock. I wish I had had five years' reading before I took to our trade.' How heartily we have heard him praise Sir Bulwer Lytton for the good example he set by being 'thoroughly *literate*!' We are not going to trench here on any such ground as Thackeray's judgements about his contemporaries. But we may notice an excellent point bearing on these. If he heard a young fellow expressing great admiration for one of them, he encouraged him in it. When somebody was mentioned as worshipping an eminent man just dead, 'I am glad', said Thackeray, 'that he worships anybody'. . . .

Few lives were more engrossed than his, discharging, as he did, at once the duties of a man of letters and a man of fashion. He dined out a great deal during the season. He went to the theatres. He belonged to three clubs – the Athenaeum, Reform, and Garrick – to say nothing of minor associations for the promotion of good fellowship. With less of this wear and tear, we should have had more work from him – should have had, perhaps, the History which long dwelt in his imagination as one of the creations of the future. As it is, he achieved a great deal during the last eight or ten years of his life. Two such elaborate novels as the *Newcomes* and *Virginians*, a second trip to America, and a ramble over Great Britain, with a new set of lectures on the *Four Georges* – not to mention a contested election, and what he did for the *Cornhill*, established on the strength of his name, and for a time directly conducted by him – these were great doings for a man who, though naturally robust, was plagued and menaced by more than one vexatious disorder of long continuance. And he did them greatly, going into the world gaily and busily to the last, and always finding time for such holy little offices of personal kindness and charity as gave him – we believe and know – more real pleasure than all his large share of the world's applause. He was much gratified by the success of *The Four Georges* . . . in Scotland. . . . He thoroughly appreciated the attention and hospitality which he met with during these lecturing tours. And if, as would sometimes happen, a local notability's adoration became obtrusive, or such a person thrust his obsequious veneration upon him beyond the limits of the becoming, his forbearance was all the more respectable on account of his sensitiveness.

Latterly he had built himself a handsome house in Kensington . . . a dwelling worthy of one who really represented literature in the great world, and who, planting himself on his books, yet sustained the character of his profession with all the dignity of a gentleman. A friend who called on him there from Edinburgh, in the summer of 1862, knowing of old his love of the Venusian, playfully reminded him what Horace says of those who, regardless of their sepulchre, employ themselves in building houses:

Sepulchri
Immemor, struis domos.[2]

'Nay,' said he, 'I am *memor sepulchri*, for this house will always let for so many hundreds (mentioning the sum) a year.' How distant, then, seemed the event which has just happened, and with which the mind obstinately refuses to familiarise itself, though it stares at one from a thousand broadsheets! Well, indeed, might his passing-bell make itself heard through all the myriad joy-bells of the English Christmas! It is long since England has lost such a son – it will be long before she has such another to lose. He was indeed emphatically English – English as distinct from Scotch – no less than English as distinct from Continental – a different type of great man from Scott, and a different type of great man from Balzac. . . . This humble tribute to his illustrious and beloved memory comes from one whom he loaded with benefits. . . .[3]

NOTES

1. A favourite fancy of Thackeray's: see J. T. Field's account, below, I, 163, 167, and *Wisdom*, p. 333.

2. Horace ('the Venusian' from his birth in Venusia), *Odes*, II, xviii. 18–19: 'Forgetful of the tomb, you build houses.' Earlier in the *Memoir*, Hannay remarks that 'A quotation from Horace was one of the favourite forms in which he used to embody his jokes' (p. 8).

3. 'There was nothing more charming about Thackeray', Hannay had written in his Preface (ibid., p. 2), ' . . . than the kindly footing on which he stood with the younger generation. He was not a man to have a little senate; he held sycophants, and all who encouraged them, in contempt; his friends and acquaintances were of all varieties of class and character, and differed from him in their ways of thinking about everything. But he made it a duty to befriend and cherish anybody in whose merit and sincerity he believed, however casual the accident which had brought them under his notice. These are the traits which endear his memory to all who knew him, and which will pleasantly connect him henceforth in their minds, with the best and greatest of the humorists and moralists to whom he is now gathered.'

A Kindly Godfather

FRANCIS ST JOHN THACKERAY

From 'Reminiscences of W. M. Thackeray', *Temple Bar*, XCVIII (1893) 374–8. Francis Thackeray (1832?–1919), a cousin of the novelist, was twenty-one years his junior, and his godson. His earliest memories of W. M. T. date from 1849, when, as a schoolboy, he used to visit his godfather every Easter.

... I instinctively felt that he was far greater than any one whom I had ever met. And looking back after an interval of forty years, I feel that I was not wrong, and that there was something in his mind and character, larger and more spacious, more liberal, with less admixture of anything petty, or unreal, or affected than it has been my fortune ever to meet. In this respect I would compare him to Tennyson. One was naturally attracted by his fine lofty figure, his bright genial smile, his pithy, amusing sentences, and his cheery greeting. There was nothing in the least deterrent or formidable in him – and most boys are quick to see if they are regarded as bores by their elders. ... I never visited, rarely saw him, at this time without having a sovereign slipped into my hand on leaving him. On one occasion, after I had my pocket picked in an omnibus, he emptied the whole of his purse into my hands. The exact amount, at this distant date, I do not remember, but it was much more than I had lost. This was when he was lying in bed, in one of his attacks of illness. On these delightful visits he would spare no pains in taking me to places of amuse-ment – the play, or the pantomime – sometimes after an excellent dinner at the Garrick Club, where I remember his checking some one in the act of blurting out an oath, the utterance of which he would not tolerate in my presence. ...[1]

In sight-seeing, whether visiting conjurors, or picture galleries, or other public places of entertainment, he was always, I think, studying faces and characters. But he must have put himself to a good deal of inconvenience; and the sacrifice of valuable time that he thus made I could under-stand afterwards, though I fear I did not appreciate it sufficiently at the time. Once, when he had taken me to the theatre and secured me a good place, after staying a little while, he said, 'Now I must leave you, and go and make a £5 note.'[2]

I saw him on the day of the opening of the Great Exhibition of 1851, on which he wrote his fine May Day Ode. He had just returned from witnessing the fairy-like scene inside the Palace, with which he had been greatly struck, and he was looking unusually happy and radiant. ...

[After that, Francis saw less of Thackeray for a few years, being preoccupied with his studies and then his teaching career at Eton: but in 1859 he received a cordial letter from

him, congratulating him on his betrothal. He illustrates
Thackeray's impulsive generosity with an anecdote.] Once
when I was walking in London with the lady who afterwards
became my wife, he came suddenly upon us as we were
looking in at the window of Lambert the jeweller. He
immediately made us go in, and purchased for her on the spot
a very handsome gold brooch. . . .

I remember his saying to me after finishing one of his books,
'I have taken too many crops out of the brain.'

NOTES

1. This principle of Thackeray's recurs in his novels. In *Esmond* (ch. 7)
'honest Dick [Steele] the Scholar' checks some soldiers in their ribaldry, 'with
a *maxima debetur pueris reverentia*' because young Henry Esmond is present.
The same tag from Juvenal (*Satires*, XVI, 7: 'Boys deserve the greatest
respect') appears in *Newcomes* (ch. 1), when 'a fellow of very kind; feeling
insists that the songs sung at 'the Cave of Harmony' be carefully selected,
because a boy is in the room.
2. A favourite saying of Thackeray's.

Goodness Showed through his
Noticeable Defects

ROBERT AND ELIZABETH BARRETT BROWNING

Sources given in notes. Thackeray was acquainted with Robert Browning
(1812–89) and his wife Elizabeth Barrett Browning (1806–61) before their
marriage in 1846, but first came to know them well in Rome, winter 1853–4,
and Paris, 1858. He invited them both to contribute to the *Cornhill* (*LPP*, IV,
165–6). Browning, averse to periodical publication, declined but his wife
offered a poem which, much to his embarrassment, Thackeray had to reject
to deference to Mrs Grundy (*LPP*, IV, 226–9). Privately he agreed with
Washington Irving in detesting Browning's poetry: 'we do not read Robert
Browning because we cannot altogether comprehend him. I have no head
above my eyes' (Wilson, I, 118). As Richard Bedingfield recalled, he saw
Browning as 'an excellent fellow, but . . . a madman', and William Alling-
ham records his opinion that Browning's poetry was unmusical and
unmanageable, and his personality uncomfortably positive (see below, I,
123; II, 283). Edward C. McAleer comments, 'Although Thackeray retained
cordial relations with the Brownings, his temperament and theirs were not

such as to make intimate friendship easy' – *Dearest Isa: Robert Browning's Letters to Isabella Blagden*, ed. McAleer (Austin, Tex., 1951) p. 22. If somewhat patronising about 'the good Brownings', Thackeray was grateful for Mrs Browning's kindness to his daughters (*LPP*, III, 333, 341), as she was moved by his goodness to her son Pen (see below). Extracts below are from the Brownings' letters.

[*30 Apr 1849*, Elizabeth Barrett Browning to Mary Russell Mitford.] ... we have just been reading *Vanity Fair*. Very clever, very effective, but cruel to human nature. A painful book, and not the pain that purifies and exalts. Partial truths after all, and those not wholesome. But I certainly had no idea that Mr Thackeray had intellectual force for such a book; the power is considerable.[1]

[*19 Dec 1853*, Robert Browning, letter from Rome.] Thackeray and daughters arrived, called on us, were very genial and kind, took tea next night or so, and are lodging close by. He became very ill suddenly.[2]

[*20 Dec 1853*, Elizabeth Barrett Browning to her sister.] Mr Thackeray ... complains of dulness – he is disabled from work by the dulness. He 'can't write in the morning without his good dinner and two parties overnight'. From such a soil spring the Vanity Fairs! He is an amusing man-mountain enough and very courteous to us – but I never should get on with him much, I think – he is not sympathetical to me.[3]

[*10 Jan 1854*, Elizabeth Barrett Browning to George Barrett: Thackeray has been ill for the second time, and talks of leaving Rome 'which doesn't agree with him!'] That is, the combination of dining out and Rome doesn't agree with him – one at a time would answer perfectly – I propose that he should give up the dinners and remain at Rome – but it's impossible he declares. He can't live without dinners – he must have his dinner and two parties at nights, or in the mornings he finds it impossible to set to work at Vanity Fairs or Newcomes. The inspiration dries without port. . . . [A few days later, John Gibson Lockhart, the biographer of Scott, offered, in 'his lean frozen voice', another explanation for Thackeray's being ill. It could not be the result of over-dining in Rome – 'Why, who *can* dine out at Rome?'] 'No, I will tell you what hurts Thackeray – Those girls [i.e. his daughters] hurt him – Those girls annoy him and teaze him. If he wants to be well, he should get a governess, or an aunt, and dispose of the girls . . . and after all Thackeray does complain that "domestic life is heavy on him –" *that*, there's no denying – and Lockhart understands why better than I pretend to do.'[4]

[*19 Feb 1854*, Elizabeth Barrett Browning to Mrs David Ogilvy.] Thackeray has left Rome. I like his two frank intelligent girls – and I like besides his own good nature and agreeableness.[5]

[*9 Mar 1854*, Elizabeth Barrett Browning to her sister.] Mr Thackeray won my heart rather by his good nature to Penini – and as to the Thackeray girls I am inclined quite to love them: they are frank, intelligent, and affectionate – three excellent qualities. I shall be glad to see them in London again this summer. . . .[6]

[Anny Thackeray recalls discussions, in the later 1850s, about spiritualism.] My father was always immensely interested by the stories told of spiritualism and table-turning, though he scarcely believed half of them. Mrs Browning believed, and Mr Browning was always irritated beyond patience . . . and then came my father's deliberate notes, which seemed to fall a little sadly – his voice always sounded a little sad – upon the rising waves of the discussion.[7]

[*8 Jan 1864*, Robert Browning to William Wetmore Story.] Poor Thackeray! I was to have met him on Wednesday 23rd at dinner – we talked about his empty chair: he was to dine next day, 24, at another friend's where I was certainly to see him. . . . He was no worse than I ever knew him, – and in higher spirits than of old, – I often met him. He never got rid of the silly way of doing himself injustice by affecting – but never mind now – one has forgotten all about it.[8]

[*19 Jan 1864*, Robert Browning to Isabella Blagden.] He was always unwell, so never inspired any sort of apprehension. Everybody feels kindly towards him now – his defects were quite noticeable enough, but of a kind to let the goodness *show through*: and I am rather struck to find how much I must have liked him, these many years. The poor girls have been at the Isle of Wight but return to town soon. Bless us all, we can't make too much of each other, while the little time lasts. I am told he looked grandly in his coffin: Thackeray with all the nonsense gone would be grand indeed, and I hope and trust that so it proves.[9]

NOTES

1. *Letters of Elizabeth Barrett Browning*, ed. Frederic G. Kenyon (1897) I, 401.

2. *New Letters of Robert Browning*, ed. William DeVane and Kenneth Leslie (1951) p. 68.

3. *Elizabeth Barrett Browning: Letters to her Sister 1846–1859*, ed. Leonard Huxley (1929) p. 196.

4. *Letters of the Brownings to George Barrett*, ed. Paul Landis (Urbana, Ill., 1958) pp. 209–10.

5. *Elizabeth Barrett Browning's Letters to Mrs David Ogilvy 1849–1861*, ed. Peter N. Heydon and Philip Kelley (1974) p. 118.

6. *Letters to her Sister*, p. 203.

7. Anne Ritchie, *Records of Tennyson, Ruskin and Browning* (1893) pp. 241–2.

8. *William Wetmore Story and his Friends*, ed. Henry James (1903) II, 147.

9. *Dearest Isa*, p. 185.

'A Great and Strange Man'

CHARLOTTE BRONTË

From *The Brontës: Their Lives, Friendships and Correspondence*, ed. Thomas James Wise and John Alexander Symington (Oxford, 1932) III, 54, 76, 117–18, 193–5, 239–47, 253; other sources specified in the notes. Charlotte Brontë (1816–55) greatly admired Thackeray, and had a copy of *Jane Eyre* (published Oct 1847) sent to him. Moved by his warm praise of the novel (letter to W. S. Williams, 23 Oct 1847, *LPP*, II, 318–19) and by her conviction that he was 'the greatest modern master [whom] I at heart reverence with all my strength' (*The Brontës*, II, 184), she dedicated to him, in fulsome terms, the second edition of her novel, published in Jan 1848. She was then much embarrassed to discover that his life bore some resemblances to her Mr Rochester's (mad wife, daughters requiring a governess). So was he, the more so when speculation arose about her having, in real life, played Jane Eyre to his Mr Rochester; Elizabeth Rigby, most culpably, gave publicity to these rumours in her review, covering both *Jane Eyre* and *Vanity Fair*, in the *Quarterly Review*, Dec 1848. (Thackeray gave a spirited reply to an enquiry about this rumour: 'Alas, Madam it is all too true. And the fruits of that unhallowed intimacy were six children. I slew them all with my own hand' – *Adversity*, p. 11.) Subsequently the two novelists met during Charlotte Brontë's visits to London, Dec 1849, June 1850, and May–June 1851, during the last of which she attended four of the six *Humourists* lectures. Further *contretemps* and awkwardnesses arose between them, and they both came to feel stronger reservations about each other's fiction. 'You see by Jane Eyre's letter dont you why we can't be very great friends?' he wrote in 1852. 'We had a correspondence – a little one; and met, very eagerly on her part. But there's a fire and fury raging in that little woman, a rage scorching her heart wh doesn't suit me' (*LPP*, III, 12), and he surmised that she was deeply affected by an unrequited passion. But he wrote of her generously in the *Cornhill*, introducing her posthumous fragment *Emma* and recalling his encounters with her ('The Last Sketch', Apr 1860, repr. in *The Roundabout Papers*). They first met at the house of her – and Thackeray's future – publisher George Smith, December 1849. 'Excitement and exhaustion together made savage work of me that evening', she reported. 'What [Thackeray] thought of me I cannot tell'; and, looking back on it later, she wrote, 'When Mr Thackeray was announced, and I saw him enter, looked up at his tall figure, heard his voice, the whole incident was truly dream-like' – Winifred Gérin, *Charlotte Brontë* (Oxford, 1967) p. 404. She was at this time still trying to preserve her *incognito; Jane Eyre* was the work of 'Currer Bell'. Thackeray, as will be seen, proved unhelpful in this regard. Extracts below are from her letters; and other witnesses are cited.

[*4 Dec 1849.*] Yesterday I saw Mr Thackeray. He dined here with some other gentlemen. He is a very tall man – above six feet high, with a peculiar face – not handsome, very ugly indeed, generally somewhat stern and satirical in expression, but capable also of a kind look. He was not told who I was, he was not introduced to me, but I soon saw him looking at me through his spectacles; and when we all rose to go down to dinner he just stepped quietly up and said, 'Shake hands'; so I shook hands. He spoke very few words to me, but when he went away he shook hands again in a very kind way. It is better, I should think, to have him for a friend than an enemy, for he is a most formidable-looking personage. I listened to him as he conversed with the other gentlemen. All he says is most simple, but often cynical, harsh, and contradictory. I get on quietly. Most people know me, I think, but they are far too well bred to show that they know me, so that there is none of that bustle or that sense of publicity I dislike. . . .

[George Smith gives a more critical account of Thackeray's conduct at this dinner.] The first time I saw Thackeray was when I called upon him to ask if he would come to dinner to meet the author of *Jane Eyre*, who was staying with my mother. Charlotte Brontë was devoured with curiosity to meet Thackeray, to whom she had dedicated the second edition of her book. I told Thackeray there would be no one with us excepting Sir John Forbes, and explained that Miss Brontë was incognita in London, and begged him not to say a word to indicate his knowledge of her identity as the authoress of *Jane Eyre*. He replied in his large way, 'I see! It will be all right: you are speaking to a man of the world.'

But unhappily it was not all right. When the ladies had left the dining-room I offered Thackeray a cigar. The custom of smoking after dinner was not common then, but I had been told he liked a cigar, and so provided for his tastes. To my dismay, when we rejoined the ladies in the drawing-room, he approached Miss Bronte and quoted a familiar and much-criticised passage from *Jane Eyre*. It was that in which she describes 'the warning fragrance' which told of the approach of Mr Rochester. . . .

The quotation, in one sense, was happy enough, and it did credit to Thackeray's memory of *Jane Eyre*; but not to his memory of his agreement with me. Miss Bronte's face showed her discomposure, and in a chilly fashion she turned off the allusion. But I was almost as much discomposed as Miss Bronte by this sudden assault on what she was so anxious to guard – her identity as the authoress of *Jane Eyre*. She cast an accusing look at me.

Thackeray, however, had no sense of either awkwardness or guilt. From my house he went to the smoking-room of the Garrick Club and said, 'Boys! I have been dining with "Jane Eyre"!' To have her identity expounded in the smoking-room of the Garrick Club was the last experience which the morbidly shy and sensitive little lady would have chosen.[1]

[*14 Feb 1850.*] Mr Thackeray ... is a man of very quiet, simple demeanour; he is however looked upon with some awe and even distrust. His conversation is very peculiar – too perverse to be pleasant ....

[*12 June 1850.*] ... an interview with Mr Thackeray. He made a morning-call and sat above two hours – Mr Smith only was in the room the whole time. He described it afterwards as a queer scene; and I suppose it was. The giant sat before me – I was moved to speak to him of some of his shortcomings (literary of course) one by one the faults came into my mind and one by one I brought them out and sought some explanation or defence – He did defend himself like a great Turk and heathen – that is to say, the excuses were often worse than the crime itself. The matter ended in decent amity – if all be well I am to dine at his house this evening.[2]

[*1 Jan 1851*, to James Taylor.] All you say of Mr Thackeray is most graphic and characteristic. He stirs in me both sorrow and anger. Why should he lead so harassing a life? Why should his mocking tongue so perversely deny the better feelings of his better moods?

[*7 Jan 1851*, to George Smith, sympathising with him over Thackeray's dilatoriness over writing and delivering *The Kickleburys on the Rhine*.] ... that promise 'really to set about writing' a book of which the publication was announced makes one's hair stand on end. May I ask whether, while the Christmas book, already advertised, was still unwritten, with all this guilt on his head and all this responsibility on his shoulders, Mr Thackeray managed to retain his usual fine appetite, to make good breakfasts, luncheons, and dinners, and to enjoy his natural rest; or whether he did not rather send away choice morsels on his plate untouched, and terrify Mrs Carmichael-Smith, Miss Truelock, and his daughters, by habitually shrieking out in the dead of the night under the visitation of a terrible nightmare, revealing two wrathful forms at his bedside menacing him with drawn swords and demanding his MS. or his life? ...

I think you did me a kindness in warding off that copy of *Pendennis* intended to be discharged at my head; the necessary note of acknowledgment would have been written by me

under difficulties. To have spoken my mind would have been
to displease, and I know, if I had written at all, my mind would
have insisted on speaking itself.

[*31 May 1851*, describing one of the *Humourists* lectures, at
Willis's Rooms.] It was delivered in a large and splendid kind
of saloon – that in which the great balls of Almack's are given.
The walls were all painted and gilded, the benches were sofas
stuffed and cushioned and covered with blue damask. The
audience was composed of the *élite* of London society.
Duchesses were there by the score, and amongst them the
great and beautiful Duchess of Sutherland, the Queen's
Mistress of the Robes. Amidst all this Thackeray just got up
and spoke with as much simplicity and ease as if he had been
speaking to a few friends by his own fireside. The lecture was
truly good: he has taken pains with the composition. It was
finished without being in the least studied; a quiet humour
and graphic force enlivened it throughout. He saw me as I
entered the room, and came straight up and spoke very
kindly. He then took me to his mother, a fine, handsome old
lady, and introduced me to her. . . . [With great lack of tact, he
introduced her in these terms: 'Mother, you must allow me to
introduce you to Jane Eyre.' George Smith reports that all eyes
turned towards Charlotte, who was 'very angry'. Mrs Gaskell,
who was present at the lecture, reports that Thackeray further
misbehaved by pointing 'Jane Eyre' out to several of his
friends – so that, when she left, people were crowding forward to see her – and that as he came down from the platform
he 'asked her for her opinion'. She later told Mrs Gaskell how
much she deplored this naive request for praise, and in *Villette*
(ch. 27) she makes M. Paul behave like Thackeray, whereupon
Lucy Snowe expresses her distaste for this 'absence of what I
considered desirable self-control. . . . He was too natural to
conceal, too impulsive to repress his wish' for reassurance.[3]
Next day Charlotte Brontë gave him his come-uppance. He
called upon her: and George Smith, who arrived a little later,
found him] looking anything but happy. Charlotte Brontë
stood close to him, with head thrown back and her face white.
The first words I heard were 'No, Sir! If *you* had come to our
part of the country in Yorkshire, what would you have
thought of me if I had introduced you to my father, before a

mixed company of strangers, as "Mr Warrington" '? Thackeray replied, 'No, you mean Arthur Pendennis.' 'No, I *don't* mean Arthur Pendennis – I mean Mr Warrington, and Mr Warrington would not have behaved as you behaved to me yesterday.' The spectacle of this little woman, *hardly reaching* to Thackeray's elbow, but, somehow, looking stronger and fiercer than.himself . . . resembled the dropping of shells into a fortress.[4]

[*2 June 1851.*] I had a long talk with him and I think he knows me now a little better than he did – but of this I cannot yet be sure – he is a great and strange man . . . .

[*June 1851.*] Mr Thackeray is in high spirits about the success of his lectures. It is likely to add largely both to his fame and purse. He has, however, deferred this week's lecture till next Thursday, at the earnest petition of the duchesses and marchionesses, who, on the day it should have been delivered, were necessitated to go down with the Queen and Court to Ascot Races. I told him I thought he did wrong to put it off on their account – and I think so still.

[*11 June 1851.*] I have seen Rachel[5] – her acting was something apart from any other acting it has come in my way to witness – her soul was in it – and a strange soul she has – I shall not discuss it – it is my hope to see her again – She and Thackeray are the two living things that have a spell for me in this great London – and one of these is sold to the Great Ladies – and the other – I fear – to Beelzebub.[6]

[*14 June 1851.*] I almost wonder the Londoners don't tire a little of this vast Vanity Fair – and, indeed, a new toy has somewhat diverted the attention of the grandees lately, viz. a fancy ball given last night by the Queen. The great lords and ladies have been quite wrapt up in preparations for this momentous event. Their pet and darling, Mr Thackeray, of course sympathises with them. He was here yesterday to dinner, and left very early in the evening in order that he might visit respectively the Duchess of Norfolk, the Marchioness of Londonderry, Ladies Chesterfield and Clanricarde, and see them all in their fancy costumes of the reign of Charles II before they set out for the Palace! His lectures, it appears, are a triumphant success. . . . Of course Mr T. is a good deal spoiled by all this, and indeed it cannot be otherwise. He has offered two or three times to introduce me to some of his great friends, and says he knows many great ladies who would receive me with open arms if I would go to their houses; but, seriously, I cannot see that this sort of society produces so good an effect on him as to tempt me in the least to try the same experiment, so I remain obscure.

NOTES

1. George Smith's 'Reminiscences', in Leonard Huxley, *The House of Smith, Elder* (privately printed, 1923) pp. 67–8.

2. The dinner that evening was a social disaster. Thackeray had invited the Carlyles, Mrs Procter, Mrs Brookfield and other friends. Charlotte Brontë, shy and withdrawn, was overwhelmed by her role as chief guest, and replied monosyllabically to all questions. Thackeray hardly helped, as host. On the way down to dinner, he addressed his guest as Currer Bell: 'She tossed her head and said She believed there were books being published by a person named Currer Bell . . . but the person he was talking to was Miss Brontë – and she saw no connection between the two' – Charles and Frances Brookfield, *Mrs Brookfield and her Circle* (1905) II, 305. Later in the evening, he unceremoniously (and very rudely) crept away to his club, leaving his guests to depart as they might – Anne Thackeray Ritchie, *Chapters from 'Some Memoirs* (1894) pp. 63–4.

3. Elizabeth Gaskell, *Life of Charlotte Brontë*, Everyman edn (1908) p. 335.

4. *George Smith: A Memoir*, by his widow (privately printed, 1902) pp. 99–100.

5. Madame Rachel (1821–58), the leading French actress of the period.

6. Thackeray and Rachel are compared in another letter (*The Brontës*, I, 253) thus: 'the one, being a human creature, great, interesting, and *sometimes* good and kind; the other . . . I think a demon'.

A Flesh and Blood Genius

RICHARD BEDINGFIELD

From 'Personal Recollections of Thackeray', *Cassell's Magazine*, n.s., I (1869) 296–9; 'Recollections of Thackeray, with Some of his Letters, Anecdotes

and Criticisms: by his Cousin', ibid., n.s., II (1870) 12–14, 28–30, 72–5,
108–10, 134–6, 230–2. Bedingfield was a distant relative of Thackeray ('His
mother's grandfather was my great-grand-sire', and before Thackeray went
to Charterhouse 'he was a pupil of my grandfather, Dr Turner, at Chiswick')
and knew him over a long period, though he specifies that he 'saw more of
Thackeray when he was about thirty years of age than at any other period of
his career. Then he was of a buoyant spirit. . . . "Michael Angelo Titmarsh"
was a far jollier fellow than he became as the famous author of *Vanity Fair*.
He was full of "madcap humour", as a critic said of him . . . .' Thackeray, in
1828, had found Bedingfield 'a very clever little chap' (*LPP*, I, 18). In the
early 1840s he attempted authorship, writing what Ray, very believably,
describes as 'indifferent fiction' (*LPP*, I, 18n). His more talented cousin
advised him that these efforts were old-fashioned and unsalable (*LPP*, II,
192), but Bedingfield dedicated his second novel to him (1844) and
'Titmarsh' was duly touched: 'he got up from his chair and made me a bow,
saying, "That's the first dedication I've had." ' Bedingfield's reminiscences
are better read in abbreviated form, as here, than *in extenso*, though either
way they provide a bumpily non-sequacious account. Rambling and prolix,
and padded out (in the original, but not here) with letters and with banal
attempts at literary criticism, they contain nevertheless some indispensable
records of conversations and anecdotes.

I recollect I asked him once the question what he wrote when
he was a lad. 'I used to write poetry', he answered, 'and it was
devilish bad; but *then* I didn't think so.' There was a dash of the
poet in him, as there was in Hood; but a generous man of the
world, quick-sighted, keen-witted, shrewd, and caustic, seldom rises to 'the vision and the faculty divine'; and I don't
believe that he saw far into anything beyond the actual; in the
actual he lived and breathed.

He told me that he read more history than anything, and
advised all authors to make historical studies the greater part
of their education. 'Read a *tremendous* lot of history', he said,
as we walked out of the Reading Room of the British
Museum. . . . I don't think latterly he read to any great extent,
for he said to a relative of ours that he thought 'books very
great lumber' except works of reference. . . .

Thackeray was often grave and reticent, especially after he
had reached middle age, when in society. The liveliness of his
youth, the keen vivacity and zest of life which he displayed at
one period, vanished after he was crowned with success. The
penalty that he paid for his popularity was heavy. He said he
had fiercely fought for it, and broken health and a jaded mind
did not allow him to enjoy his good fortune. But he always

made a good fight for the victory over his gloomy feelings; so manly and firm-hearted was he by nature. Once I called on him, when he told me that he had not the power of writing at all; he feared it was going from him; and then, indeed, he appeared most wretched. . . .

When I was writing works of fiction in my juvenile days, my kinsman Thackeray invited me on one occasion to dine with him at the Rose Cottage, Richmond, and we were talking on the subject of style. Like most very young fellows, I admired a more ornate and a less simple and Saxon phraseology than I do *now*. 'The more simple and the more natural a style, the better', my entertainer observed; to which I objected that in the highest works of art, the most ideal and poetical works, 'this simple style – such as Goldsmith's, for instance – was not appropriate'.

'Dickens persuaded me to admire Tennyson,' said Thackeray; 'but I don't care for idealism. Beware of it! *Englishmen like roast beef*'[1]. . . .

The genius of Thackeray was all flesh and blood. He is one of the most literal, one of the least imaginative of authors. I heard a certain bishop, and a fine scholar, on one occasion remark that he 'had everything but imagination'. Fancy, doubtless, he possessed. He delighted in pretty, charming, and whimsical things. He had a great respect for Shakespeare; but he said to me, 'he did not *always* write naturally'. . . .

The mighty passions which shake the world, Thackeray, I suspect, was sceptical of. The tremendous, the awful, and the harrowing, he did not seek to penetrate. When I asked him what he meant in a certain illustration in which 'Becky' is 'Clytemnestra', he replied, 'I meant she had committed murder; but I didn't want anything *horrible.*' . . .

His mother, who was a Miss Becher, and his and my great-grandmother's grandchild, was a lady of remarkable beauty . . . very tall, very graceful, and decidedly sarcastic. . . . He greatly admired his mother's beauty. No man had a more artistic perception of feminine charms than Thackeray. I suspect that in his incipient manhood he was attracted by the external fascinations of woman far more than by mental excellence. Clever women, it is possible, did not at any time influence his fancy as much as those who, with a natural and an easy manner, combined expressive features with a certain

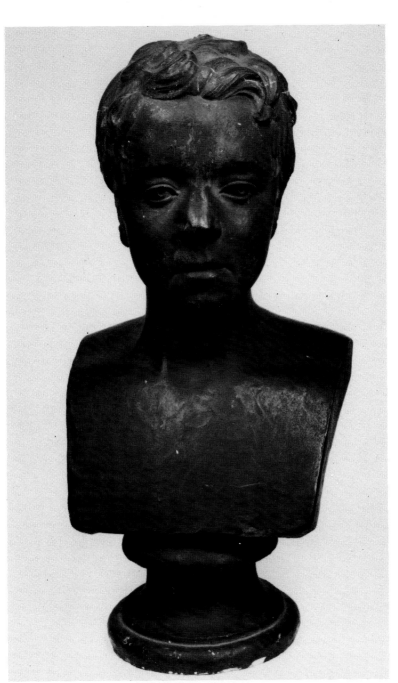

1. Bust by Joseph Edgar Boehm, after J. S. Deville, *c.* 1824

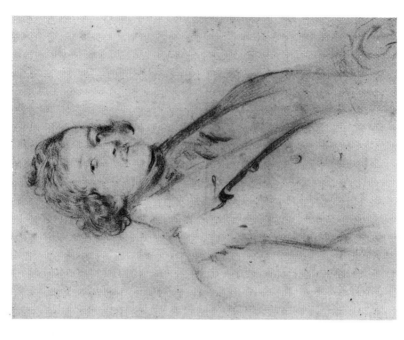

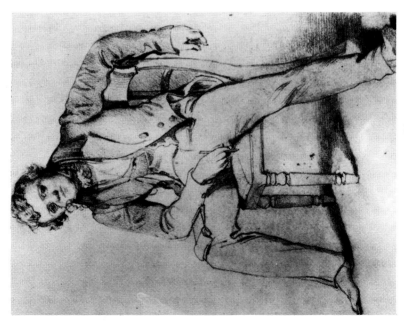

2. Sketches of Thackeray by Daniel Maclise, 1832 and c. 1840

3. 'The Fraserians' by Daniel Maclise, 1834

Fraser's Magazine, established 1830, was the first periodical of importance with which Thackeray was prominently associated. Distinguishable by his monocle, he is seated fourth to the right of its first editor (standing), William Maginn. Like other periodicals of its time, *Fraser's* promoted convivial occasions such as this formalised one, at which contributors could forgather and carouse.

4. Caricature, by Thackeray, of himself and his wife in early married life

5. Portrait by Frank Stone, 1839

6a. *(above left)* Thackeray, self-caricature in *Vanity Fair,* 1847: see Dr John Brown's comment (I, 148)

6b. *(above right)* Thackeray's monogram, carved into the *Punch* Table

6c. *(below)* 'Authors' Miseries. No. VI' (*Punch,* 4 November 1848): cartoon by Thackeray, depicting himself and Douglas Jerrold – presumably with some expectation that one or both of the 'Two Authors' would be recognised by a fair number of readers.

Old Gentleman. Miss Wiggets. Two Authors.

Old Gentleman. "I AM SORRY TO SEE YOU OCCUPIED, MY DEAR MISS WIGGETS, WITH THAT TRIVIAL PAPER 'PUNCH.' A RAILWAY IS NOT A PLACE, IN MY OPINION, FOR JOKES. I NEVER JOKE—NEVER."
Miss W. "SO I SHOULD THINK, SIR."
Old Gentleman. "AND BESIDES, ARE YOU AWARE WHO ARE THE CONDUCTORS OF THAT PAPER, AND THAT THEY ARE CHARTISTS, DEISTS, ATHEISTS, ANARCHISTS, AND SOCIALISTS, TO A MAN? I HAVE IT FROM THE BEST AUTHORITY, THAT THEY MEET TOGETHER ONCE A WEEK IN A TAVERN IN SAINT GILES'S, WHERE THEY CONCOCT THEIR INFAMOUS PRINT. THE CHIEF PART OF THEIR INCOME .IS DERIVED FROM THREATENING LETTERS WHICH THEY SEND TO THE NOBILITY AND GENTRY. THE PRINCIPAL WRITER IS A RETURNED CONVICT. TWO HAVE BEEN TRIED AT THE OLD BAILEY ; AND THEIR ARTIST—AS FOR THEIR ARTIST . . . ."
Guard. "SWIN-DUN ! STA-TION !" *[Exeunt two Authors.*

7. Caricature, by Thackeray, of himself and Anny, 1848

From a note to John Leech. The text reads: 'Dear Leech/This has just occurred to me
& I think might be utilised by your pleasing though satiric pencil. WMT/The little
darlings/'Anny. Papa, I think that sketch of you by [Count Dorsay *deleted*] Leech is
uglier than you are./Papa. Thank you dear.' Leech seems not to have used the idea
for a *Punch* cartoon, but evidently Thackeray worked at this joke, because a similar
sketch appears in an 1848 letter *(LPP,* II, 388, to a correspondent unknown, but
doubtless Leech), depicting himself flanked by a son as well as a daughter, with the
legend: *'Little Darling.* Papa, Tommy has just made a drawing of you. But I think it's
uglier than you are./*Tommy.* O not it's not.'

8. Caricature by John Leech, 1851

'Mr Michael Angelo Titmarsh, as he appeared at Willis's Rooms in his celebrated character of Mr Thackeray.' *The Month,* reproducing (July 1851) this impression of the opening of the *English Humourists* series, remarked that the audience was 'as brilliant and fashionable, as intelligent and judicious – in fact, after the lecturer, the agreeable sight of the excellent set of people who gathered about him with such thoughtful attention, was really an attraction'. Dr John Brown thought this 'extravaganza . . . excessively funny and not unlike. . . . He is reproduced lecturing, when certainly he looked his best.'

amount of beauty. Probably, he would always have despised *'imperial* charms', though his mother was of the commanding order of women. 'She is *natural*', meant the highest compliment that he could utter. This is what he said to me about Miss Becher, who is related to us, and is now the wife of the Bishop of Gloucester and Bristol. Nature was to him a goddess – in books, men, and women.

'Who is this wonderful actress, Mrs Stirling, about whom William raves?' said his mother to me. It was the natural style of that excellent performer which delighted him. I don't suppose the greatest effort of ideal art gave him the pleasure that he felt in the presence of a picture by Wilkie or Hogarth, or when perusing a book by Fielding, Goldsmith, etc. He expressed to me the highest admiration of Cooper's *Leatherstocking*. He once also told me that after finishing *The Three Musketeers* of Dumas, he could read the work again. He almost always felt disposed to ridicule anything pretentious. ...

The sense of the ridiculous and the *outré* in any author, overpowered in him the perception of his talent. If he saw a 'celebrity' with a turn-down collar (now so general), a moustache and a beard (now worn by half the population), he set him down as an ass. He liked nothing out of the way – either in manner, dress, or style.

Most Englishmen deify common sense. Thackeray was a thorough Briton – liked to be British to the core, liked all the pluck and doggedness of our nationality. 'He was ever a fighter' at school. ...

Thackeray was not devoid of pride, but was the kindest of men to inferiors. 'I always write to him "Dear John" ', he said, speaking of an old attached servant in his mother's house. It was only to the presumptuous that he displayed anything like *hauteur*. ...

He was of a buoyant spirit, and the organ of hope, if phrenology be correct, must have been largely developed in his head. That head, as we know, was of great dimensions. He had a capacity for the apocryphal blessing of taking more wine than the generality can swallow without any intoxicating effect. Once I recollect hearing him rally one of his friends, who came to visit him in his chambers, because the latter had succumbed to the power of wine while he was sober.

His habit was to write in bed – so he told me – and to put off the work that he had in hand till the last; for then, he considered, the high pressure urged him to his best speed. I asked him why he called that work *Pendennis*. 'I don't know', he replied. 'I wish I had called it "Smith", but I didn't think of it.' He added that he thought *Pendennis* a failure. . . .

Jerrold, of whom Thackeray said to me, 'He is the wittiest man I ever knew', had not half his knowledge of manners and society: neither had he his racy humour and quaint shrewdness of remark. Thackeray was also a fine critic, and not an ungenerous one. He was a man of fastidious taste and delicacy. Speaking on the subject of pathos to me, he said that he did not think it should be excluded from a book, but that it should be used very sparingly. . . .

When I mentioned to him that I had recently been to hear Thomas Cooper lecture on Christ,[2] he rejoined, 'Oh, Cooper the Chartist! I suppose he only makes Christ a reformer! *I don't know what to think!*'

Reverential scepticism must have been strong in his mind. The doubt and the reverence were perhaps *equally* strong. His masculine intellect and his veneration of the Creator had not solved the problem of Reconciliation, as Browning appears to have done. There is hardly a vestige in the writings of Thackeray suggestive of a theological dogma. We know but little more thereby of the state of his religious belief, than we knew of Shakespeare's by his dramatic works. This reticence was not merely from prudential motives; or why did he say to me, 'I think scepticism a very humble state of mind'? When I told him that I had heard Robert Montgomery[3] in the pulpit, expressing himself on the subject of Adam's transgression, saying, 'The squalling of an infant is an illustration of original sin', he observed, 'Did he say so? by Jove! He must be a beast! But he is a clever fellow to have said it!' . . .

When I told him I had been to hear Emerson lecture, he informed me that he had been invited to meet him, but that he had not felt a desire to do so, 'as he supposed he *ought*'.

He had no sympathy with transcendentalism, but he admired Thomas Carlyle. He has also expressed his reverence for 'the grand old Goethe'. When he was talking of the poets to me, he said, 'Yes, Milton was a great poet; but he is such a d——d bore, no one can read him!' He was persuaded that a poet *must* be appreciated (if there be anything in him) in twenty years; but admitted that 'Wordsworth was before his time.' He liked lyrical poetry, and praised a little song of mine. . . .

Thackeray's mother told my own mother that when her son thought of being a painter, he used to lie awake for hours conceiving pictures – he could conceive, but he could not execute, he said. The executive brilliancy of his literary works, the extreme elaboration and finish one recognises therein, he seemed to achieve with less trouble than would have been necessary in the pictorial department. But when he found that his pen would not serve him well, he informed me that he was in the habit of sketching those little illustrations which we find in his books. 'They are a great relief to my mind,' he said; 'I can *always* do *them*.'

The artistic excellence of Thackeray was not perceived to any extent when he was but a magazine contributor. He soon despised some of his own early attempts; but they are so fresh, genial, and graphic, that they will always afford pleasure. Of the *Yellowplush Papers*, when I told him I did not like them so much as his other works, he said, 'They are horrid rubbish; but I get well paid for them. A man must live.' He thought at that time '*Punch* paid nobly', and the 'Fat Contributor' was doubtless of very great service to the facetious satirist and showman; but I suspect that he never intended to remain on the staff of *Punch*. He told me that he wished *one day* to be ranked with 'classical writers'. That he *is*. No more 'classical' writer than Thackeray ever existed.

I called on him when he lived in Young Street, Kensington, and I saw a bust of George IV on his mantelpiece. I expressed my astonishment at seeing it. Thackeray laughed, and replied, 'Yes, the other day I noticed it in a friend's house, and exclaimed, "What! have you got that snob?" The next morning I found it here. My friend had sent it.' He told me George IV could not write English. He had seen letters of his 'full of bad grammar, incorrect spelling, and execrable French'. He had the greatest contempt for 'the first gentleman in Europe'. I don't think he admired monarchs, good or bad. That Thackeray was a violent democrat, however, I utterly deny.[4] At heart he was a bit of an aristocrat. His mother admired Feargus O'Connor. I don't think he did; and when defeated by Mr Cardwell at Oxford, how generously and with what magnanimity he spoke of him! When I expressed dislike of Daniel O'Connell, he replied, 'He may be a humbug, but he is a great man. We owe to him Catholic emancipation.' Of Disraeli (opposed to him in politics, as he was) he said, 'I think he has great talents.' Clearly, if Thackeray had become a senator, and were now alive, he would be supporting our great minister, Mr Gladstone. . . .

'I like your cousin Mr Thackeray, very much', said the authoress of *John Halifax*'[5] to me. 'He came with Mrs Procter the other day to call on me. He's not at all what I fancied he was.' Of Miss Mulock, Thackeray said to me, *not* disparagingly, 'I think she writes very prettily', and the 'pretty' had a charm for him. Whether he thought highly of the feminine mind I do not undertake to say. He was convinced that a man ought to be superior in intellect to his wife. I mentioned some persons related to us, where the lady had most brains, and who had lived happily together. 'I don't know how that was,' he replied; 'but, depend upon it, at one time the old gentleman ran some rigs.' We were also talking of Captain —— and his wife, and he said he had heard they did not always agree; 'but', he added, 'a man shouldn't be much at home. He's sure to quarrel with a woman if he is.' Yet I was told by a lady, who lived for years under the same roof with him, that 'William had the sweetest possible temper'. She also said that the want of money, when he was a young fellow, did not seem to weigh on his mind; for in Paris he would come to her and say, 'Polly, can you lend me a franc? I want some cigars!' Those were his artist days, and probably his happiest. . . .

When I asked him, just before *Vanity Fair* was published, whether it was 'funny', he replied, 'It will be humorous.' Mere fun, mere farcical nonsense, he did not value very highly.

I used to meet Thackeray frequently at the Reading Room of the British Museum, whither he had advised me to go, and where he was a diligent student. I don't think his reading was immense, but he had many things at his fingers' ends. . . .

Heterodox he was on many subjects, and I recollect he once defended the views of the polygamists to me, remarking, 'I think polygamy a good institution.' When I replied, that if men are to be allowed a plurality of wives, it is only just that women should have a similar privilege as to husbands, he repudiated the latter notion. . . .

When one thinks of the club life of London, and the society that Thackeray for many years was thrown into, the wonder is that he was not more utterly a man of the world than he was. He affected no cynicism; there was no amateur bitterness in his conversation, no grim contempt for the life that heaven has given us, in his works. 'Make the best of it!' is his, *in fact*, optimist view of existence. One day he observed that there were times when he thought he had been unhappy in losing a wife, as he *had* lost her, by a misfortune worse than death. 'But what should I have done', he added, 'with an immense family? No doubt everything is for the best.' . . .

He hated 'Jack Ketch' and his worse than 'bloody trade', he hated all things unmerciful and ruthless.[6] He sees 'no hint of damning' in the universe; he inveighs against the lash in the army; he has a loathing detestation of bullies, small and big; he would shake hands with many an outcast and an outlaw, male and female; and he once told me that a class to whom one can only refer by a glance at the 'woman' forgiven by a great authority many centuries ago, he believed to be 'very good people'. . . .

The restless spirit of our novelist was always taking him into various scenes and strange society. I have heard that he would disappear for a day or two, and his family in London would then receive an intimation from the Continent that he was on his way to Rome. He turned up in the most unexpected places, and at the strangest times. . . .

How altered he was, some time before he died! Once I said to him, 'You must weigh very heavy.'

'I suppose I do', was the reply.

'Do you know what you weigh?'

'Yes; but I'm not obliged to tell you.'

I laughed, and said, 'Sixteen stone?'

'No; if you come to *that* – fifteen', he rejoined. But he was quite thin at fifty; his appetite was gone; and he ceased to relish the choicest dishes.

I asked him once if he was strong. 'No', he answered. 'I *should* be; but I don't give the muscles fair play.' . . .

It was evidently Thackeray's ambition to be one of our legislators. He said to me once, pointing to such a consum-

mation as admission into Parliament, 'The bore of the thing is,
I can't speak. I was at a dinner the other day, and I had to say
something. Thinking, of course, I could do it, I got on my legs,
and broke down in the middle. I never felt such a fool in my
life. The fellows cheered and vociferated to cover my retreat;
but I won't do it again.' . . .

He expressed his aversion, I recollect, in conversation with
me, to the exaggeration and gross caricature of French
novels. He could not bear 'Paul de Kock', he once remarked to
me, and he could not bear Boucicault's plays; the morality of
both these writers being, to his mind, more than problematical. . . .

The habits of Thackeray were those of a 'clubman'. I have
met at his chambers some of those who doubtless transgressed
many of the rules of our present social etiquette. 'How soon
you were *gone* after the dinner at ——'s, the other day!' said
Thackeray to one of his friends, who looked as if he still
suffered from the effects of headache. 'I think we should stick
to one wine only!' . . .

The last time I ever spoke to Thackeray was on an
afternoon in summer. I met him near Trafalgar Square, and
was shocked to see him looking so ill. 'Now that I have won all I
want,' he said, 'I can't enjoy it. That's what we must expect, I
suppose. We lose one thing and gain another. I shall never be
any better, and have no appetite – no energy. I sometimes
envy a poor beggar.'

The world-weariness, the 'vanity and vexation of spirit'
which he endured could be read in his pale face – once so
ruddy. The famous author, whom I recollected struggling
with difficulties, and as obscure as others, desponding in the
midst of luxuries – now a broken man in health and heart –
had paid the price exacted by Fortune, and was not destined to
survive many months. . . .

I remarked, in conversation with Thackeray, that when we
got to the mightiest questions of existence it was always with
him, 'I don't know.' And yet I suspect that, whenever he was
out of society, the great 'maybe' of a future life was frequently
in his mind. He said on one occasion to me that materialism is
the necessary stage at which the superficial mind arrives in
investigating the truth.

There was no jealousy, as there was no mean pride, in

Thackeray. How he admired Dickens – how honestly, heartily, and entirely he paid a tribute to the modest merit of Thomas Hood, and was ready to call his 'Song of the Shirt' the finest lyric ever written! I think he sometimes over-rated the merit of his contemporaries. When he admired, he did so with his whole being. . . .

I have heard that Thackeray was able to imitate Edmund Kean admirably. He evidently considered that meteoric tragedian superior to Macready. When I remarked to him, once, that Mrs K—— was a capital actress, he responded, 'Yes; but she's so deucedly ugly!' Thackeray had much reverence for all beauty – it appealed to his weak side. 'She is so beautiful!' he once said of his mother, when she had done something that kindled a momentary ire. I think he loved her very sincerely, but he said to me, 'We differ about a thousand things. Those of a past generation can't feel with us.' Though she had some Asiatic blood (not visible in him), few women could be compared to her in personal attractions. She really looked as young as her son when she was fifty. . . .

An American lady, an authoress, of Roman Catholic opinions, told me she was once rather offended with Thackeray, because she was 'snubbed' (that was her expression) by the satirist, when she informed him that she went to the 'oratory' at Brompton – 'Oh! you go to that *shop*, do you?' That was what he thought of Popery. I suspect that Thackeray was a sort of Christian sceptic, like Carlyle. On the subject of religion, however, he was always reverential, and when we were speaking of the late W. J. Fox[7] and his talents (which Thackeray confessed), he remarked to me, 'He has such a way of patronising God Almighty!'

He always spoke with the profoundest veneration for Christ; and I fancy that, latterly, he was of Unitarian (that is, modern Unitarian) views in theology. He once remarked to me, that he considered scepticism 'a very humble state of mind'. . . .

He had an Englishman's abhorrence of lax continental notions on the subject of morality, and said to me, 'France will never be politically regenerated while the social notions of the French are so degraded.' Balzac and George Sand he disliked (admitting their brilliant abilities) because of their gross profligacy (if I remember, those were his words). Of Mrs

Gore, personally, he said, 'She is as clever as somebody else, and as wicked.'[8]

I once asked him to a party, and he would have accepted the invitation; but when he heard that Mrs Trollope would be present, he ejaculated, "Oh, by Jove! I can't come. I've just cut up her *Vicar of Wrexhill* [1837] in a review. I think she tells lies.' . . .

When he mentioned Dickens to me, I said I did not fancy he was a deep thinker. 'No; but he has a clear and a bright-eyed intelligence, which is better than philosophy', he said. I rejoined that I thought he a little over-rated Dickens. 'I think he is equal to Fielding and Smollett – at any rate, to Smollett. He is not a scholar as Fielding was', he replied. He told me he thought 'Dickens wrote the most charming extravaganza in world', which seems to me a fine and a just criticism. I asked him what writer of all living authors he most admired. 'Macaulay is about the most brilliant', was the answer. No doubt he was captivated by Lord Macaulay's style, but I was surprised that he cared for him so much. . . .

The singular mixture of perfect charity with a shade of cynicism in Thackeray – the latter, the result of his keen perception, for he knew 'all qualities with a learned spirit of human dealings' – can hardly be questioned. He was a cynic in theory, not in practice; and even his theory was but skin-deep. The word 'humbug' was always in his mouth, rarely in his heart. I was telling him that [Sheridan] Knowles, whom I had opinion of most Irishmen, for he said to me, They are a the most agreeable persons I ever saw. 'He's a most charming old humbug', said Thackeray. And I think that was his opinion of most Irishmen, for he said to me, 'They are a nation of liars!'[9] . . .

I believe Thackeray hardly ever would accept the return of money which he had lent to poor authors. He told me that he thought it very probable he might come to want 'the same thing' himself; and I was surprised that he was able to lay by money, as he did. . . .

Thackeray did not like to be always discussing politics or grave subjects, and assured me that it was quite 'refreshing' to escape to his wife sometimes – who was not political. He said, with a sigh to me, after she became hopelessly insane, 'Poor thing! I was as happy as the day was long with her.' . . .

Authors in general may not like to hear Thackeray's
opinion, which he expressed to me, that but few of them were
gentlemen, and that they were the *least* well-informed men he
knew. I believe he had a great fancy for the society of the
'swells', as he sometimes called the nobility; but he would also
laugh at his own weakness. He was walking with an uncle of
mine in Brighton, and a gentleman spoke to him; but they did
not remain long in conversation.

'That was the Duke of Dèvonshire', said Thackeray, a
minute afterwards. 'I did not wish to say much to him, for fear
of being asked to dinner; and I am obliged to live very plainly.'
The next day, however, a Brighton paper informed the public
that the author had dined with the Duke.

I think Thackeray lived too well, and shortened his days,
perhaps, by a relish for made dishes and rare wines – most of
us do who can get them. But after all he did his work. The
mission of Thackeray was not merely that of a detective of
literature. He hated flunkeys of the pen, but he loved genius.
Once he told me that he thought 'Browning is an excellent
fellow, but seems to me a madman.'[10]

NOTES

1. A surprising story (if true – but Bedingfield assures his readers that
'All that I state in these pages may be relied upon as strictly correct'):
surprising that Thackeray had to be urged to admire his Cambridge
contemporary and friend Tennyson by Dickens, who was much less close to
Tennyson, culturally and socially, than he was. Dickens, though not much
given to reading poetry, did indeed greatly admire Tennyson's 1842 *Poems*,
and later the *Idylls*.

2. Thomas Cooper (1805–92), working-class poet, journalist, lecturer
and later preacher, was an eminent Chartist in the early 1840s. By the later
1840s he had become a popular lecturer, promulgating a sceptical anti-
supernaturalism derived from Strauss's *Life of Jesus*, translated from the
German by the future George Eliot (1846). See her associate John
Chapman's remarks on Thackeray's religious position – or disbelief –
below, I, 138. Chapman reports Thackeray as being a discreetly silent
unbeliever, but Bedingfield, wandering round to this matter again later,
opines, 'I think there is no doubt at all that Thackeray believed in a future
life' – though, he continues, Thackeray had no pretensions to philosophy,
and what he said to Bedingfield about Dickens was true also of himself: 'He
has a clear, bright-eyed intelligence' (but no deeper pretensions).

3. Montgomery (1807–55), 'poetaster' (*Dictionary of National Biography*): author of some much-praised religious poems, he officiated at the Percy Chapel, St Pancras, from 1843.

4. It is curious, but noteworthy, that Bedingfield should feel impelled, in 1870, so emphatically ('utterly') to deny that Thackeray was 'a violent democrat'. Such accusations have become rare during the century since then.

5. Dinah Mulock, later Mrs Craik (1826–87), whose novel *John Halifax, Gentleman* (1856) was very popular.

6. Later in these reminiscences, Bedingfield remarks that he once praised, to Thackeray, his abolitionist article 'Going to See a Man Hanged' (*Fraser's Magazine*, Aug 1840), and 'His observation was: "I think I was wrong. My feelings were overwrought. Those murderers are such devils, after all." Nevertheless, he did not like the idea of capital punishment.' Thackeray's distinguished editor George Saintsbury comments, 'The anti-capital-punishment fad was one of the special crotchets of mid-century Liberalism, and [Thackeray] kept to it for some time: but in his later and wiser days admitted that he was wrong' – *A Reconsideration of Thackeray* (1931) p. 56.

7. W. J. Fox (1786–1864), reviewer, M.P. and preacher, became so unorthodox in behaviour and doctrine as to alienate even the Unitarians, to whom he belonged.

8. Mrs·Catherine Gore (1799–1861), novelist and dramatist.

9. James Sheridan Knowles (1784–1862), much-admired poetic dramatist, was an Ulsterman. John Westland Marston (1819–90) was another poetic dramatist.

10. Bedingfield, having dedicated these 'Recollections' to Browning, duly contests his kinsman's underestimate of the poet. See above, I, 103, for Thackeray's relationship with Browning.

The Reluctant Lecturer

FANNY KEMBLE AND OTHERS

(1) From Frances Anne Kemble, *Records of Later Life* (1882), III, 360–2; (2) from 'Mr Thackeray's Lectures', *Spectator*, 24 May 1851, pp. 493–4; (3) from [William Cullen Bryant], 'Mr Thackeray's Lecture', *Evening Post* (New York), 20 Nov 1852; (4) from *The Journal of Richard Henry Dana, Jr*, ed. Robert F. Lucid (Cambridge, Mass., 1968) p. 527; (5) from Richard Henry Stoddard, *Recollections, Personal and Literary* (New York, 1903) pp. 215–16; (6) an unnamed young lady's account of the 'Charity and Humour' lecture,

in Coventry, 1855, *Biog. Intros*, VIII, xxvii; (7) from Charles A. Cooper, *An Editor's Retrospect: Fifty Years of Newspaper Work* (1896) pp. 41–4. Lecturing, and other such 'personal appearances' by major authors were just coming into fashion in the 1850s, but Thackeray was among the pioneers in exploiting American enthusiasm for paying big money to star performers from Britain. His 1851–2 *Humourists* lectures in England and Scotland were explicitly a try-out for the real thing – dollars, duly earned in the States during the winter of 1852–3. The *Four Georges* series had their debut in America, 1855–6, and were then repeated in Britain, winter 1856–7. Thackeray did not much enjoy lecturing, and came to hate repeating his scripts. He undertook this chore mainly to amass a nest-egg for his dependent women-folk; like Dickens with his paid Public Readings (1858–70), he could earn more, more quickly, by personal appearances than by writing. Moreover, these personal appearances enhanced his popularity and thus his sales and fees. His worrying about his debut as a lecturer (London, 22 May 1851) was witnessed by the actress Fanny Kemble (1809–93), with whom he had long been acquainted, though he never greatly liked her. She, however, tells this anecdote to illustrate 'his great kindness and amiability, his *sweetness* of temper and disposition'. He had met her shortly before his debut, and asked her to come to it, telling her 'that he was so nervous about it, that he was afraid he should break down'. She was engaged that night, but promised to visit and cheer him before the lecture.

(1) He was to lecture at Willis Rooms, in the same rooms where I read,[1] and going thither before the time for his beginning, I found him standing like a forlorn disconsolate giant in the middle of the room, gazing about him. 'Oh, Lord,' he exclaimed, as he shook hands with me, 'I'm sick at my stomach with fright.' I spoke some words of encouragement to him, and was going away, but he held my hand, like a scared child, crying, 'Oh, don't leave me!' 'But,' said I, 'Thackeray, you mustn't stand here. Your audience are beginning to come in', and I drew him from the middle of his chairs and benches, which were beginning to be occupied, into the retiring-room adjoining the lecture-room, my own readings having made me perfectly familiar with both. Here he began pacing up and down, literally wringing his hands in nervous distress. 'Now,' said I, 'what shall I do? Shall I stay with you till you begin, or shall I go, and leave you alone to collect yourself?' 'Oh,' he said, 'if I could only get at that confounded thing' (his lecture), 'to have a last look at it!' 'Where is it?' said I. 'Oh, in the next room on the reading-desk.' 'Well,' said I, 'if you don't like to go in and get it, I'll fetch it for you.' And remembering well the position of my reading-table, which had been close to the door of the retiring room, I darted in, hoping to snatch the

manuscript without attracting the attention of the audience, with which the room was already nearly full. I had been used to deliver my reading seated, at a very low table, but my friend Thackeray gave his lectures standing, and had had a reading-desk placed on the platform, adapted to his own very tall stature, so that when I came to get his manuscript it was almost above my head. Though rather disconcerted, I was determined not to go back without it, and so made a half jump, and a clutch at the book, when every leaf of it (they were not fastened together), came fluttering separately down about me. I hardly know what I did, but I think I must have gone nearly on all fours, in my agony to gather up the scattered leaves, and retreating with them, held them out in dismay to poor Thackeray, crying, 'Oh, look, look, what a dreadful thing I have done!' 'My dear soul,' said he, 'you couldn't have done better for me. I have just a quarter of an hour to wait here, and it will take me about that to page this again, and it's the best thing in the world that could have happened.' With which infinite kindness he comforted me, for I was all but crying, at having, as I thought, increased his distress and troubles. So I left him, to give the first of that brilliant course of literary historical essays with which he enchanted and instructed countless audiences in England and America.

(2) What are his lectures like? good of course, exceedingly worth hearing, but like *what*? – Well, they are like his conversation, like his books, like himself; probably very near to what was expected by that audience, fit though not few, which assembled to answer the question for itself on Thursday.

We all knew before, how Thackeray handles the follies which he satirises – with what gentleness and tenderness. . . . He is a satirist, but *not* supercilious. . . . Thackeray in the rostrum is not different from the Thackeray at the table or in the printed page, except that he *is* in the rostrum. His lecture is a long soliloquy, giving you Thackeray's idea of his subject. . . . But the look and manner of the man! Thackeray in the rostrum, we say, is not different from Thackeray anywhere else; a thought graver, perchance because he is reading, or is nervous at the idea of sustaining, himself alone, a colloquy with that distinguished assemblage. But the form which rises before you in that crimson desk is unaltered; it is the same strange, anomalous, striking aspect; the face and contour of a child – of the round-cheeked humorous boy, who presumes so saucily on being liked, and liked for his very impudence – grown large without losing its infantile round-ness or simplicity; the sad grave eyes looking forth – through the spectacles that help them but baffle you with their blank dazzle – from the deepest vaults of that vast skull, over that gay, enjoying smile; the curly hair of youth, but grey with years brought before their time by trouble and thought.

(3) Everyone who saw Thackeray last evening for the first [lecture in New York], seemed to have had their impressions of his appearance and manner of speech, corrected. Few expected to see so large a man; he is gigantic, six feet four at least; few expected to see so old a person; his hair appears to have kept its silvery record over fifty years; and then there was a notion in the minds of many that there must be something dashing and 'fast' in his appearance, whereas his costume was perfectly plain; the expression of his face grave and earnest; his address perfectly unaffected, and such as we might expect to meet with, in a well-bred man somewhat advanced in years. His elocution, also, surprised those who had derived their impressions from the English journals. His voice is a superb tenor, and possesses that pathetic tremble which is so effective in what is called emotive eloquence, while his delivery was as well suited to the communication he had to make as could well have been imagined.

His enunciation is perfect. Every word he uttered might have been heard in the remotest quarters of the room, yet he scarcely lifted his voice above a colloquial tone. The most striking feature in his whole manner was the utter absence of affectation of any kind. He did not permit himself to appear conscious that he was an object of peculiar interest to the audience, neither was he guilty of the greater error of not appearing to care whether they were interested in him or not. In other words, he inspired his audience with a respect for him, as a man proportioned to the admiration, which his books have inspired for him as an author.

Of the lecture itself, as a work of art, it would be difficult to speak too strongly. Though written with the utmost simplicity and apparent inattention to effects, it overflowed with every characteristic of the author's happiest vein. There has been nothing written about Swift so clever . . . .[2]

(4) [Journal of R. H. Dana, Jr,[3] 31 Dec 1852.] Went to Thackeray's lecture. Subject – Prior, Gay and Pope. He is a tall strong built man, with that well-bred awkwardness which characterises most Englishmen in good society, hair prematurely grey, voice strong, clear & melodious, manner natural & conversational, without any attempt at rhetorical effect. Prior & Gay, & indeed Pope, too, as he ought to have treated him, were entirely within his range, but when he undertook to say that the close of the *Dunciad* was unsurpassed for grandeur of imagery, thought & language by anything in English poetry, he displayed his incapacity to judge of a great poetic theme. Yet, within his range, the lecture was very entertaining, & delivered with that manliness, independence & clearness wh distinguish the best specimens of Engl. gentlemen.

(5) Every characteristic of Thackeray was noted [in the American press, writes Richard Henry Stoddard[4]] and once, at least, he was well described: 'As for the man himself who has lectured us, he is a stout, healthful, broad-shouldered specimen of a man, with cropped greyish hair, and keenish grey eyes, piercing very sharply through a pair of spectacles that have a very satiric focus. He seems to stand strongly on his own feet, as if he would not be easily blown about or upset, either by praise or pugilists; a man of good digestion, who takes the world easy, and scents all shams and humbugs (straightening them between his thumb and forefinger) as he would a pinch of snuff.'
There was something in Thackeray's reading which no one caught. It defied analysis, and evades memory. His voice, as I recall it, was at once low and deep, with a peculiar and indescribable cadence; his elocution was matchless in its simplicity. His attitude was impressive and tranquil, the only movement of his hands being when he wiped his glasses as he turned over the leaves of his manuscript. He read poetry exquisitely.

(6) [The 'Charity and Humour' lecture] was quietly and well delivered – no action – read as a book. He gave a slight sketch

of the early Humourists, but when he came to Dickens, he spoke with affectionate enthusiasm, saying, 'I have a little maid at home who is never happy without one of his books beneath her pillow.' His benediction on Dickens became almost a thanksgiving, so devout was it. He also read from *Punch* an extract from 'The Curate's Walk' so touching and humorous that is alone would almost prove the principle that true 'humour is always charitable'. He had written it himself as he told us very simply.

(7) [In 1857 Thackeray gave his *Four Georges* series in Hull. After the first lecture, he sent for Charles Cooper, a young journalist who had reported it in the local newspaper. 'Do you know, sir,' he said, 'that you have done your best to deprive me of a living?' – readers provided with such full and accurate reports would feel no need to attend the lectures.[5] The reporter apologised, and was departing when Thackeray asked what he had thought of the lecture.] 'I thought it very clever,' I replied; 'but I thought you had used a great deal of cleverness in trying to hide a kindly heart under cover of cheap cynicism.'

'Confound it,' he said, 'you are frank enough. What do you mean by cheap cynicism?'

'Well, I am scarcely prepared to answer that question off-hand.'

'I think you should try to tell me what you mean. It sounds like harsh criticism!'

'Please remember, it is the criticism of a very young man. Perhaps it is impertinent.'

'I am sure you did not mean to be impertinent, and I should like to know what was in your mind.'

'I thought the lecture was cynical. You will, I think, admit that it is.'

He nodded: and I went on. 'It struck me that the cynicism was what any clever man who chose to give his mind to it could produce, and therefore I spoke of it as "cheap cynicism."'

'Thank you', he said, with a smile. 'Perhaps you are right. But no one has ever said such a thing to me before. Don't imagine I am offended. *Ex oribus parvulorum* ['Out of the mouths of babes and sucklings...']: you know the rest.'

I did, and I felt a little mortified. But the kindness of the tone soon removed all that feeling. I was a babe, to him; and I had been a venturous babe.

NOTES

1. The Willis Rooms, King Street, St James's, were a frequent venue for such events as Fanny Kemble's Shakespearean recitals.
2. According to General Wilson (I, 23), this critique was written by the poet William Cullen Bryant (1794–1878). Thackeray was evidently pleased with it; he sent a cutting of it to Mrs Brookfield (*LPP*, III, 124).
3. R. H. Dana, Jr (1815–82), American author and man of affairs, best remembered for *Two Years before the Mast* (1840).
4. Richard Henry Stoddard (1825–1903), American poet, critic and journalist. His *Recollections* contains a pleasant account of social meetings and talk with Thackeray (pp. 216–25).
5. At Hull, in fact, his takings were guaranteed. When a deputation from its Literary and Philosophical Society had called upon him in London, he had brusquely replied, 'You won't pay me my price' – 'so brusquely, indeed [recalls one of the officers], that my companion was completely taken aback, and hardly knew what to say.' They were, in fact, quite willing to pay the 100 guineas Thackeray demanded for the course, and made £50 profit. At an impromptu supper he met 'what, measured by Hull standards, was a distinguished body of savants' and retrieved his reputation for politeness: he 'soon warmed up; his conversation was full of interest, with a plentiful spice of satire, and any unfavourable impression that his brusqueness may have made was completely obliterated' – James Samuelson, *Recollections* (1907) pp. 116–20.

His Arch-tormentor Arcedeckne

F. C. BURNAND

From '*Punch* Notes. II', *Pall Mall Magazine*, XVII (1899) 327–9. For Burnand, editor of *Punch* (1880–1906) see below, II, 323. Andrew Arcedeckne, clubman and man-about-town, was 'the original of Foker', Thackeray confided, 'don't say so though' (*LPP*, IV, 109). Many stories are told of his teasing Thackeray, though his famous 'pianner' crack has been attributed to others. Burnand confirms that Arcedeckne was indeed the perpetrator.

... I, personally, had this very story from Andrew Arcedeckne himself: he told it me at the Garrick Club, and with it
several other anecdotes of passages between himself and
Thackeray, in which Arcedeckne as a matter of fact, on the
testimony of credible witnesses, invariably had the best of it.
This sounds strange, as, in the fitness of things, Thackeray
ought to have been the victor; but Arcedeckne was a most
eccentric character, a genuine low comedian off the stage, and
nothing of an actor, even for an amateur, when on the
'boards', where he sometimes appeared, only to be chaffed by
all his friendly audience, who would throw coppers into his
hat on his assuming Robson's celebrated part of Jem Bags in
The Wandering Minstrel. During the last years of his comparatively short life, Arcedeckne and myself were great 'chums'.
He used to amuse me immensely, especially with his Garrick
Club stories and his reminiscences of Thackeray. Finding that
in me he had a ready listener, he 'let himself go', and in his own
quaint, dry way he would recount to me, when we happened
to be alone in the smoking-room, stories, not only of Thackeray, but also of many literary and theatrical celebrities
whom he had personally known. Arcedeckne 'owed' Thackeray 'one' on account of his having used him as his model for
Foker in *Pendennis*,[1] and he never lost an opportunity of
scoring off the great novelist, of whom, however, he invariably
spoke with affectionate familiarity as 'Old Thac'. Occasionally, and only when in a very mischievous yet genial mood,
would Arcedeckne address him as 'Thac my boy!' He would
select a moment when Thackeray, towering above little podgy
Arcedeckne, was standing in the smoking-room with his back
to the fire and his coat-tails spread out, his mind occupied with
some work the proofs of which were probably in the pockets
he was warming, when Arcedeckne would furtively enter,
look round, pretend not to see him, and then, as he reopened
the door preparatory to taking his departure, he would look
back and say, in his grating, nasal voice, 'Hallo! Thac my boy!
gettin' inspiration, eh?' and then *'exit quickly'*. It was a
delightful illustration of 'dignity and impudence'. At other
times Arcedeckne would wait until Thackeray had comfort-
ably settled himself with a cigar in a large armchair, and just
when he had assumed his favourite attitude of lounging back,
head in air, and right leg crossed over his left, the sole of his

boot being well *en evidence*, the original of Foker would sneak in, humming to himself some popular air – his favourite was the song of 'Villikens and his Dinah' – while carrying an unlighted cigar in his left hand and a match in his right. Then, as he passed the peacefully meditative giant, pigmy Arcedeckne, pausing awhile in his humming, would exclaim, with a sort of cheery grunt, 'Hallo! Thac my boy!' and, as if obeying an irresistible inspiration, would sharply strike the match on the sole of Thackeray's boot, light his cigar, and then hurriedly limp out of the room (he was a bit gouty) without saying another word, leaving Thackeray speechless at this 'confounded liberty'. 'Awfully good chap was old Thac', Arcedeckne used to say, when subsequently narrating this and similar anecdotes: 'Lor' bless you, he didn't mind me a bit. But I *did* take it out of him now and again. Never gave him time for a repartee.'

I have, by way of preamble, been at some pains to describe the style and manner of 'Merry Andrew' Arcedeckne in order to show how perfectly in keeping with his peculiar humour was his observation on the absence of a 'pianner' from Thackeray's lectures. It was in this way: on Thackeray's expressing his fear lest his lecture should not prove a success, as his first start had seemed to him a comparative failure, Arcedeckne, who among others had been listening to him, sidled up to the door (his usual 'safe move', reminding me of the pugilist's dodge of 'going down to avoid a blow') and, looking back sorrowfully as he went out, croaked, '*Ah! Thac my boy! you ought to ha' 'ad a pianner*', with which 'exit speech' he disappeared, chuckling.[2] This was Arcedeckne down to the ground; but surely it is not Jerrold. However, Arcedeckne, as I have said, told it to me of himself: and certainly 'it was just like him', as was the other story, so well known, of his asking Thackeray with what he was going to follow up *The Four Georges*. 'There's plenty for you to do, Thac my boy,' observed Arcedeckne thoughtfully, 'there's the two Charleses, the eight Henries, and the sixteen Gregories.' After delivering himself of this valuable suggestion he, as usual, vanished. Imagine Thackeray on such an occasion! especially as it must have flashed across him that 'Foker' was being avenged. There are many good Garrick stories about Andrew Arcedeckne. . . .

NOTES

1. Various acquaintances of Arcedeckne state, however, that he was rather pleased than otherwise by being immortalised as Foker – and that the portrait rather flattered him, Foker being a more estimable and socially a more distinguished character than the man himself was.

2. Music – an accompanied vocalist or a trio – often featured in poetry recitals, one-man-shows, and similar events, to provide some variety in the programme and to give the recitalist's voice a rest. See Philip Collins, *Reading Aloud: A Victorian Métier* (Lincoln: Tennyson Society, 1972) pp. 14, 24.

Recollections of a Secretary

EYRE CROWE

(1) from *Thackeray's Haunts and Homes* (1897) pp. 23–4, 52–6; (2) from *With Thackeray in America* (1893) pp. 34–5, 45–7, 110–11, 171–3. Thackeray became intimate with the family of Eyre Evans Crowe (1799–1868), historian, novelist and Paris correspondent of the *Morning Chronicle*, during his mid-1830s sojourn in Paris; he used to visit them and play with the children every Saturday, joining in Mrs Crowe's musical At Homes, where a song from him was regarded as the highlight of the ·evening – Sir Joseph Crowe, *Reminiscences of Thirty-five Years of My Life* (1895) pp. 10–11. In his later and more prosperous days, he remained very friendly and was able to help two of the Crowe boys, Joseph (1825–96) and Eyre *fils* (b. 1824); and their sister Amy (1831–65) was for eight years a member of Thackeray's household, after her mother's death and until her marriage in 1862. Eyre *fils*, struggling to become an artist – eventually he became an A.R.A. – was engaged as his amanuensis and researcher while he was writing *Esmond*, and in 1852 was persuaded to accompany him on the American *Humourists* lecture tour. 'I dont think you'd make the best and cutest Secretary that a man could find anywhere,' Thackeray wrote to him: 'yet to me you would be valuable as you know from old affection and entire confidence wh I couldn't give to a stranger who might be a hundred times more spry than you' (*LPP*, III, 79). As Thackeray expected, Crowe proved imperfect as a secretary but very 'pleasant as a companion, and always agreeable gentlemanlike and trustworthy'. His letters from the States often refer to his being the 'fondest best-humoured affectionate fellow', 'my immensest comfort; I could not live without someone to take care of me, and he is the kindest and most affectionate henchman ever man had' (*LPP*, III, 82, 121, 184). Unfortunately Eyre's account of the tour is dull and uninformative, more concerned

with America and with his own drawings than with Thackeray's doings – no match for the account of Dickens's American readings tour by his 'henchman' George Dolby (*Charles Dickens as I Knew Him*, 1884). Though affectionate, the two men were not uncritical of each other. In 1856, Thackeray wrote that 'poor Eyre gets no work, paints no better, half starves, has himself to thank for his poverty', and, the same month, Crowe was writing of him, 'Thackeray, afflicted with fever & ague, is at home in a bad temper & making every one around him feel the dampening effect of his low spirits. He shuns society at one moment, then rushes into it the next with a rapidity which brings on his illness again. He wants quietness & I suppose a certainty for his old days. Don't we all wish for that. His daughters go out a great deal, but he is disappointed at their not meeting with more success. I fear that the high places to which he brings them won't make them particularly happy' (*LPP*, III, 613 and n).

(1) [Crowe recalls, as a boy, visiting Great Coram Street, where Thackeray lived intermittently from 1838 to 1843.] The sentences which caught my juvenile ear were Thackeray's noble acknowledgement of the great powers of 'Boz', whose *nom de plume* covered the walls of London at that time. Without acerbity, but as plain matter-of-fact, Thackeray added plaintively, 'he sells thousands of copies to my small hundreds'. . . .[1]

Besides works of comparatively slow growth he produced [in the years before *Vanity Fair*] the weekly lucubrations for *Punch*'s pages, which charm as a rule by their natural ease, suggestive of spontaneous rapid conception. That this was not always the case was once made clear, when at the appointed time for collecting manuscript, the printer's boy was announced and was told to wait in the hall. Thackeray, pacing the room in which the brain-cudgeling was taking place, exclaimed, 'Well, I must be funny in five minutes.' With pluck he sat down at his desk and shortly after the printer's devil was off with the needed copy. . . .

I was in Paris when the first numbers of *Vanity Fair* came out, and like the equally immortal *Pickwick Papers*, the preliminary chapters were not accepted with the enthusiasm accorded to the future developments. Toward the closing months, on my return to England, and in rambles in the evening from Young Street, accompanied by Thackeray, and others, the talk was generally not alone about the prodigious success already achieved, but as to the probable *dénouement* of the story. It was Thackeray's humour to baffle enterprising inquisitiveness by evolving different lines and modes of winding up the career of Becky, Dobbin, and the others, having doubtless already well settled mentally how they were finally to be allotted their dues. One exceptional instance I remember in which a suggestion was accepted as valuable. It occurred in June 1848, one day when Thackeray came at lunch-time to my father's Hampstead house. Torrens Mc-Cullagh[2], happening to be one of the party, said across the table to Thackeray, 'Well, I see you are going to shut up your puppets in their box!' His immediate reply was, 'Yes; and, with your permission, I'll work up that simile.' How skilfully that chance phrase was worked up in the prefatorial 'Before the Curtain', all his readers well know. . . .[3]

(2) [On the train from Boston to New York a child book-merchant] accosted him with his own volumes, and called out 'Thackeray's Works!' quite unaware that he was addressing the author himself. He therefore re-read his *Shabby Genteel Story*, of a dozen years before, as we were whisked along the undulating territory of Massachusetts. I expended twenty-five cents in the purchase of *Uncle Tom's Cabin*, and was properly harrowed by the tale told by Mrs Beecher-Stowe. But Thackeray declined to plunge into its tale of woe; his opinion expressed upon it being that stories founded upon such painful themes were scarcely within the legitimate purview of story-telling. Besides, judicious friends had dinned well into his ears the propriety of his not committing himself to either side of the Slavery Question, then a burning one, if he wished his career as a lecturer not to become a burthen to him. He dwelt in preference upon the blithe aspects of American life, such as the group of children in the cars, eight in number, every one of whom he wished there and then to present with a dollar tip a-piece. . . .

[His New York debut took place in a Unitarian chapel.] I shall not easily forget the author's expression of wonder when he looked athwart the long, dark, wainscoted benches, and saw the pillared nave and the oak pulpit. He seemed fascinated by the idea of his lay-sermonising in this place. Then looking at the communion table . . . he asked, 'Would not the sacred emblems be removed from the altar?' followed by the query: 'Will the organ strike up when I enter?' Then, peering into the side room, he further inquired, 'I suppose I shall have to enter by the sacristy?' To sum up the matter, it was determined that this was the eligible resort.... The lecturer ascended the somewhat high rostrum, which had been erected fronting the pulpit; along with him came the secretary, Mr Willard Felt, who, on the warm greetings of welcome subsiding, introduced the lecturer in a few well-chosen sentences, and sat down on a chair at the side. All went cheerily to the end. As was the case in England, the reporters had been asked not to give *in extenso* or even too liberally the subject-matter of the lectures. This intent was honourably adhered to; but to eke out their paragraphs – which Thackeray read with interest the next morning – the manipulation of his coat-tails, varied with his favourite posture of diving his hands in his side-pockets, was dwelt upon facetiously, as well as the unusual fact that he indulged in no particular form of gesticulation. The first and only intimation anyone had that these humoristic details tickled the author's fancy was on the arrival in New York in mid-January, a month after date, of the January number of *Fraser's Magazine*, containing his unsigned, yet palpably his own, description of this quaint form of personal characterisation.[4]

Neither the prevailing gloom of the place (the lights, as usual wherever there is dark wainscot, proving powerless to diffuse brightness), nor inclement weather, such as that on the occasion of the second lecture, could daunt the intrepid ladies and gentlemen, the *élite* of New York fashion, from coming and applauding throughout the double courses. . . .

Thackeray has himself put on record the originating source of his lecture on 'Humour and Charity', about this time, when we returned once more to New York. Some friends wished to benefit a 'Ladies' Society for the Employment and Relief of the Poor', and he volunteered to write a new discourse to be delivered for that purpose. He took a whole day for the task, lying down in his favourite recumbent position in bed, smoking, whilst dictating fluently the phrases as they came. I took them down, with little or no intermission from breakfast-time till late in the dusk of the evening. The dinner-gong sounded, and the manuscript was then completed. I remember his pleased exclamation at this *tour de force* – not usual with him – 'I don't know where it's all coming from!'

. . . Doubtless the incentive of a benevolent motive was inspiriting to the author. . . .

The signal for departure [from America] took place with the suddenness of a thunder-clap. I visited Thackeray in his room in the early morning. He had a newspaper in his hand, and he said, 'I see there's a Cunarder going this morning', which happened to be 20 April. 'I'll go down to Wall Street to see whether I can secure berths in her; meanwhile, try and see all the traps packed up and ready.' As we were old campaigners, the thing was done and the bills paid in the nick of time. The only people we had time to shake hands with were the friendly family of the Baxters.[5] One of the ladies, I regret to say, wrote wittily afterwards to this effect, 'We shall never forgive Mr Crowe for the cheerful expression upon his face the day he went away!' Who does not sigh for home at the end of six months, wherever that domicile may be? At about eleven o'clock we were speeding down Broadway; we got into a boat on the East River, and were greeted by the shipping agent's shout, 'Hurry up – she's starting!' and we had hardly had time to get on board when we were going full steam on to Sandy Hook. . . .

NOTES

1. The Young Street period (1838–43) might seem implausibly early for Thackeray to be measuring himself for size beside the leader of the profession; by then, he had published only one book, *The Paris Sketch Book* (1840), and had yet to write a novel. But twice in letters of July 1842 he made comparisons – if half-jokingly as well as ruefully – between himself and Dickens (*LPP*, II, 60, 66).
2. William Torrens McCullagh, later surnamed Torrens (1813–94), Irish author and politician; M. P. for Dundalk 1847–54, and later for English constituencies.
3. The 'shut up the puppets in their box' phrase is of course used in the novel's final sentence.
4. 'Mr Thackeray in the United States', by 'John Small', *Fraser's Magazine*, Jan 1853.
5. On the Baxters see below, I, 172.

A Discreetly Silent Freethinker?

JOHN CHAPMAN AND ANOTHER

From Gordon S. Haight, *George Eliot and John Chapman* (New Haven, Conn., 1940) pp. 177–9. Chapman (1821–94), bookseller, publisher and journalist, was a freethinker and freeliver, and edited the *Westminster Review* (1852–94). Marian Evans, the future 'George Eliot', whose translation of Strauss's *Life of Jesus* he had published in 1846, was his assistant on the *Westminster*, 1852–4. His 1851 diary mentions two encounters with Thackeray.

[*12 June 1851.*] Heard Thackeray lecture on Steele and was much disappointed. The lecture was more like a long sermon than anything, and did not gain by being read. [Thornton] Hunt introduced me to him. He said he wanted to buy at the 'trade price' some of my 'atheistical' publications.

[*14 June 1851.*] Thackeray called, I proposed to him to write an article on the Modern Novelists for the *Westminster* (Jany N°); he declined, alleging that his writings were so much more valuable, pecuniarily, if published in other ways; that he, from his position, could not criticize his cotemporaries, and that the only person he could thoroughly well review and cut up would be himself! He complained of the rivalry and partizanship which is being fostered, I think chiefly Fo(r)ster'd, in respect to him and Dickens by foolish friends.[1]

I find that his religious views are perfectly *free*, but he does not mean to lessen his popularity by fully avowing them; he said he had debated the question with himself whether he was called upon to martyrize himself for the sake of his views and concluded in the negative. His chief object seems to be the making of money. He will go to America for that purpose. He impresses me as much abler than the lecture I heard, but I fear his success is spoiling him.

[Thackeray's religious views appeared less 'perfectly *free*' to another observer. When lecturing in Coventry in 1855 he visited Charles Bray (1811–84), author of the sceptical *Philosophy of Necessity* (1841), who, as the future George Eliot's mentor in her earlier years, had helped persuade her to translate Strauss. An unnamed young lady who was present recorded their conversation.] They talked of orthodoxy, and whether there was any talented person on the orthodox side. [Thackeray] said he was going to spend the next day with —— of Birmingham.[2] 'A good fellow – O Heavens, if I could write three lines of that man's orthodoxy I could make £20,000, but I couldn't do it.' The conversation then turned upon personal piety, and Thackeray gave us his own beautifully simple faith – in conclusion saying, half in way of apology for his oldfashioned belief (for the Brays were of very different ways of thinking, as he was aware), 'But I have a dear old Gospel mother who is a good Christian, and who has always chapter and verse to prove everything. Poor dear!'

Talked of [John Henry] Newman. Called him a saint, in a way that was a blessing to hear, so heartily and truly did he utter it. Said that somewhere in his heart he (Newman) was a sceptic, but that he had shut it down and locked it up as with Solomon's Seal, and went on really believing in the Catholic faith.   (*Biog. Intros*, VIII, xxxvii)

NOTES

1. A commonly-made play on the name of John Forster (1812–76), Dickens's friend, adviser and bottle-holder.

2. The Hon. and Revd Grantham Munton Yorke (1809–79), Rector of St Philip's, Birmingham, 1844 to 1874. Thackeray was friendly, over many years, with him and his family ('such a nice family'). Visiting him in 1855 he wrote to his mother, 'Yorke a perfect prize parson – pious humble merry orthodox to the most lucky point liked by everybody. How I should like to be like Yorke! – not for the being liked – but for that happy orthodoxy wh is as natural with him as with Addison and other fortunate people, and wh wd make my dear old Granny so happy if I had it' (*LPP*, III, 438).

The Jester with a Melancholy Face

SIR WILLIAM FRASER

From *Hic et Ubique* (1893) pp. 149–61, 166–74. Fraser (1826–98), 4th Baronet, spent some years in the Life Guards, and later became an M. P. and author of anecdotal collections about Wellington and Disraeli. He first met Thackeray in Paris, and became friendly with him.

Thackeray said to me in Paris that the best French literary authorities had told him that the character of Becky Sharp was so common in France that it would have excited no sensation there.[1] He also told me, with evident, and deserved satisfaction, that they were lecturing in the principal colleges in Paris on *Vanity Fair* as the most perfect English of the period.

Thackeray's resentment towards the trade of publishers was deeply rooted. I believe that sixteen publishers[2] refused him the pittance required to print his immortal work, *Vanity Fair*. Not one of them was capable intellectually of appreciating it.

He pours out the vials of his wrath upon them in *Pendennis*: painting them to the world as the most stupid, the most selfish, and the most vulgar, class of tradesmen. This appears to me to be not worthy of his dignity. To trample upon them when they came in his way, after their contemptuous treatment of his genius, might have been right: he steps from the path of real dignity, when, in his lofty position, he lavishes his sarcasm on beings unworthy of his satire. *Aquila non captat muscas* ['The eagle does not chase flies'], particularly such dirty flies as he paints them.

Calling on a publisher, Thackeray waited with a friend, who told me the story: the carpet of the drawing-room was of a gaudy design of red and white: on the host appearing, the author of *Vanity Fair* said, 'We have been admiring your carpet: it is most appropriate! You wade in the blood and brains of authors.'

I remember in Germany saying to Thackeray, 'It must be a fine thing to be a successful author.' He grimly replied, 'You had better break stones on a road.'

I went with him, soon after our first acquaintance, to the Théâtre Francais. Regnier, the great actor, was playing. The applause in that cultivated audience was vociferous. I turned to Thackeray, and said, 'That must be nice: you get the money at the moment you want it': he answered sadly, 'Quite right! better than writing ever so many books.'

One practice I discussed with Thackeray: that of repeating the same characters and names in successive works. Balzac does this: but with bad effect: Balzac was a much more voluminous writer: and this may account for the necessity of his so doing: in Thackeray I feel sure that it was a mistake. I remember his lightly sketching a character in a projected book to me; I inadvertently said, 'Like Warrington.' I observed a slight spasm in his face. On reflection I was sorry that I had said this; I felt that it suggested an impression in my mind that his powers of invention might be failing: this was not the case.

Thackeray told me that he intended to write three great novels, in which Simon Lord Fraser of Lovat, beheaded in 1747, was to be the central figure: I deeply regret that he did not live to accomplish this work. I am not surprised that so dramatic a character as Lord Lovat's charmed him: he would have revelled in the intrigues carried on in that curious epoch of our national history.

Dining with him in Young Street, Kensington, and sitting at some distance from him at table, he said to me, 'I am everlastingly indebted to you': I expressed my pleasure to hear this; and asked, 'Why?' 'You taught me to love *Rockingham.*' At this moment I observed a lady sitting opposite to me raise her eyes from her plate: and I saw, without a glance, that she and Thackeray had read the book together. *Rockingham* was a novel [published in 1849] which I had read alternately with a chapter of *Vanity Fair*: a work of an extremely romantic character; written, in English, by Count Jarnac. . . .

On the same evening Thackeray courteously conducted me to the door. He said, 'A few nights ago Mrs Crowe', the author of the first, and admirable, sensational novel *Susan Hopley*, 'was here. I took her to her fly: there were two more waiting: she turned to me; and in a voice of deep enthusiasm said, pointing to the flies, "Mr Thackeray, this is a great success! a great social success"!!' . . .

I must honestly say that I was woefully disappointed in Thackeray, as regards his powers of conversation. I saw him on this occasion [of their first meeting, in 1851], and at other times, under circumstances in which he had every opportunity, and inducement, to speak well. In no society in which I saw him, in spite of every wish, and effort, to discern what was original, and worth remembering, could I find anything to repay the interest which I took in him. Perfectly kind; utterly without affectation; amused, and somewhat interested by my enthusiasm, I listened in vain for the oracular words which I had fondly hoped would come from his mouth. On one occasion Count D'Orsay, with whom he had been intimate for many years, and other distinguished Frenchmen; he was a perfect master of the language; were present: but no spark was emitted: nor indeed up to the time of his death, on the occasions when I was thrown with him, was there a sentence that rose much above commonplace. I do not think that a word passed from his lips that I cannot recall.

I remember at the dinner in Paris of which I have spoken that I asked him if it were true that he had said that all men were 'Georges': alluding to the commonplace character in *Vanity Fair*.[3] He said, 'Yes: or would like to be; I have said so; and I think so.' I ventured to suggest that he was in error: that though the character of 'George' was a common one, he must have met with far higher types. I frequently observed that he had a way of uttering somewhat shallow cynicisms; far below the grand generalisations which appear in his works: this saying as to 'George Osborne' is a specimen. It appeared to me as if he thought that the person with whom he was talking expected him to say cynical things: that his interlocutor would be disappointed if he did not. I formed the opinion after long observation; and think, that though he had an extraordinary power of reading human nature in the mass, he had hardly any power of reading the individual. I have seen this in others; Whyte Melville for instance: but I was extremely struck with it in Thackeray. That he could not discriminate: that he had a general idea of young men, middle aged men, and old men: a generic, not a specific power.

One of the first things that he said to me at the Duchess de

Gramont's [in Paris] was, 'You are in the Life Guards.' 'Yes; in the First.' 'Are they clever enough for you?' 'Quite.' A few years later I asked him to dine with the Mess of my regiment; then quartered in the Regent's Park. Fortunately there was a small party: and still more fortunately all who were present were good specimens of an exceptionally intelligent set of officers. Both the regimental field-officers were happily absent: they would have terribly reduced the average of intellect. Major Biddulph subsequently 'Master of the Household' and 'Privy Purse' to the Queen, was there; and Captain Lord William Beresford; the finest type of man intellectually, and physically, that I have ever met with. The conversation turned upon Ireland: Thackeray gave his views: they were courteously, but most admirably, controverted by Lord William. No officer knew that Thackeray was coming but myself; the party was a chance one. Lord William Beresford showed him not only that he knew more about Ireland than he did, but that Thackeray's own work, the *Irish Sketch Book*, was better known to Lord William than to its author. Nothing could be more polite than the way in which the conversation was carried on. I was not surprised at the effect produced upon the great author. When he came up to my room to put on his cloak, he exclaimed, 'I am astonished! I am bewildered! I will never write another word against soldiers.' I said, 'My dear Thackeray, you have described men about whom you know little, or nothing: you have painted the British officer with about as much truth as if you were to paint me, a North Devon M.P., with the features of "Squire Western". Now you see what officers really are.' He bluntly answered, 'Well I will never do it again: trust me.' ...

I found Thackeray at the hotel at Folkestone having tea with his daughters: one of the young ladies said, 'Do you know, Sir William, what has happened to Papa?' 'No.' 'A young lady has fallen in love with him.' 'Can you be surprised?' 'But you don't know how old she is.' 'I don't.' 'Just six.' Thackeray put on a face of intense grief: and said, 'It is a very sad business: the less said about it the better!' This is the only occasion which I can recall where he imitated an expression of a feeling; or showed anything approaching comic dramatic power.

Like most men of great minds he was occasionally playful. I

give an instance of his playfulness. I dined with him at the old 'Beef-steak Club', at six o'clock, in a room at the back of the Lyceum Theatre: then owned by Mr Arnold. Never can I forget that dinner: morsels of beef-steak, about a mouthful and a half each, were brought from the fire in an adjoining room: the folding doors being open, and the fire visible. Each morsel, instead of diminishing your appetite, increased it: the term 'tickling the palate' was illustrated. We adjourned from dinner to Mr Arnold's box, in the Lyceum, a proscenium box on the level of the stage. The piece was a burlesque; what the French call a *piece aux jambes*. The box held half-a-dozen. Thackeray and myself were in the rear. Miss L. T. who was, and still is particularly well endowed with the necessary adjuncts of burlesque, was leaning against the proscenium, and displaying a splendid pair of legs, tightly fitted in elastic red silk. Thackeray gazed upon them; and said, without pause, 'Surely, surely; is this to hold the mirror up to Nature? to show Virtue her own image, Scorn her own feature? will any gentleman in front oblige me by pinching those legs?'

The only portrait like Thackeray is that by Laurence. I have examined carefully all the likenesses, painted, engraved, and in sculpture; I am unable to see any resemblance to him in the others. They give a dead, inanimate, look, which he never had. His eyes were exceedingly bright under his spectacles: his flesh had a soft look, with colour: not I should say over healthy: rather wanting in substance....

The only occasion on which I saw Thackeray, I cannot say laugh, but display in his countenance the signs of inward merriment; was when I told him this story. [A lengthy and not very funny anecdote about a misadventure of the Miss Berrys follows.]

Dining with Thackeray, he told me that he considered *Tom Jones* as by far the finest romance ever written. He added, 'If you had to write for your bread, you would know that the fable is unapproachable.'...

I asked Thackeray which of all his writings he *liked* the best: he answered at once 'George de Barnwell', the quiz of *Eugene Aram*, Lord Lytton's novel.[4] ... He told me that he thought the *best* thing that he had written was the Surgeon's Song in 'Harry Rollicker', and that he had written it when on board an Austrian Lloyd's Steamer; very seasick.... Of Thackeray's good nature I give an instance. He delighted, as I have said, in his 'Harry Rollicker' or the 'Onety-oneth'; particularly in the Surgeon's Song: he told me that he had avoided quizzing Lever about his bad French: he knew that that would annoy him. He makes fine fun of Lever's jumble of military terms; as he deserved. . . .

The dominant idea which Thackeray wished to present to the public of his idiosyncrasy was that depicted in his vignettes of himself: the poor jester, with a flat, and melancholy, face; holding the grinning mask in his hand: no doubt this accurately represented the tone of his mind; which, like that of every man of genius, was melancholy. Nothing can be more touching than the suggestiveness of the little picture on the original yellow covers: the sad, and humble, humorist; signifying his own pathetic fate.

NOTES

1. This neatly justifies the contention of Elizabeth Rigby (Lady Eastlake), in her review of *Vanity Fair* (*Quarterly Review*, Dec 1848), that 'the author has almost disarmed [criticism] by making [Becky's] mother a Frenchwoman. The construction of this little clever monster is diabolically French. . . . France is the land for the real Syren, with the woman's face and the dragon's claws' (*TCH*, p. 85).

2. The highest figure known to me, in this much-repeated (and increasingly mythical) story of Thackeray's difficulty in finding a publisher for *Vanity Fair*. See above, I, 45, 51, 82.

3. That is, men are, or tend to be – like Captain George Osborne – vain, selfish, flirtatious and snobbish.

4. In *'Punch's* Prize Novelists', as is 'Harry Rollicker', mentioned below, a lampoon upon Charles Lever, author of *Harry Lorrequer*, etc.

The Depths of his Great Nature

JOHN BROWN

(1) from Alexander Peddie, *Recollections of Dr John Brown* (1893) pp. 50–2;
(2) from [John Brown], 'Thackeray', *North British Review*, XL (1864) 260–5.

'We shall never see such a man and such a friend again, never!' wrote
Dr John Brown to Mrs Brookfield, on Thackeray's death – C. and F.
Brookfield, *Mrs Brookfield and her Circle* (1905) II, 504. Brown (1810–82),
Edinburgh physician and essayist, best known for his *Rab and his Friends*
(1859) and *Horae Subsecivae* (1858, 1861, 1882), was one of Thackeray's
closest and most admiring friends in later years. In 1849 he organised a gift
to Thackeray, by eighty Edinburgh admirers, and the novelist was deeply
moved by this gesture (see *LPP*, II, 538–9). They met during Thackeray's
first lecturing stint in Edinburgh, 1851 (see (1), below), and became intimate
friends. During a later visit, 1856, Brown writes, 'We have seen a great deal
of him; he comes and sits for hours, and lays that great nature out before us,
with its depths and bitternesses, its tenderness and desperate truth. It is so
sad to see him so shut out from all cheer and hope' – John Taylor Brown,
Dr John Brown (1903) p. 110. He contributed an obituary of Thackeray to the
Scotsman, and his *North British Review* recollections of the novelist were later
incorporated into his essay 'Thackeray's Death', *Horae Subsecivae*, 3rd Ser.
(1882) pp. 187–96.

(1) With the author of *Vanity Fair* friendship dated, I believe
[writes Alexander Peddie], from the occasion of Thackeray's
lectures in Edinburgh on the English Humourists, after which
time Dr Brown held resolutely to the opinion that Thackeray's
true character was much misunderstood by the general
public. Indeed, he could not endure the comparisons frequently drawn between him and the rival novelist of the day.
The following letter from Dr Brown to his warmly attached
friend, the late Andrew Coventry Dick, appears to have been
written at this time:

> . . . I wish you had been here for the last fortnight to have
> seen, heard, and known Thackeray, – a fellow after your
> own heart, – a strong-headed, sound-hearted, judicious
> fellow, who knew the things that differ, and prefers Pope
> to Longfellow or Mrs Barrett Browning, and Milton to
> Mr Festus,[1] and Sir Roger De Coverley to *Pickwick*, and
> David Hume's *History* to Sheriff Alison's; and the 'verses by
> E. V. K. to his friend to town'[2] to anything he has seen for a
> long time; and 'the impassioned grape' to the whole works
> prosaic and poetical of Sir Bulwer Lytton. I have seen a
> great deal of him and talked with him on all sorts of things,
> and next to yourself I know no man so much to my mind.
> He is much better and greater than his works. . . . He is 6
> feet 3 in height, with a broad kindly face and an immense
> skull. Do you remember Dr Henderson of Galashiels? He is

ludicrously like him, – the same big head and broad face, and his voice is very like, and the same nicety in expression and in the cadences of the voice. He makes no figure in company, except as very good-humoured, and by saying now and then a quietly strong thing. I so much wish you had met him. He is as much bigger than Dickens as a three-decker of 120 guns is bigger than a small steamer with *one* long-range swivel-gun. He has set everybody here a-reading *Stella's Journal, Gulliver, The Tatler, Joseph Andrews,* and *Humphrey Clinker*. He has a great turn for politics, right notions, and keen desires, and from his kind of head would make a good public man. He has much in him which cannot find issue in mere authorship.

Then when Thackeray lectured on the Four Georges in 1856, there is the following letter to the same friend, not dated, but probably in December of that year:

> . . . Thackeray has been here and a great deal with us, and I like him more than ever, – he is so natural and unforced in his ways and talk. The lecture on George the III. was very noble. . . . He made 2000 men and women weep by reading old Johnson's lines on poor Levett the surgeon. . . .

(2) We have seen no satisfactory portrait of Mr Thackeray. We like the photographs better than the prints; and we have an old daguerreotype of him without his spectacles which is good; but no photograph can give more of a man than is in any one ordinary – often very ordinary – look of him; it is only Sir Joshua and his brethren who can paint a man liker than himself. Laurence's first drawing has much of his thorough-bred look, but the head is too much tossed up and *vif*. The photograph from the later drawing by the same hand we like better: he is alone, and reading with his book close up to his eyes. This gives the prodigious size and solidity of his head, and the sweet mouth. We have not seen that by Mr Watts, but if it is as full of power and delicacy as his Tennyson, it will be a comfort.

Though in no sense a selfish man, he had a wonderful interest in himself as an object of study, and nothing could be more delightful and unlike anything else than to listen to him on himself. He often draws his own likeness in his books. In the 'Fraserians' by Maclise, in *Fraser*, is a slight sketch of him in his unknown youth; and there is an excessively funny and not unlike extravaganza of him by Doyle or Leech, in the *Month*, a little short-lived periodical, edited by Albert Smith. He is represented lecturing, when certainly he looked his best. We give below what is like him in face as well as in more.[3]

The tired, young, kindly wag is sitting and looking into space, his mask and his jester's rod lying idly on his knees.

The foregoing estimate of his genius [omitted in the present selection] must stand instead of any special portraiture of the man. Yet we would mention two leading traits of character traceable, to a large extent, in his works, though finding no appropriate place in a literary criticism of them. One was the deep steady melancholy of his nature. He was fond of telling how on one occasion, at Paris, he found himself in a great crowded *salon*; and looking from the one end across the sea of heads, being in Swift's place of calm in a crowd,[4] he saw at the other end a strange visage, staring at him with an expression of comical woebegoneness. After a little he found that this rueful being was himself in the mirror. He was not, indeed, morose. He was alive to and thankful for everyday blessings, great and small; for the happiness of home, for friendship, for wit and music, for beauty of all kinds, for the pleasures of the 'faithful old gold pen'; now running into some felicitous expression, now playing itself into some droll initial letter; nay, even for the creature comforts. But his persistent state, especially for the later half of his life, was profoundly *morne* – there is no other word for it. This arose in part from temperament, from a quick sense of the littleness and wretchedness of mankind. His keen perception of the meanness and vulgarity of the realities around him contrasted with the ideal present to his mind could produce no other effect. This feeling, embittered by disappointment, acting on a harsh and savage nature, ended in the *saeva indignatio* of Swift; acting on the kindly and too sensitive nature of Mr Thackeray, it led only to compassionate sadness. In part, too, this melancholy was the result of private calamities. He alludes to these often in his writings, and a knowledge that his sorrows were great is necessary to the perfect appreciation of much of his deepest pathos. We allude to them here, painful as the subject is, mainly because they have given rise to stories – some quite untrue, some even cruelly injurious. The loss of his second child in infancy was always an abiding sorrow – described in the *Hoggarty Diamond* [ch. 12], in a passage of surpassing tenderness, too sacred to be severed from its context. A yet keener and more constantly present affliction was the illness of his wife. . . .

His sense of a higher Power, his reverence and godly fear, is felt more than expressed – as indeed it mainly should always be – in everything he wrote. It comes out at times quite suddenly, and stops at once, in its full strength. We could readily give many instances of this. [He gives one.] In ordinary intercourse the same sudden 'Te Deum' would occur, always brief and intense, like lightning from a cloudless heaven; he seemed almost ashamed – not of it, but of his giving it expression.

We cannot resist here recalling one Sunday evening in December, when he was walking with two friends along the Dean road, to the west of Edinburgh – one of the noblest outlets to any city. It was a lovely evening, such a sunset as one never forgets; a rich dark bar of cloud hovered over the sun, going down behind the Highland hills, lying bathed in amethystine bloom; between this cloud and the hills there was a narrow slip of the pure aether, of a tender cowslip colour, lucid, and as if it were the very body of heaven in its clearness; every object standing out as if etched upon the sky. The north-west end of Corstorphine Hill, with its trees and rocks, lay in the heart of this pure radiance, and there a wooden crane, used in the quarry below, was so placed as to assume the figure of a cross; there it was, unmistakable, lifted up against the crystalline sky. All three gazed at it silently. As they gazed, he gave utterance in a tremulous, gentle, and rapid voice, to what all were feeling, in the word 'Calvary!' The friends walked on in silence, and then turned to other things. All that evening he was very gentle and serious, speaking, as he seldom did, of divine things – of death, of sin, of eternity, of salvation; expressing his simple faith in God and in his Saviour.

There is a passage at the close of the *Roundabout Paper* No. XXIII, 'De Finibus', in which a sense of the ebb of life is very marked; the whole paper is like a soliloquy. It opens with a drawing of Mr Punch, with unusually mild eye, retiring for the night; he is putting out his high-heeled shoes, and before disappearing gives a wistful look into the passage, as if bidding it and all else good-night. He will be in bed, his candle out, and in darkness, in five minutes, and his shoes found next morning at his door, the little potentate all the while in his final sleep. The whole paper is worth the most careful study; it reveals not a little of his real nature, and unfolds very curiously the secret of his work, the vitality, and abiding power of his own creations. . . . But what we chiefly refer to now is the profound pensiveness of the following strain, as if written with a presentiment of what was not then very far off: 'Another *Finis* written; another milestone on this journey from birth to the next world. Sure it is a subject for solemn cogitation. Shall we continue this story-telling business, and be voluble to the end of our age?' 'Will it not be presently time, O prattler, to hold your tongue?' And thus he ends: '. . . Yet a few chapters more, and then the last; after which, behold *Finis* itself comes to an end, and the Infinite begins'. . . .

He fixed with his friend and surgeon to come again on Tuesday; but with that dread of anticipated pain, which is a common condition of sensibility and genius, he put him off with a note from 'yours unfaithfully, W. M. T.' He went out on Wednesday for a little, and came home at ten. He went to his room, suffering much, but declining his man's offer to sit with him. He hated to make others suffer. He was heard moving, as if in pain, about twelve. . . . Then all was quiet, and then he must have died – in a moment. Next morning his man went in, and opening the windows found his master dead, his arms behind his head, as if he had tried to take one more breath. . . . Long years of sorrow, labour, and pain had killed him before his time. It was found after death how little life he had to live. He looked always fresh with that abounding, silvery hair, and his young, almost infantine face, but he was worn to a shadow, and his hands wasted as if by eighty years.[5]

NOTES

1. That is, *Festus: A Poem* (1839, 1845), an 'epic' by Philip James Bailey (1816–1902), which was for a while much admired.
2. Published in the *Horae Subsecivae*, 3rd ser., pp. 406–12 [Peddie's footnote].
3. Thackeray's woodcut sketch of himself appears at the end of ch. 9 of *Vanity Fair*.
4. 'An inch or two above it' [Brown's footnote].
5. Brown's last two paragraphs rely heavily on a letter received from Theodore Martin, Thackeray's neighbour (see below, II, 205), lately published in *Thackeray Newsletter*, No. 14, November 1981, pp. 1–2.

A Most Agreeable Man

JOHN EVERETT MILLAIS

From John Guille Millais, *Life and Letters of Sir John Everett Millais* (1899) I, 160, 276–7, 376–7. Millais (1829–96), painter, President of the Royal Academy, created Baronet 1885, was one of the originators of the Pre-Raphaelite Brotherhood, 1848. Thackeray was among his early admirers, and they became good friends. Lord Redesdale (1837–1916), who several times met Thackeray at the Millais household, 'when he and I would be the only guests, making up a quartette with the genial, handsome host and his no less handsome wife', recalls Thackeray's fondness for Millais: 'He admired his art, and the great painter's large, honest, bluff and rough nature, his innocence of all humbug or affectation, which Thackeray loathed above all things, appealed to him. The two were perfectly happy together, so in that studio Thackeray was at his best. And what a best it was!' – *Memories* (1915) pp. 208–9. They first met in 1852, when Millais found Thackeray 'most agreable'.

As to Thackeray [writes Millais's son] my father and mother always regarded him as one of the most delightful characters they ever met.[1] Though in dealing with the infirmities of human nature his works now and then show traces of cynicism, the man himself was no cynic – was rather, indeed, to those who knew him best, a most sympathetic friend, and tender-hearted almost to a fault. For some years he entertained and brought up as one of his family the daughter of a deceased friend; and so grieved was he at the thought of parting from her that on her wedding-day he came for consolation to my father's studio, and spent most of the afternoon in tears.[2] They met so frequently – he and Millais – that but little correspondence of any interest appears to have passed between them. . . .

Of Thackeray, Millais and Carlyle, William Millais tells an interesting story illustrative of the littleness of earthly fame, however highly we may regard it. He says, 'I was sitting with my brother [John Everett] in the Cromwell Place studio when Thackeray suddenly came in all aglow with enthusiasm at my brother's fame. Every window in every shop that had the least pretension to art-display, he said, was full of the engravings of his popular works. On his way he had seen innumerable *Orders of Release, Black Brunswickers*, and *Huguenots*; in fact, he had no hesitation in affirming that John Millais was the most famous man of the day. He then alluded to his own miserable failure at first, and told us how he had taken some of his works, which have since been acknowledged to be the finest specimens of English literature, to the leading publishers, and how they had one and all sneeringly hinted that no one would read his works after Dickens. . . .'

The sudden death of Thackeray, the bright and genial novelist, cast a deep gloom over the household, both my father and mother being devotedly attached to him. They had noticed with distress his failing health and loss of appetite, when dining with them shortly before their annual migration to the North; but neither of them ever dreamt that this was the last time that they and he would meet. In a letter to my mother on Christmas Day my father wrote, 'I am sure you will be dreadfully shocked, as I was, at the loss of poor Thackeray. I imagine, and hope truly, you will have heard of it before this reaches you. He was found dead by his servant in the morning, and of course the whole house is in a state of the utmost confusion and pain. They first sent to Charlie Collins and his wife, who went immediately, and have been almost constantly there ever since. I sent this morning to know how the mother and girls were, and called myself this afternoon; and they are suffering terribly, as you might expect. He was found lying back, with his arms over his head, as though in great pain. I shall hear more, of course.[3] Everyone I meet is affected by his death. Nothing else is spoken of.' . . .

In another letter, on 31 December, he added, 'I went yesterday to the funeral, in Theodore Martin's carriage. It was a mournful scene, and badly managed. A crowd of women were there – from curiosity, I suppose – dressed in all colours; and round the grave scarlet and blue feathers shone out prominently! Indeed, the true mourners and friends could not get near, and intimate friends who were present had to be hustled into their places during the ceremony of interment. We all, of course, followed from the chapel, and by that time the grave was surrounded. There was a great lack of what is called "high society", which I was surprised at. None of that class, of whom he knew so many, were present. The painters were *nearly all* there – more even than the literary men. . . .'[4]

NOTES

1. In 1855 Millais married Effie (Euphemia), whose marriage with Ruskin had been annulled. She had known Thackeray during her years with Ruskin, and had then (1850) found him 'loud and vulgar and fond of good living', also 'a handsome man' but for his broken nose – Sir William James, *The Order of Release* (1948) pp. 159, 163.

2. Amy Crowe, daughter of Eyre Evans Crowe and sister of Eyre Crowe. She joined the Thackeray household in 1854, after her mother's death, and stayed there until her marriage to a cousin of Thackeray's in 1862.

3. Some years later, Millais 'lamented that he had been called in by the immediate relatives of the two novelists [Thackeray and Dickens] to paint the lifeless forms of his two illustrious friends. "I cannot refuse," he said, "cost me what it may" ' – Arthur Coleridge, *Reminiscences* (1921) p. 155. Charlie Collins's wife, mentioned above, was Dickens's daughter Kate: see below, II, 306.

4. W. H. Russell, in the next item, makes the same point. As other commentators pointed out, however, most members of 'high society' were out of town in December, when the funeral took place.

'No Ortolans for Pendennis!'

WILLIAM HOWARD RUSSELL

From John Black Atkins, *The Life of Sir William Howard Russell* (1911) I, 113–14, 375; II, 120. Russell (1820–1907), journalist, knighted 1895, became famous through his reports in *The Times* on the Crimean War, and was a familiar figure in literary circles. Reflecting, years afterwards, on Thackeray, he wrote (14 Mar 1899), 'But oh! the pity of it! He never had a chance of being at his best. He suffered the greatest tortures. He told me of his sufferings sometimes when he was obliged to write "funny" papers for *Punch*. . . . Yes! It was a "privilege" to know him – to love him as I did' (*Life of Russell*, II, 438). His biographer remarks that 'there are touching entries in the diaries which suggest briefly, but completely, the unwavering friendship of Thackeray', particularly valued when Mrs Russell was suffering from a painful terminal illness. Thackeray used often to walk past his house at appointed times, 'and Russell would appear at the window and if he felt unable to leave his wife would wave Thackeray away, or, in the contrary case, would signal that he was coming down for a walk' (ibid., I, 386). The first extract from Russell's diary provides a pleasant instance of Thackeray's ability to take with good humour an invidious comparison between Dickens and himself. It also exemplifies his habit of publicly identifying himself with his character Pendennis.

[Russell's diary, Apr 1852.] X. asked a party to Watford to shoot. There were only hares and rabbits to be sure, but what more could be expected in April? The sportsmen among whom I had the honour to be numbered were of the Winkle order: Thackeray, Dickens, John Leech, Jerrold, Lemon, Ibbotson, and others were invited and carriages were reserved to Watford. As we were starting, a written excuse was brought from Dickens to be conveyed to Mrs X. by Thackeray. The party drove up to the house, and, after compliments, Thackeray delivered the billet. The effect was unpleasant. Mrs X. fled along the hall, and the guests heard her calling to the cook, 'Martin, don't roast the ortolans; Mr Dickens isn't coming.' Thackeray said he never felt so small. 'There's a test of popularity for you! No ortolans for Pendennis!'

[In a fragmentary autobiography, Russell describes his venturing into writing leading articles for *The Times*, in 1859, anonymously of course. He was somewhat nervous of this new activity.] Thackeray was one of the few who knew my secret, and as he strolled round from his house in Onslow Square, with his cigar, to Sumner Place [Russell's house] after breakfast I was anxious for his opinion, and I knew when he said 'I have not read my *Times* very carefully this morning' that he was not quite content with me. He could always guess what was mine. He was, I think, averse to my course of life. 'Don't wrap yourself up in *Times* foolscap. You have escaped now. Try work for yourself!' But alas! There were the various little reasons at home, and the twelve hundred reasons a year on the other side of the question.

One day some years afterwards I went to the office with Thackeray and others to look at a new printing machine; the old one was at work, whirling round and round, and throwing off the long riband of printed paper with the satisfied hum of wheel and fly, and the buzz of life within its iron rollers peculiar to well-organised machinery. Thackeray, with his hand in his breeches pockets, his glasses on his nose, stood before it for a moment, then putting his right hand forth with menacing finger toward the press he exclaimed, 'Heartless! insatiable! bloody! destroying monster! What brains you have ground to pulp! What hopes you have crushed, what anxiety you have inflicted on us all!'

On 24 December [1863, Atkins records] he wrote in his diary, 'My dear friend Thackeray died this morning. Oh, God, how soon and untimely! Had to do my *Army and Navy Gazette* work. Dined with O'Dowd at the Club; the talk all of Thackeray – of him alone.' On 30 December comes the entry, 'This day followed the remains of my dear friend Thackeray to the grave at Kensal Green. Such a scene! Such a gathering! Dickens, thin and worn, so rejoiced me by saying he had lately been speaking to Thackeray of familiar topics. John Leech, Doyle, Millais, O'Dowd, O'Shea, J. C. Deane, Shirley Brooks, etc. The Garrick almost whipped of its cream, but not a swell, not one of the order. Little he cared!'

Russell's affectionate nature, as we have seen before, was not easily reconciled to the loss of friends, and the loss of

Thackeray was such a blow as he had not suffered since Douglas Jerrold's death. Again and again he returned to the subject in his private letters and diaries. Here is a character-istic entry more than three months after Thackeray's death: 'Read to-day an article about Thackeray. Lord, how I wish the man who wrote it were dead and he of whom it was written were alive! No more will the world be to me as once it was. No, not with all the happiness of wife and children, or even if fame and fortune came instead of this dull, dead, inglorious struggle with the present, and no hope in the future.'

As Playful as a Schoolboy

J. T. FIELDS

From *Yesterdays with Authors* (1872) pp. 15–23, 27–35. James T. Fields (1817–81), partner in the Boston publishing firm of Ticknor & Fields, and Editor (1861–70) of the *Atlantic Monthly*, was instrumental in getting Thackeray to lecture in America, and made many of his business arrange-ments for him. He did like service for Dickens, one of whose most intimate friends he was, for his American tour of 1867–8. He and his enchanting young wife Annie (1834–1915), whom he married in 1854, were among Thackeray's closest and most valued American friends. In *A Shelf of Old Books* (1894) Annie Fields fondly recalls his 'kindly face – large, full of humour, full of human sympathies' and his kindness to her when she was a young bride 'and very much afraid of him. Afraid, let me say, rather of the idea of him, the great author and famous lecturer, who was making his crowded audiences laugh or cry at his simple word every evening; the great man of the moment whom everybody was "running after", yet of whom they said that he liked his friends so much better than all their noise about himself that he was always trying to escape from it, and here he was! coming to see – whom? Well, it appears it did not so much matter, for he was bent on kindnesses, and he took it all in at a glance, and sat down by the window and drew me to him and told me about his "little girls" at home. . . . Thackeray loved the great world and the strange, noble, and even ignoble creatures it contains; he loved delightful women always, and "liked to see them straight" as he says somewhere; and would have said to his favourites, as Dr Johnson said to Mrs Thrale, "Be brisk, and be splendid, and be publick"; but he loved above all his fireside-corner and his "little girls" and the friends they drew about them' (pp. 205, 213). James Fields's is among the most lively and vivid accounts of Thackeray, and has been much quoted by his biographers.

They first met in London in 1852, to discuss the possibility of an American tour of *The English Humourists*. Friends of Thackeray, whom Fields had consulted, 'all said he could never be induced to leave London long enough for such an expedition'. In fact, Thackeray had had his eyes on American dollars long before the series was given in Britain (*LPP*, II, 692; *Wisdom*, pp. 138–9), so Fields's embassage prospered. Anny Thackeray, it may be mentioned, sharply reprimanded Fields for overemphasising her father's playful and uproarious aspects (*Adversity*, pp. 2–3, 436).

I had the opportunity, both in England and America, of observing the literary habits of Thackeray, and it always seemed to me that he did his work with comparative ease, but was somewhat influenced by a custom of procrastination. Nearly all his stories were written in monthly instalments for magazines, with the press at his heels. He told me that when he began a novel he rarely knew how many people were to figure in it, and, to use his own words, he was always very shaky about their moral conduct. He said that sometimes, especially if he had been dining late and did not feel in remarkably goodhumour next morning, he was inclined to make his characters villanously wicked; but if he rose serene with an unclouded brain, there was no end to the lovely actions he was willing to make his men and women perform. When he had written a passage that pleased him very much he could not resist clapping on his hat and rushing forth to find an acquaintance to whom he might instantly read his successful composition. Gilbert Wakefield, universally acknowledged to have been the best Greek scholar of his time, said he would have turned out a much better one, if he had begun earlier to study that language; but unfortunately he did not begin till he was fifteen years of age. Thackeray, in quoting to me this saying of Wakefield, remarked, 'My English would have been very much better if I had read Fielding before I was ten.' This observation was a valuable hint, on the part of Thackeray, as to whom he considered his master in art. . . .

One day, in the snowy winter of 1852, I met Thackeray sturdily ploughing his way down Beacon Street with a copy of *Henry Esmond* (the English edition, then just issued) under his arm. Seeing me some way off, he held aloft the volumes and began to shout in great glee. When I came up to him he cried out, 'Here is the *very* best I can do, and I am carrying it to Prescott as a reward of merit for having given me my first dinner in America. I stand by this book, and am willing to leave it, when I go, as my card.'

As he wrote from month to month, and liked to put off the inevitable chapters till the last moment, he was often in great tribulation. I happened to be one of a large company whom he had invited to a six-o'clock dinner at Greenwich one summer afternoon, several years ago [Sep 1859]. We were all to go down from London, assemble in a particular room at the hotel, where he was to meet us at six o'clock, *sharp*. Accordingly we took steamer and gathered ourselves together in the reception-room at the appointed time. When the clock struck six, our host had not fulfilled his part of the contract. His burly figure was yet wanting among the company assembled. . . . This untoward state of things went on for one hour, still no Thackeray and no dinner. . . . It was confidentially whispered by a fat gentleman, with a hungry look, that the dinner was utterly spoiled twenty minutes ago, when we heard a merry shout in the entry and Thackeray bounced into the room. He had not changed his morning dress, and ink was still visible upon his fingers. Clapping his hands and pirouetting briskly on one leg, he cried out, 'Thank Heaven, the last sheet of *The Virginians* has just gone to the printer.' He made no apology for his late appearance, introduced nobody, shook hands heartily with everybody, and begged us all to be seated as quickly as possible. His exquisite delight at completing his book swept away every other feeling, and we all shared his pleasure, albeit the dinner was overdone throughout.

The most finished and elegant of all *lecturers*, Thackeray often made a very poor appearance when he attempted to deliver a set speech to a public assembly. He frequently broke down after the first two or three sentences. He prepared what he intended to say with great exactness, and his favourite delusion was that he was about to astonish everybody with a remarkable effort. It never disturbed him that he commonly made a woeful failure when he attempted speech-making, but he sat down with such cool serenity if he found that he could not recall what he wished to say, that his audience could not help joining in and smiling with him when he came to a stand-still. Once he asked me to travel with him from London to Manchester to hear a great speech he was going to make at the founding of the Free Library Institution in that city. All the way down he was discoursing of certain effects he intended to produce on the Manchester dons by his eloquent appeals to their pockets. This passage was to have great influence with the rich merchants, this one with the clergy, and so on. He said that although Dickens and Bulwer and Sir James Stephen, all eloquent speakers, were to precede him, he intended to beat each of them on this special occasion. . . . The occasion was a most brilliant one[1]. . . . As he rose [to speak], he gave me a half-wink from under his spectacles, as if to say, 'Now for it; the others have done very well, but I will show 'em a grace beyond the reach of their art.' He began in a clear and charming manner, and was absolutely perfect for three minutes. In the middle of a most earnest and elaborate sentence he suddenly stopped, gave a look of comic despair at the ceiling, crammed both hands into his trousers' pockets, and deliberately sat down. Everybody seemed to understand that it was one of Thackeray's unfinished speeches and there were no signs of surprise or discontent among his audience. He continued to sit on the platform in a perfectly composed manner; and when the meeting was over he said to me, without a sign of discomfiture, 'My boy, you have my profoundest sympathy; this day you have accidentally missed hearing one of the finest speeches ever composed for delivery by a great British orator.' And I never heard him mention the subject again.

Thackeray rarely took any exercise, thus living in striking contrast to the other celebrated novelist of our time, who was remarkable for the number of hours he daily spent in the open air. It seems to be almost certain now, from concurrent testimony, gathered from physicians and those who knew him best in England, that Thackeray's premature death was hastened by an utter disregard of the natural laws. His vigorous frame gave ample promise of longevity, but he drew too largely on his brain and not enough on his legs. *High* living and high *thinking*, he used to say, was the correct reading of the proverb.

He was a man of the tenderest feelings, very apt to be cajoled into doing what the world calls foolish things, and constantly performing feats of unwisdom, which perform-ances he was immoderately laughing at all the while in his books. No man has impaled snobbery with such a stinging rapier, but he always accused himself of being a snob, past all cure. This I make no doubt was one of his exaggerations, but there was a grain of truth in the remark, which so sharp an observer as himself could not fail to notice, even though the victim was so near home. . . .

[Arriving in Boston, in November 1852] he seemed greatly to enjoy the novelty of an American repast. In London he had been very curious in his inquiries about American oysters, as marvellous stories, which he did not believe, had been told him of their great size. We apologised – although we had taken care that the largest specimens to be procured should startle his unwonted vision when he came to the table – for what we called the extreme *smallness* of the oysters, promising that we would do better next time. Six bloated Falstaffian bivalves lay before him in their shells. I noticed that he gazed at them anxiously with fork upraised; then he whispered to me, with a look of anguish, 'How shall I do it?' I described to him the simple process by which the free-born citizens of America were accustomed to accomplish such a task. He seemed satisfied that the thing was feasible, selected the smallest one in the half-dozen (rejecting a large one, 'because', he said, 'it resembled the High Priest's servant's ear that Peter cut off'), and then bowed his head as if he were saying grace. All eyes were upon him to watch the effect of a new sensation in the person of a great British author. Opening his mouth very wide, he struggled for a moment, and then all was over. I shall never forget the comic look of despair he cast upon the other five over-occupied shells. I broke the perfect stillness by asking him how he felt. 'Profoundly grateful,' he gasped, 'and as if I had swallowed a little baby.' . . .

We had many happy days and nights together both in England and America, but I remember none happier than that evening we passed with him when the *Punch* people came to dine at his own table with the silver statuette of Mr Punch in full dress looking down upon the hospitable board from the head of the table.[2] This silver figure always stood in a conspicuous place when Tom Taylor, Mark Lemon, Shirley Brooks, and the rest of his jolly companions and lifelong cronies were gathered together. . . .

Thackeray's playfulness was a marked peculiarity; a great deal of the time he seemed like a schoolboy, just released from his task. In the midst of the most serious topic under discussion he was fond of asking permission to sing a comic song, or he would beg to be allowed to enliven the occasion by the instant introduction of a brief double-shuffle. Barry Cornwall [B. W. Procter] told me that when he and Charles Lamb were once making up a dinner-party together, Charles asked him not to invite a certain lugubrious friend of theirs. 'Because', said Lamb, 'he would cast a damper even over a funeral.' I have often contrasted the habitual qualities of that gloomy friend of theirs with the astounding spirits of both Thackeray and Dickens. They always seemed to me to be standing in the sunshine, and to be constantly warning other people out of cloudland. During Thackeray's first visit to America his jollity knew no bounds, and it became necessary often to repress him when he was walking in the street. I well remember his uproarious shouting and dancing when he was told that the tickets to his first course of readings were all sold, and when we rode together from his hotel to the lecture-hall he insisted on thrusting both his long legs out of the carriage window, in deference, as he said, to his magnanimous ticket-holders. An instance of his procrastination occurred the evening of his first public appearance in America. His lecture was advertised to take place at half-past seven, and when he was informed of the hour, he said he would try and be ready at eight o'clock, but thought it very doubtful. Horrified at this assertion, I tried to impress upon him the importance of punctuality on this, the night of his first bow to an American audience. At a quarter past seven I called for him, and found him not only unshaved and undressed for the evening, but rapturously absorbed in making a pen-and-ink drawing to illustrate a passage in Goethe's *Sorrows of Werther*, for a lady, which illustration – a charming one, by the way, for he was greatly skilled in drawing – he vowed he would finish before he would budge an inch in the direction of the (I omit the adjective) Melodeon. A comical incident occurred just as he was about leaving the hall, after his first lecture in Boston. A shabby, ungainly looking man stepped briskly up to him in the anteroom, seized his hand and announced himself as 'proprietor of the Mammoth Rat', and proposed to exchange season tickets. Thackeray, with the utmost gravity, exchanged cards and promised to call on the wonderful quadruped next day.

Thackeray's motto was 'Avoid performing today, if possible, what can be postponed till tomorrow.' Although he received large sums for his writings, he managed without much difficulty to keep his expenditures fully abreast, and often in advance of, his receipts. His pecuniary object in visiting America the second time was to lay up, as he said, a 'pot of money' for his two daughters. . . .

I once made a pilgrimage [in London] with Thackeray (at my request, of course, the visits were planned) to the various houses where his books had been written; and I remember when we came to Young Street, Kensington, he said, with mock gravity, 'Down on your knees, you rogue, for here *Vanity Fair* was penned! And I will go down with you, for I have a high opinion of that little production myself.' He was always perfectly honest in his expressions about his own writings, and it was delightful to hear him praise them when he could depend on his listeners. . . .

He told me he was nearly forty years old before he was recognised in literature as belonging to a class of writers at all above the ordinary magazinists of his day. 'I turned off far better things then than I do now,' said he, 'and I wanted money sadly (my parents were rich but respectable, and I had spent my guineas in my youth) but how little I got for my work! It makes me laugh', he continued, 'at what *The Times* pays me now, when I think of the old days, and how much better I wrote for them then, and got a shilling where I now get ten.'

One day he wanted a little service done for a friend, and I remember his very quizzical expression, as he said, 'Please say the favour asked will greatly oblige a man of the name of Thackeray, whose only recommendation is, that he has seen Napoleon and Goethe, and is the owner of Schiller's sword.' . . .

One of the most comical and interesting occasions I remember, in connection with Thackeray, was going with him to a grand concert given fifteen or twenty years ago by Madame Sontag. We sat near an entrance door in the hall, and every one who came in, male and female, Thackeray pretended to know, and gave each one a name and brief chronicle, as the presence flitted by. It was in Boston, and as he had been in town only a day or two, and knew only half a dozen people in it, the biographies were most amusing. As I happened to know several people who passed, it was droll enough to hear this great master of character give them their dues.... There is one man still living and moving about the streets I walk in occasionally, whom I never encounter without almost a shudder, remembering as I do the unerring shaft which Thackeray sent that night into the unknown man's character....

It was a treat to hear him, as I once did, discourse of Shakespeare's probable life in Stratford among his neighbours. He painted, as he alone could paint, the great poet sauntering about the lanes without the slightest show of greatness, having a crack with the farmers, and in very earnest talk about the crops. 'I don't believe', said Thackeray, 'that these village cronies of his ever looked upon him as the mighty poet,

> Sailing with supreme dominion
> Through the azure deep of air

but simply as a wholesome, good-natured citizen, with whom it was always pleasant to have a chat. I can see him now,' continued Thackeray, 'leaning over a cottage gate, and tasting good Master Such-a-one's home-brewed, and inquiring with a real interest after the mistress and her children.' Long before he put it into his lecture, I heard him say in words to the same effect, 'I should like to have been Shakespeare's shoe-black, just to have lived in his house, just to have worshipped him, to have run on his errands, and seen that sweet, serene face.'[3] To have heard Thackeray depict, in his own charming manner, and at considerable length, the imaginary walks and talks of Shakespeare, when he would return to his home from occasional visits to London, pouring into the ready ears of his unsophisticated friends and neighbours the gossip from town which he thought would be likely to interest them, is something to remember all one's days.

The enormous circulation achieved by the *Cornhill Magazine*, when it was first started with Thackeray for its editor-in-chief, is a matter of literary history. The announcement by his publishers that a sale of 110,000 of the first number had been reached made the editor half delirious with joy, and he ran away to Paris to be rid of the excitement for a few days. I met him by appointment at his hotel in the Rue de la Paix, and found him wild with exultation and full of enthusiasm for excellent George Smith, his publisher. 'London', he exclaimed, 'is not big enough to contain me now, and I am obliged to add Paris to my residence! Great heavens,' said he, throwing up his long arms, 'where will this tremendous circulation stop! Who knows but that I shall have to add Vienna and Rome to my whereabouts? If the worst comes to the worst, New York, also, may fall into my clutches, and only the Rocky Mountains may be able to stop my progress!' Those days in Paris with him were simply tremendous. We dined at all possible and impossible places together. We walked round and round the glittering court of the Palais Royal, gazing in at the windows of the jewellers' shops, and all my efforts were necessary to restrain him from rushing in and ordering a pocketful of diamonds and 'other trifles', as he called them; 'for', said he, 'how can I spend the princely income which Smith allows me for editing the *Cornhill*, unless I begin instantly somewhere?' If he saw a group of three or four persons talking together in an excited way, after the manner of that then *riant* Parisian people, he would whisper to me with immense gesticulation, 'There, there, you see the news has reached Paris, and perhaps the number has gone up since my last accounts from London.' His spirits during those few days were colossal, and he told me that he found it impossible to sleep, 'for counting up his subscribers'.

I happened to know personally (and let me modestly add, with some degree of sympathy) what he suffered editorially, when he had the charge and responsibility of a magazine. With first-class contributors he got on very well, he said, but the extortioners and revilers bothered the very life out of him. He gave me some amusing accounts of his misunderstandings with the 'fair' (as he loved to call them), some of whom followed him up so closely with their poetical compositions, that his house (he was then living in Onslow Square) was never free of interruption. 'The darlings demanded', said he, 'that I should rewrite, if I could not understand their —— nonsense and put their halting lines into proper form.' 'I was so appalled,' said he, 'when they set upon me with their "ipics and their ipecacs", that you might have knocked me down with a feather, sir. It was insupportable, and I fled away into France.' ...

He took very great delight in his young daughter's first contributions to the *Cornhill*, and I shall always remember how he made me get into a cab, one day in London, that I might hear, as we rode along, the joyful news he had to impart, that he had just been reading his daughter's first paper, which was entitled 'Little Scholars'. 'When I read it,' said he, 'I blubbered like a child, it is so good, so simple, and so honest; and my little girl wrote it, every word of it.' . . .

Overhearing me say one morning something about the vast attractions of London to a greenhorn like myself, he broke in with, 'Yes, but you have not seen the grandest one yet! Go with me today to St. Paul's and hear the charity children sing.' So we went, and I saw the 'head cynic of literature', the 'hater of humanity', as a critical dunce in *The Times* once called him, hiding his bowed face, wet with tears, while his whole frame shook with emotion, as the children of poverty rose to pour out their anthems of praise. . . .

I parted with Thackeray for the last time in the street, at midnight, in London, a few months before his death. The *Cornhill Magazine*, under his editorship, having proved a very great success, grand dinners were given every month in honour of the new venture. We had been sitting late at one of these festivals, and, as it was getting toward morning, I thought it wise, as far as I was concerned, to be moving homeward before the sun rose. Seeing my intention to withdraw, he insisted on driving me in his brougham to my lodgings. When we reached the outside door of our host, Thackeray's servant, seeing a stranger with his master, touched his hat and asked where he should drive us. It was then between one and two o'clock – time certainly for all decent diners-out to be at rest. Thackeray put on one of his most quizzical expressions, and said to John, in answer to his question, 'I think we will make a morning call on the Lord Bishop of London.' John knew his master's quips and cranks too well to suppose he was in earnest, so I gave him my address, and we went on. When we reached my lodgings the clocks were striking two, and the early morning air was raw and piercing. Opposing all my entreaties for leave-taking in the carriage, he insisted upon getting out on the sidewalk and escorting me up to my door, saying, with a mock heroic protest to the heavens above us, 'That it would be shameful for a full-blooded Britisher to leave an unprotected Yankee friend exposed to ruffians, who prowl about the streets with an eye to plunder.' Then giving me a gigantic embrace, he sang a verse of which he knew me to be very fond; and so vanished out of my sight the great-hearted author of *Pendennis* and *Vanity Fair*. But I think of him still as moving, in his own stately way, up and down the crowded thoroughfares of London, dropping in at the Garrick, or sitting at the window of the Athenaeum Club, and watching the stupendous tide of life that is ever moving past in that wonderful city.

Thackeray was a *master* in every sense, having as it were, in himself, a double quantity of being. Robust humour and lofty sentiment alternated so strangely in him, that sometimes he seemed like the natural son of Rabelais, and at others he rose up a very twin brother of the Stratford Seer. There was nothing in him amorphous and unconsidered. Whatever he chose to do was always perfectly done. There was a genuine Thackeray flavour in everything he was willing to say or to write. He detected with unfailing skill the good or the vile wherever it existed. He had an unerring eye, a firm understanding, and abounding truth. 'Two of his great master powers', said the chairman at a dinner given to him many years ago in Edinburgh, 'are *satire* and *sympathy*.' George Brimley remarked that 'He could not have painted Vanity Fair as he has, unless Eden had been shining in his inner eye.'[4] He had, indeed, an awful insight, with a world of solemn tenderness and simplicity, in his composition. Those who heard the same voice that withered the memory of King George IV repeat 'The spacious firmament on high' have a recollection not easily to be blotted from the mind, and I have a kind of pity for all who were born so recently as not to have heard and understood Thackeray's lectures. But they can read him, and I beg of them to try and appreciate the tenderer phase of his genius, as well as the sarcastic one.

NOTES

1. For an account of this illustrious occasion, 2 Sep 1852, when the speakers also included Lord Shaftesbury, John Bright, R. M. Milnes and other notabilities, see *The Speeches of Charles Dickens*, ed. K. J. Fielding (1960)

pp. 151–4. Mrs Gaskell, to whom Dickens had given reserved seats 'near to the speakers', got very bored by so many long speeches – 'we went at ½ p. 9, & did not get out till ¼ to 4, which was too much of a good thing' – her 'only comfort being seeing the caricatures Thackeray was drawing which were very funny. He & Mr Monckton Milnes made plenty of fun, till poor Thackeray was called on to speak & broke down utterly, after which he drew no more caricatures' – *Letters of Mrs Gaskell*, ed. J. A. V. Chapple and Arthur Pollard (Manchester, 1966) p. 197.

2. Eighty Edinburgh admirers had given him this statuette in 1849: a gesture which greatly moved him and evoked an eloquent letter of thanks; see *LPP*, II, 538–9, and above, I, 146.

3. *The English Humourists*, 'Swift'. As is noted above (I, 101) Thackeray often indulged in this fancy about Shakespeare's years of retirement. This iteration is significant in its insistence upon diminishing Shakespeare (*sc.* the great author) by positing him as an ordinary sociable citizen, simply out to make a decent living. 'He knew all about Shakespeare, he "understood him"', Horace Howard Furness, later editor of the *Variorum Shakespeare*, heard him assert: Shakespeare, he knew by intuition, 'wrote solely for money and when he had made enough he returned to Stratford, sat at his door and *sassed* passengers' – a confident pronouncement over which Furness 'laughed fit to split' (Wilson, I, 210). Records of eminent scholars' laughing fit to split are so rare and salutary as to be always welcomed and, in this case, saluted as being well occasioned. Thackeray's remarks on Shakespeare never rise above the banal, and are often silly.

4. *Spectator*, 6 Nov 1852 (*TCH*, p. 140).

A High-bred and Considerate Gentleman

GEORGE LUNT

From 'Recollections of Thackeray', *Harper's New Monthly Magazine*, LIV (1877) 256–64. Lunt (1803–85), United States district attorney for Massachusetts, 1848–53, was later a newspaper editor. He met Thackeray, through a friend, on the day after his arrival in Boston in 1852.

Our conversation turned principally upon the subject of the city [of Boston], which evidently struck Mr Thackeray with the most unqualified amazement. 'Why,' said he, 'there is nothing that looks new about it; it has every appearance of solidity, just like an English city.' . . . I ventured jokingly to inquire if he expected to see log-huts, wigwams, or buildings of rough boards. 'Not that, of course,' he said; but he 'certainly had no idea of finding every thing in such a settled and improved condition, so that he should not have known but what he was actually in Europe.' . . .

With [Boston] society, after a while, Mr Thackeray became familiarly acquainted, and received from it every possible attention, but not so much at first as on his second visit. Indeed, outside the lecture-room, when he came in 1855, his life in Boston was one round of dinner parties and evening entertainments. On both occasions I sat by him at dinner at the Tremont House almost every day when he was not engaged abroad, and had the pleasure of his conversation there and in his apartments [and he did not find in him the 'outward austerity' which Blanchard Jerrold and others had alleged sometimes came over him[1]].

In fact, Thackeray seemed to me a highbred, conscientious, and considerate man, a gentleman in sentiment and feeling, deeply thoughtful, introspective, as well as keenly and constantly observant of outward things; and any seeming 'austerity' which I might have observed I attributed to the absorption of his mind in his literary pursuits and contemplations. This sort of abstraction, however, could hardly have been permitted to him while in the United States, since, with the true spirit of a gentleman, making it a point to write nothing about us or our concerns while accepting our hospitality and making profit out of our attendance upon his lectures, he was at leisure to enjoy himself in society as he saw fit. Indeed, I think he felt himself quite at home, and sometimes, in a festive mood, indulged in certain off-hand private remarks, not always well taken by sensitive persons to whom they happened to be addressed. In this way offence was on some occasions given when certainly none could have been intended. They were examples of English bluntness, in cases where I think an American gentleman would have scarcely given way to a personal allusion. . . .

We took various walks together, in which he enjoyed the exercise, as I certainly did the conversation upon literary topics and upon persons and things which he had seen or expected to see in this country. His remarks, with an occasional touch of satiric humour, were in their general spirit genial and benevolent; and it was easy to see that his disposition was charitable, however shrewd and even caustic his expressions may sometimes have been. I do not think he struck me as being what is technically called a *conversationist* – that is, one who would be invited to dinner for the purpose of keeping up the round of talk – and there was not the least shadow of attempt to show himself off; and though what he said was always sensible and to the point, it was the language of a well-bred and accomplished gentleman, who assumed no sort of superiority, but seemed naturally and simply at ease with his companions of the moment. . . .

On Thackeray's second visit to the United States, in the winter of 1855, I saw him still more familiarly than on the occasion of his first lecturing tour. . . . After dinner I sometimes went with him to his apartments, consisting of a parlour and bedroom, the most agreeable of any in the Tremont House, for a little social chat. On one of these occasions he recited to me his 'Ballad of Bouillabaisse'. . . . He gave those touching verses forth with emphatic expression and every manifestation of the tender feeling which must have inspired them. 'But', said he, 'they made no mark' – referring to the fact that they had formerly appeared in some London periodical. . . . I expressed my own gratification at the sentiment and spirit of the verses, which seemed to give him pleasure. . . .

I once asked Thackeray which he considered his best novel, and he said, without hesitation, he thought *Esmond* superior to either of the others. . . .

It was a subject of amusement with Thackeray, that he, a grave gentleman past middle life, a philosopher and a moralist, not beautiful certainly, with white hair and in spectacles, dignified and somewhat reserved in manner, should be exposed to [the] personal adulation [showered upon some celebrities]. I am afraid he had occasion sometimes to set down the demonstrations in question to the disadvantage of the manners of some of the freer of our American girls, compared with the more staid demeanour of English young ladies with whom he was acquainted. Of course no imputations of a moral nature could arise, except so far as manners are in themselves the external indications of the inner moral sense. I know that one very pretty young lady actually followed him to Boston from a distant city, whose respectable father came and reclaimed her from this Quixotic undertaking. Her countenance was known to me, and one day, walking with Thackeray on Beacon Street, we met this infatuated young person coming from the opposite direction. He accosted her politely, and passed on without pause, remarking, as if to himself, with a sort of sigh of relief, 'Well, thank Heaven, that pipe is smoked out.' I was a good deal struck by the more than ordinary freedom of the expression from such a man and on such an occasion. Surely it was not in the best taste; but I am not attempting to describe Thackeray as other than he was, according to his several moods of mind. . . .

Mr Thackeray was an admirer – as what man of taste and true sentiment is not? – of female beauty. Certainly he saw in Boston many cultivated and attractive ladies; but I think he admired, more than others, one married lady whom he knew in private life rather than in general society, and in whose parlour I often met him.[2] It was a domestic scene in which he seemed completely at home, and where he conversed freely of his own household ties in England, which he so sorely missed in another land. Of this lady, distinguished for her personal attractions and her unpretending good sense, he used to say, 'She would be a countess anywhere'; which was taken as a remark of no little significance from one who had the *entrée* into aristocratic English society, and was sufficiently well acquainted with countesses and duchesses at home.

Of course Thackeray studied character wherever he observed any of its eccentricities. There were idiosyncrasies enough in Boston, if he had had the leisure to look them up; but his associations there and in other American cities, I imagine, were with an altogether different class from the persons he may have sometimes met at 'Caves of Harmony', or the like, in his more familiar home life in London, sitting up till four o'clock in the morning and singing his 'Reverend Dr Luther'. But among his casual acquaintances were two or three whose society he occasionally enjoyed. . . . They were persons with whom he might have been on easy terms at the 'Cave' aforesaid, had there been any such place in Boston (though there are lower dens enough), where gentlemen of slightly Bohemian tastes and manners might resort for occasional relaxation.... He appeared to like their society once in a while better than that of persons in Boston of more formal ways and habits. ... They got up small supper parties for him, and sometimes they did me the honour to invite me to form one of a small party with him at Porter's to partake of game, for which that place of entertainment in the neighbourhood of Boston was then famous....

Our primitive dinner hour at the Tremont House was half past two o'clock. On these occasions we generally had the company of an excellent lady, already referred to; and I believe he really preferred these not very pretentious repasts to the formal feasts, at hours so much later, in fashionable London society; for it was easy to see that his tastes in this respect were simple enough, and that his personal wants were easily satisfied. We had wine, commonly sherry, of which he moderately partook, to which was not unfrequently added a modest half bottle of Champagne. As our talk at table turned a good deal on literary subjects, he inquired of me, one day, if I had ever seen some verses of his upon Charlotte and Werther; to which I was ashamed to make a negative reply, but begged him to repeat them; which he did, with unmoved gravity of tone and feature, as if it were some especially solemn recitation, though relieved a little by the sly twinkle of his eyes through his spectacles.[3] ...

I expressed my honest liking for these odd stanzas, and ventured to ask for a copy. He said nothing, but at tea-time – that is, about half past six or seven o'clock – he came down with a sheet of paper in his hand, and a little bustle, as though he had accomplished something, and handed me the verses, copied out in his wonderfully fine handwriting, illustrated at the top by one of his incomparable ink drawings. I looked upon it with the most unaffected admiration. I was astonished at the rapidity as well as the excellence of the execution . . . .

NOTES

1. For Blanchard Jerrold's remarks, see below, II, 356.
2. Mrs George B. Jones, wife of a Boston jeweller (*LPP*, III, 259n).
3. 'The Sorrows of Werther'. The drawing referred to below is reproduced at the head of Lunt's article.

The Kind, Sympathetic Side of his Great Nature

LUCY BAXTER

From *Thackeray's Letters to an American Family*, introduced by Lucy W. Baxter (New York and London, 1904) pp. 3–15. Lucy (b. 1836) was one of the two daughters of Mr and Mrs George Baxter, his frequent visits to whose New York house became one of his most treasured American experiences. He enjoyed its domestic atmosphere, and with Sally Baxter (1833–62), he developed a semi-avuncular, semi-sentimental, relationship: she had an *amour de tete* for him (*LPP*, III, 523). Her marriage in 1855 rather upset, and her early death in 1862 much grieved, him (see below, I, 185, and *Wisdom*, pp. 206–11). To prevent any suggestion of impropriety, however, he would never enter the house if the girls' mother was not at home. George Baxter was a warehouse-owner, not a literary man, and it was an unexpected honour for him to meet, let alone become so intimately acquainted with, Thackeray. A young Englishman who was courting Sally Baxter had met Thackeray in London, and introduced her father to him after one of the *Humourists* lectures, in November 1852. Thackeray immediately took to Baxter and, soon afterwards, to his household. His warm friendship with the family, evidenced also in the *Letters* here introduced, continued all his life and was maintained by his daughters after his death.

... he came to us whenever he could, with perfect freedom and informality. He begged to dine with us before the lectures, which even at first bored him greatly, and in the end became a real burden. The monotony of saying the same things over and over again, and the constraint of being obliged to be ready at a given time, whether he felt in a talking mood or not, were very trying to him. He became greatly attached to my mother, whose quiet sympathy soothed him, and his place at her right hand, with the claret-pitcher ready for him, was an established arrangement before a lecture. He would sometimes stop in the midst of the desultory conversation then in progress, and roll out in a deep voice, with an exaggerated accent, the opening sentences of the lecture next to be delivered, making us all laugh at his comic distaste for the performance. He did not like the lecture platform, and had it not been for the abundant shower of 'American dollars', assuring the future of the much-loved daughters, he would doubtless have refused many of the invitations which came to him from all parts of the country. Indeed, his letters will show that he was often sorely tempted to throw up his engagements and run off to England by the next steamer.

He entered with great interest into all our plans and amusements, and on one occasion, when my eldest brother's costume for a juvenile fancy ball was under discussion, he took pen and paper as he sat chatting among us, and drew little sketches of the proper dress for a page of various periods, being well versed in all the details belonging to each costume. He said that the quaint little figure with the big cuffs and broad brim to his hat was like little melancholy Harry Esmond when the kind Lady Castlewood first saw him and smiled so sweetly in his grave face. [*Esmond*, Bk I, ch. 1]. . . .

After dinner Mr Thackeray often sat chatting while my sister was dressing for a ball to which he himself might be going. It was on one of these occasions that, turning over the leaves of *Pendennis* as it lay on the table beside him, he said, smiling, from time to time, 'Yes, it is very like – it is certainly very like.'

'Like whom, Mr Thackeray?' said my mother.

'Oh, like me, to be sure; Pendennis is very like me.'

'Surely not,' objected my mother, 'for Pendennis was so weak!'

'Ah, well, Mrs Baxter,' he said, with a shrug of his great shoulders and a comical look, 'your humble servant is not very strong.'

An American ball-room amused him greatly. The bright, gay talk, the lively girls full of enjoyment, which they did not fear to show, made a contrast to the more conventional entertainments of London. My sister was at that time going much into society – she was not yet twenty and had both wit and beauty. In his picture of Ethel Newcome, as she holds a little court about her at one of the great London balls, Thackeray reproduces some impressions made by the New York girl.[1] Some of Ethel's impatience for the disillusions of society, its spiteful comment and harsh criticism, might well be reflections from discussions with my sister in the Brown House library, where Mr Thackeray passed many an hour talking of matters grave and gay.

With December came the course of lectures in Boston, and his first letters told us of the people he met there.... In one of his letters Mr Thackeray speaks of meeting Mrs Stowe and being pleasantly impressed by her looks and manner.[2]

When the return from Boston was at hand, my mother suggested to the younger members of the family that, should Mr Thackeray appear during the day at Brown House, it were best not to ask him to dine. 'I have not just such a dinner as I like to give him', she said.

Whatever was the deficiency, my mother had to overlook it, as the sequel proved. As she stood in the dining-room just before the dinner-hour, giving some orders to the maid, a summons came from the front door. After it was opened, steps were heard coming steadily through the hall to the dining-room. As my mother turned in surprise to see who could be coming at so late an hour, there in the doorway stood the tall figure with kind eyes and silvery hair which had become so familiar to us [with some pictures to show her].

Then, turning to my mother, he said, 'Now you will give me some dinner, won't you?'

The younger people were greatly delighted by my mother's discomfiture. I doubt if Mr Thackeray discovered anything amiss in the dinner. He always laughed at our American idea of making a 'feast' for a guest, saying that we did not understand at all 'just to fetch a friend home to a leg of mutton'....

With the New Year Mr Thackeray started to fulfil his Southern engagements, and his letters brought us little sketches of the negroes, whose ways and sayings amused him greatly.... Before going to Charleston, he ran back to New York to give a lecture for the benefit of the Sewing Society of the Unitarian Church, in which the mother of Mr Felt was much interested.[3] He wrote an introduction, in the course of which he repeated Hood's poem, 'The Bridge of Sighs'. No one who heard him would easily forget the pathos of his voice in the verse:

Take her up tenderly,
Lift her with care!
Fashioned so slenderly,
Young, and so fair!

No more tender appreciation of distress could be found than that which always responded in the great author (cynic as he has been called) to any tale of trouble or want. His purse was constantly at the service of his friends, or often mere acquaintances, much to his own pecuniary detriment, and his glasses were dimmed when he spoke of the sorrows which day after day came to his knowledge. His liberality to those who served him was unfailing.

After his return from the South, Mr Thackeray found there was to be a little celebration of my seventeenth birthday. There was to be music, dancing, and flowers, for what was called in those days a 'small party'. Mr Thackeray made the occasion memorable by the verses he sent with some flowers. With them came also the quaint little rhymed note, striking a lighter key. The verses have always been very precious to me, but the first form[4] ... I think more attractive than the shorter lines used in the published poem. The month of May carried Mr Thackeray back to England, and he was not again in America until 1855.

The second course of lectures, on the Four Georges, was not, I think, as well received in America as that on the English Humourists. He speaks of this in one of his later letters, when he mentions that the lectures were much more popular in England than in 'the States'. . . . We saw him but seldom during this last visit, compared with the earlier one. There were changes in the circle of the Brown House. My sister had, as he said, 'slipped away smiling, on her husband's arm', and the gap thus made could not be filled. In February we met in Charleston, where I had gone to be with my sister and brother-in-law, and he writes most kindly to my mother of us there. One experience of what was another side of Mr Thackeray's temper came to me in Charleston. Up to this time we had never seen anything of the roughness sometimes attributed to him when he was annoyed.

At a certain dinner-party where I went alone with him, my sister not being well, a lady was present who from their first meeting had antagonised Mr Thackeray. She was clever and rather brilliant, but had written some very trashy novels, whose reputation had certainly not extended beyond her native city. On this and other occasions she seemed determined to attract Mr Thackeray's attention, to his great annoyance. At last when something was said about the tribulations of authors, the lady leaned across the table, saying in a loud voice, 'You and I, Mr Thackeray, *being in the same boat*, can understand, can we not?' A dead silence fell, a thunder-cloud descended upon the face of Mr Thackeray, and the pleasure of the entertainment was at an end. The hostess was no doubt grateful when the novelist had to excuse himself for the lecture and take his departure. Certainly one of the guests was, for the first time in her experience, relieved to see the door close upon her kind friend. This annoyance on the part of the lady was the culmination of numerous attacks, and struck just the wrong chord. She is referred to as the 'Individual' in a letter to my mother.[5]

In all *our* intercourse with Mr Thackeray we saw only the kind, sympathetic, loving side of his great nature. It was always impossible for us to feel afraid of his cynicism, his sharp criticism, of which others speak. He could not help seeing the weakness of human nature, but he did the fullest justice – as he would say, he 'took off his hat' – to whatever was fine or noble in man or woman. He was, too, very patient with weakness of character, but he hated and despised pretence and humbug. All this has been said before, but I feel I must add my confirmation of such a view of his character from our personal experience.

In May, as will be seen from his letters, Mr Thackeray took a sudden resolution and went off, without warning, to England. It was a real distress to my mother, as to all of us, that he should go thus, without a word of goodbye; but that was just what he wanted to avoid.[6] We never saw him again, but letters came from time to time. . . . In the last years he wrote in full and affectionate sympathy with our great anxiety and sorrow [during the Civil War, when Sally lived in the South, and fell ill and died].

NOTES

1. This is somewhat at variance with what Lucy Baxter told General Wilson in June 1900: "'It is not true, as has been often said, that the character of Ethel Newcome was drawn from my sister, although some of the scenes in *The Newcomes* are no doubt suggested by seeing my sister holding her court in New York ball-rooms." To this it may be added [Wilson remarks] that in Mrs Julia Ward Howe's *Reminiscences*, speaking of Mrs Hampton [*nee* Sally Baxter], the sister-in-law of General Wade Hampton, the venerable lady writes, "She told me that she recognised bits of her own conversation in some of the sayings of Ethel Newcome; and I have little doubt that in depicting the beautiful and noble though wayward girl Thackeray had in mind something of the aspect and character of the lovely Sally Baxter." The novelist, in a note to an American friend, described the latter as being "eighteen and brilliantly beautiful"' (Wilson, I, 152–3). Lucy Baxter also told Wilson that Thackeray 'used to call my mother Lady Castlewood and my sister Miss Beatrix' (ibid., p. 152), but both these characters in *Esmond* had of course been created before he met the Baxters. Ray notes that Blanche Airlie as well as Sally Baxter was a model for Ethel Newcome (*Wisdom*, p. 242).

2. He wrote to Mrs Baxter, 3 June 1853, that he found Mrs Stowe 'a gentle almost pretty person with a very great sweetness in her eyes and smile' (*LPP*, III, 273).

3. The 'Charity and Humour' lecture was first given on 31 January 1853 at the Church of the Messiah, Broadway. Willard L. Felt, as chairman of the Lecture Committee of the New York Mercantile Library Association, had been instrumental in bringing Thackeray to the United States.

4. See *LPP*, III, 256–8. The poem, 'Lucy's Birthday', was published in *Ballads and Poems* (1855). His letter accompanying the poem and the bouquet was in doggerel verse, written out as prose.

5. *LPP*, III, 569. The obnoxious 'Individual' was Mrs Henry King (1826–75), author of *Busy Moments of an Idle Woman* (1854), *Lily* (1855) and other novels. Ray writes, 'She and her friends appear to have regarded her encounter with Thackeray as a triumph, for Charleston tradition has it that "the celebrated English author . . . undertook a tilt with her and was badly discomfited"' (*LPP*, III, 569n).

6. Thackeray sailed from New York, not in May, but on 25 April 1856. His secretary, Eyre Crowe, contradicts Lucy's account: 'The only people we had time to shake hands with were the friendly family of the Baxters . . .' (see above, I, 137). The terms of Thackeray's letter to Mrs Baxter, written during the voyage (*LPP*, III, 603–4), though indefinite, makes Lucy's account sound rather the more likely to be true.

Animated but Sensitive and Sad

'A. Z.'

From 'Some Recollections of Thackeray', *Lippincott's Magazine*, VII (1871) 106–10. An American, and apparently a Bostonian: but I have not been able to discover his identity. He writes (p. 106), 'I saw [Thackeray] for the first time a day or two after his arrival in America on his first visit [in Boston, on 12 Nov 1852], and I saw him for the last time a few weeks before his death.' If the letter, quoted below, about 'another bottle of the '35!' survives and comes to light (it is not in *LPP*), it will identify 'A. Z.' His host on the first occasion of his meeting Thackeray was the historian W. H. Prescott (1796–1859), the crossed swords on whose library walls feature in the opening sentence of *The Virginians*, referred to below (see Prescott's letter to Thackeray, 30 Nov 1857, *Biog. Intros*, X, xxxiv).

Good portraits of Thackeray are so common, and so many of your readers saw him in the lecture-room, that I need not describe his person. The misshaped nose, so broad at the bridge and stubby at the end, was the effect of an early accident. His near-sightedness, unless hereditary, must have had, I think, a similar origin, for no man had less the appearance of a student who had weakened his sight by application to books. In his gestures – especially in the act of bowing to a lady – there was a certain awkwardness, made more conspicuous by his tall, well-proportioned and really commanding figure. His hair, at forty, was already grey, but abundant and massy; the cheeks had a ruddy tinge and there was no sallowness in the complexion; the eyes, keen and kindly even when they wore a sarcastic expression, twinkled sometimes through and sometimes over the spectacles. What I should call the predominant expression of the countenance was courage – a readiness to face the world on its own terms, without either bawling or whining, asking no favours, yielding, if at all, from magnanimity. I have seen but two faces in which this expression, coupled with that of high intellectual power, was equally striking – those of Daniel Webster and

Thomas Carlyle. But the former had a saturnine gloom even in its animation, and the latter a variety and intensity of expression, which were absent from Thackeray's.

On the evening of which I speak I sat beside him some time in the library – an apartment of which he has made mention in the opening sentence of *The Virginians*. A variety of topics, chiefly literary, were discussed. His own manner soon made it impossible, even for one who in every sense looked up to him, to be otherwise than familiar in tone. No one was more thoroughly high-bred, but no one more averse to formality, and there was consequently no fencing required before one could feel at ease with him. His expressions at times were tolerably blunt. Speaking of Carlyle, he said, 'Why don't he hang up his d——d old fiddle?' adding, however, in reference to the *Life of Sterling*, then recently published, 'Yes, a wonderful writer! What could *you or I* (!) have made of such a subject?' He went on to praise Carlyle's dignity of character: '*He* would not go round making a show of himself, as I am doing.' 'But he *has* lectured.' 'He did it once, and was done with it.'

When I was going away, and had reached the farther end of a vacant drawing-room, a voice, which had already grown familiar to my ear, called after me from the half-opened glass door of the library, 'I say! come and dine with me tomorrow at two-thirty.' While I was gladly accepting the invitation the host came out and took us both back to smoke, the ladies and other guests having in the meantime left. We sat till a late, or rather early, hour. Thackeray was at that time a furious smoker, choosing the strongest cigars and despatching them in rapid succession. Part of the talk ran on Dickens, of whom he spoke in a somewhat different strain from what he used in public. Our host had introduced the subject by saying, after some censure of that popular novelist's extravagancies, 'But I like Dickens personally: he is so genial and frank.' 'Genial, yes,' was the reply; 'but frank' – and a twinkle came from over the spectacles – 'well, frank as an oyster.' 'Dickens,' he said afterward, apropos of some remarks on literary genius, 'is making £10,000 a year. He is very angry at me for saying so, but I *will* say it, for it is true. He doesn't like me: he knows that my books are a protest against his – that if the one set are true, the other must be false.[1] But *Pickwick* is an exception: it is a capital book. It is like a glass of good English ale. I wish I had it to read before going to bed tonight.' And he made a slight inaudible motion with his lips, as if tasting the beverage he had mentioned.

During his stay in Boston at that time, as well as on his second visit, I saw a good deal of him, both in company and *tête-à-tête*. In his general manner he gave one the impression of having a very large amount of vitality, without that excess which makes some people restless and others boisterous. I never heard him laugh heartily or talk vehemently, nor do I believe that breeding or a deep experience of life had so much to do with this as natural temperament. But neither was there any appearance of ennui, though a lassitude – the effect of ill-health, from which, though you would never have suspected it, he was seldom free – came over him at times, especially in the small hours. In society he was almost always animated, and he had the power of diffusing animation over a somewhat frigid circle.

One evening, when he was expected at a large dinner-party, where the other guests were already assembled, a general conversation sprung up – we were sitting in a semi-circle before a bright coal fire – in reference to his lectures. Two or three extremely well-read men, of a rather formal turn of mind, did most of the talk, and indulged in a good deal of carping criticism. It was not his depreciation of Swift and Sterne, or his exaggerated laudation of Addison, of which they complained, but of his calling Sir William Temple a prig – whereas Temple was in truth the very model of a gentleman, who had written in a style which was charming, though a little incorrect – his talking of 'a place in the Pipe Office' in evident and deplorable ignorance of what the Pipe Office was or had been, and similar matters. At the height, or rather depth, of the discussion the subject of it entered, and going round the circle shook hands with those he knew, and finding they were by far the greater number, turned back to exchange the same greeting with those to whom he had merely bowed when introduced. In a moment it seemed as if a new spirit had taken possession of the company. It was not that the theme was changed: on the contrary, though dropped for a moment, most of the mooted points were again taken up. But there was a life in the conversation which it had wanted before. It was no longer a dry debate. On some of the questions Thackeray owned himself wrong. He admitted with a quizzical look his lack of information in regard to the Pipe Office. But he stuck to the assertion that Stella was a natural daughter of Temple, went over the facts from which the inference was drawn, and in answer, not to a counter-statement, but a demand for more sufficient proof, said, 'I cannot prove it: it is apparent, like the broken nose in my face.'

The French draw a distinction between *l'homme de génie* and *l'homme d'esprit*, meaning by the latter term not so much the witty man, or the man of talent or even of intellect, but rather the man whose powers, without being great or profound, are always at his service, who is never embarrassed or at a loss in his particular line, which line, in a land where the salon is an institution, always includes sparkling conversation. Thackeray was a man of genius, but he possessed as much of *esprit* as is compatible with genius. If seldom brilliant, he was always self-possessed and ready. It is doubtful whether those who knew him best and longest could make out a list of his *bon mots* which would bear repeating; but he could always say a thing sufficiently good for the occasion, and in a manner which set it off to advantage. Being challenged by a lady for a rhyme to '*liniment*', he replied immediately, with a reference to the customary physician's fee in England.

> When the doctor writes for liniment,
> There is nothing but a guinea meant.

Another fair one going into raptures, on shipboard, over the appearance of the foam-crested waves, and demanding a simile in default of imagination on her own part, he said, 'They look like white ponies racing over green fields.' . . .

Such things, I well know, are not at all worth citing for themselves, but, like his bright look and springing gait, they were, in their abundance, indications of a quality which is obvious enough in Thackeray's writings – at least in the earlier ones – but which was more conspicuous in his conversation – a quality which, for lack of a better term, I must call animal spirits, though this carries with it a notion of effusiveness and loud gaiety that would not at all suit the description. When a subject was seriously discussed he could talk gravely, though with diminished fire, and was apt, when pressed, to have recourse to banter. I doubt whether anyone ever induced him to say much about matters of religious belief or feeling. What is called his cynicism showed itself occasionally. He defined the difference between Shakespeare and an ordinary mind as a difference in the length of two maggots. But much of his light talk was intended, not so much to conceal as to keep down a sensibility amounting almost to womanliness which belonged to his nature, and which contrasted, one might almost say, struggled, with the manliness which was equally its characteristic. He could not read anything pathetic without actual discomfort, and was unable, for example, to go through with the *Bride of Lammermoor*.[2] I have heard him allude to some early sorrows, especially the loss of a child, in a way which showed how sharp and painful was the recollection after the lapse of many years. That he could sympathise warmly with others I infer from much that I have heard. His well-known sensitiveness sprung perhaps from the same root as his sensibility. 'I like Thackeray,' an English critic once said in my hearing, 'but I cannot respect him – he is so sensitive.' But his sensitiveness made harsh things distasteful to him even when he was not himself the object of them. 'You fiend!' he said to a friend who was laughing over a sharp attack on an acquaintance of both, and refused to hear or read a word of it.

Hawthorne says in his *English Notebooks* that he had heard Thackeray could not endure to have servants about him, feeling uneasy in their presence, and he goes on, *à la Hawthorne*, to analyse the feeling.[3] On his second visit to America he brought with him an attendant who looked like a good specimen of the best English domestics. 'I don't call him my servant,' he told me: 'I call him my companion. I found he didn't like the company downstairs' (this was at a hotel), 'so I make him sit beside me at the *table d'hôte*.' Yet Thackeray was a man of aristocratic feelings, and the last person in the world to be *hail fellow well met* with everyone who chose to accost him. A touch on the shoulder from a railway conductor – after the manner of those 'gentlemanly' officials – made the blood tingle in his finger-ends, and left a feeling of indignation which burned anew as he recounted the occurrence. He demanded civil treatment, but hauteur or condescension was

not in his disposition. Standing in no awe of the highest, he
had no wish to inspire awe in the lowest. One day, after we had
lunched together at Parker's, he handed a gold-piece to the
waiter, saying, 'My friend, will you do me the favour to accept
a sovereign?' 'I am very much obliged to you, *Mr Thackeray*',
was the man's reply: he had not read *Vanity Fair* or *Esmond*, I
imagine, but he had probably tasted their author's bounty on
former occasions. Yet Thackeray would sometimes be whim-
sically economical for others. 'Don't leave this bit of paper,' he
would say to a visitor who was laying down a card on the table;
'it has cost you two cents, and will be just as good for your next
call.'

It was on a bright day, though the month was November
and the place London, in 1863, that I called upon Thackeray
at his red-brick house – the only one of the kind (so he
thought) in the metropolis – looking out on the old oaks of
Kensington Gardens. There had been no correspondence
between us since I had seen him last, but two or three kindly
messages had reached me, and I had read a passage in a letter
to a friend at whose house we had met, in which he wrote,
'How often I think I should like to be sitting with you and Z. at
the table in —— street, with that old butler putting on another
bottle of the '35!' It was a little past noon, and I was shown up
to his bed-room, a large and cheerful apartment, with little
furniture besides the bed – the bed in which so shortly after he
was to be found lying calm in death. There was a dressing-
room behind, to which he went at times while making his
toilette, keeping up the conversation through the open door.
His appearance showed a change for which I was not
prepared. It is hard to understand how his medical men
should have allowed him to continue writing with signs of
impending apoplexy so apparent to the unprofessional eye.
In answer to my inquiries about his health, he said he felt
'infernally old'. What was missing in his manner was a sort of
light glee with which in former days he had been wont to tell
an anecdote or say a good thing. The twinkle, too, was less
bright, the lassitude more decided, and the sadness which lay
deep in his nature, and against which, I think, he always
fought, seemed to be gaining the upper hand. However, the
sarcastic power was not extinct, and he expended several
flings on the editor of a well-known literary paper – a person

of infinite conceit and of never-failing ignorance. The war in America formed, of course, one of the topics of talk. Thackeray expressed no decided opinion, but his leanings were evidently on the side of the South. Speaking of letter-writing, 'I had left off', he said, 'corresponding with everybody but Sally Fairfax, and you have killed her – sweet creature!'[4] He asked whether I thought the North would ultimately beat, and on my assurance that its superior resources, combined with its persistent spirit, admitted of little doubt on that point, answered, with a half sigh, 'I suppose so: you will tire them out at last.' He took a volume from a book-case to show me the autograph of Washington on the fly-leaf. 'You have forgotten all about *him*,' he said: 'you care nothing now for his warnings.' I laughed, reminding him that I had always protested against his idolatry for Washington. After chatting for an hour or more, he changed his dressing-gown for a coat and asked me to go down to his library – or rather to the room he had built for this object, but which was not well suited to it, making him consequently discontented ·with the house. An old lady in black entered: 'My mother', he said, and presented me to her. There was no strong resemblance that I noticed; but her face had a look of placid resoluteness inherent, I fancy, in the stock, and she gave a vigorous description of a combat she had carried on in the night with the agile insects that disturb slumber. She was the widow of a second husband, and bore the name of Smyth. She looked likely to survive her son, and did in fact, though only by a few months. After a while she went out, and Thackeray produced a box of Manillas, but did not smoke himself. 'I envy you', he said – and I cannot help thinking, if the doctors had taken away his pen instead of his cigar, they would have done at least equally well. It was on this occasion that he mentioned the child who had died so many years before. 'Even now,' he said, 'I cannot bear to think of it.' When he shook hands with me on the doorstep, he pointed to the oaks and said, 'You have no such trees in America; but they are dying.' The appearance of the top branches indicated as much; and he too, from indications not less apparent – he in whose character and intellect the strength of the oak was united with the beauty and the sweetness of the lily – he too was dying.

It was with a shock, but not of surprise, that going into

Galignani's on Christmas morning I received the announcement that Thackeray was dead.

NOTES

1. I know of no evidence that, at this period, Dickens 'did not like' Thackeray, or that he saw Thackeray's fiction as 'a protest' against his own. Prescott had met Dickens during his American visit of 1842.

2. 'A. Z.' in a footnote refers, however, to Hawthorne's surprise over some lack of sensibility here: Russell Sturgis, in 1855, talked about 'the last number of *The Newcomes* – so touching that nobody can read it aloud without breaking down – he mentioned that Thackeray himself had read it to James Russell Lowell and William Story, in a cider-cellar!' – *The English Notebooks by Nathaniel Hawthorne*, ed. Randall Stewart (New York, 1962) p. 225. On this episode, see below, II, 213–16, 218.

3. '*12 August 1855*. Thackeray has a dread of servants, insomuch that he hates to address them, or to ask them for anything. His morbid sensibility, in this regard, has perhaps led him to study and muse upon them, so that he may be presumed to have a more intimate knowledge of the class than any other man' (ibid., p. 190). The servant Thackeray brought to America, mentioned below, was Charles Pearman.

4. For 'Fairfax' understand 'Hampton'. Sally Baxter – on whom see above, I, 172 – had married a Southerner, Frank Hampton, in 1855, and had gone to live in South Carolina. By 1862 she was dying (see her pathetic last letter to Thackeray, *Wisdom*, pp. 317–19), but her father and sister were not allowed through the Confederate lines to visit her. She died in September 1862; see *LPP*, IV, 278–9 for Thackeray's letter of condolence to her family. The historian Henry Adams (1838–1918), who knew Sally, recalls an encounter in London with Thackeray after her death. He had been laughing, but 'his tone changed as he spoke of [her] . . . whom he had loved as Sally Baxter and painted as Ethel Newcome. Though he had never quite forgiven her marriage, his warmth of feeling revived when he heard that she had died of consumption at Columbia while her parents and sister were refused permission to pass through the lines to see her. In speaking of it, Thackeray's voice trembled and his eyes filled with tears. The coarse cruelty of Lincoln and his hirelings was notorious. He never doubted that the Federals made a business of harrowing the tenderest feelings of women – particularly of women – in order to punish their opponents. On quite insufficient evidence he burst into violent reproach . . .' – *The Education of Henry Adams: An Autobiography* (Boston, Mass., and New York, 1918) p. 131.

His Simple Naturalness

WILLIAM BRADFORD REED

From *Haud Immemor* (Philadelphia: privately printed, 1864) pp. 3–7, 10, 25–7; later reprinted in *Blackwood's Magazine*, CXI (1872) 678–90, and elsewhere. Reed (1806–76), lawyer, scholar and politician, was a distinguished citizen of Philadelphia, with whom Thackeray became very intimate during his first visit in 1853. Their warm friendship and correspondence continued, as is here described.

Mr Thackeray (who that has heard him, with sweetness of voice unequalled, speak of *Mr* Joseph Addison, and *Mr* Congreve, and *Mr* Fielding, and *Mr* Atterbury; who that has read *Henry Esmond*, or *The Virginians*, will find fault with me for so describing him?) came to Philadelphia, on his first visit to America, in the month of January 1853. My impression is that he brought very few letters of personal introduction, and was rather careless of what may be called 'social success', though anxious about the work he had in hand – his course of lectures on *The English Humourists* – and, as he used to say, the dollars he wished to make, not for himself, but for those at home. With, or without letters, he soon made friends, on the hearts of whom the news of his death has struck a sharp pang. As one of them, I venture to record a few memories of him who is gone.

The lectures were very successful here. There are two classes of people in every American microcosm – those who run after celebrities, and those, resolute not to be pleased, who run, as it were, against them. All were won or conquered by his simple naturalness; and, as I have said, the lectures were a great success.

My personal relations to him happened to become very intimate. He seemed to take a fancy to me and mine; and I certainly loved him. He used to come to my house, not the abode of wealth or luxury, almost every day, and often more than once a day. He talked with my little children, and told them odd fairy-tales; and I now see him (this was on his second visit) one day in Walnut Street, walking slowly along with my little girl by the hand; the tall, grey-headed, spectacled man, with an effort accommodating himself to the toddling child by his side; and then he would bring her home; and one day, when we were to have a great dinner given to him at the Club, and my wife was ill, and my household disarranged, and the bell rang, and I said to him, 'I must go and carve the boiled mutton for the children, and take for granted you do not care to come'; and he got up, and, with a cheery voice, said, 'I love boiled mutton, and children too, and I will dine with them', and we did; and he was happy, and the children were happy, and our appetite for the Club dinner was damaged. Such was Thackeray in my home. . . .

It was a bright moonlight night on which we (Thackeray and I) walked home from that dinner [at the house of a friend]; and I remember well the walk and the place, for I seem to localise all my associations with him, and I asked him, what perhaps he might have thought, the absurd question, 'What do you honestly think of my country; or, rather, what has most struck you in America? Tell me candidly, for I shall not be at all angry, or hurt if it be unfavourable, or too much elated, if it be not?' And then his answer, as he stopped (we were walking along Penn Square), and turning round to me said, 'You know what a virtue-proud people we English are? We think we have got it all to ourselves. Now, that which most impresses me here is, that I find homes as good as ours; firesides like ours; domestic virtues as gentle and pure; the English language, though the accent be a little different, with its home-like melodies; and the Common Prayer Book in your families. I am more struck by pleasant resemblances than by anything else.' And so I sincerely believe he was.

There was a great deal of dining out while 'the great satirist', as we used to address him, was here; but although always genial, I do not think, according to my recollection, he was a brilliant conversationist. Those who expected much were often disappointed. It was in close, private intercourse, he was delightful. Once – it was in New York – he gave a dinner, at which I happened to be a guest, to what are called 'literary men': authors, and lawyers, and actors (two very accomplished ones, and most estimable gentlemen, still living), and editors, and magazine men. There he made what seemed to be an effort. He talked for the table. He sang some odd post-prandial songs; one, in a strange sort of 'recitative', about Dr Martin Luther. But, as I have said, it was an effort, and I liked him better at home and alone. It was on this occasion, or, rather, on our return journey to Philadelphia, that, on board the steamboat (here again am I localising) he spoke to me of domestic sorrows and anxieties too sacred to be recorded here. He referred to a friend whose wife had been deranged for many years, hopelessly so;[1] and never shall I forget the look, and manner, and voice with which he said to me, 'It is an awful thing for her to continue so to live. It is an awful thing for her so to die. But has it never occurred to you, how awful a thing the recovery of lost reason must be, without the consciousness of the lapse of time? She finds the lover of her youth a grey-haired old man, and her infants young men and women. Is it not sad to think of this?' And yet it was this man whom vulgar-minded people called heartless! As he thus talked to me, I thought of lines of tenderness, often quoted, which no one but he could have written:

> Ah me! how quick the days are flitting;
>   I mind me of a time that's gone,
> When here I'd sit, as now I'm sitting,
>   In this same place, but not alone.
> A fair, young form was nestled near me;
>   A dear, dear face looked fondly up,
> And sweetly spoke and smiled to cheer me –
>   There's no one now to share my cup![2]

It is no part of this little memorial to refer to what may be called his public relations to Philadelphia, and his success as a lecturer. I merely record my recollection of the peculiar voice and cadence, the exquisite manner of reading poetry, the elocution, matchless in its simplicity, his tranquil attitude – the only movement of his hands being when he wiped his glasses as he began and turned over the leaves of his manuscript – his gentle intonations. There was sweet music in his way of repeating the most hackneyed lines, which freshened them anew. I seem still to hear him say,

And nightly to the listening earth
Repeats the story of her birth.

Or, in his lecture on Pope:

Lo! thy dread empire, Chaos! is restored;
Light dies before thy uncreating word.
Thy hand, great Anarch! lets the curtain fall,
And universal darkness buries all!

But to resume my personal recollections. He was too sincere a man to talk for effect, or to pay common compliments; and on his first visit to America, he seemed so happy, and so much pleased with all he met, that I fancied he might be tempted to come and, for a time, live amongst us. The British consulate in this city became vacant, the incumbent, Mr William Peter, dying suddenly, and it seems from the following note, written at Washington, that I had urged him to take the place, if he could get it. . . .

[Thackeray replied, 14 Feb 1853, kindly declining (*LPP*, III, 201–3). Reed then prints various letters from Thackeray. As a preface to one, he relates 'a little incident which was very illustrative of his generous temper'.]

On his return to Philadelphia, in the spring of 1856, from the south and west, a number of his friends – I as much as any one – urged him, unwisely as it turned out, to repeat his lectures on the Humourists. He was very loath to do it, but finally yielded, being, I doubt not, somewhat influenced by the pecuniary inducements accidentally held out to him. A young bookseller of this city offered him a round sum – not very large, but, under the circumstances, quite liberal – for the course, which he accepted. The experiment was a failure. It was late in the season, with long days and shortening nights, and the course *was* a stale one, and the lectures had been printed, and the audiences were thin, and the bargain was disastrous, not to him, but to the young gentleman who had ventured it. We were all disappointed and mortified; but Thackeray took it good-humouredly: the only thing that seemed to disturb him being his sympathy with the man of business. 'I don't mind the empty benches, but I cannot bear to see that sad, pale-faced young man as I come out, who is losing

money on my account.' This he used to say at my house when
he came home to a frugal and not very cheerful supper after
the lectures. Still the bargain had been fairly made, and was
honourably complied with; and the money was paid and
remitted, through my agency, to him at New York. I received
no acknowledgement of the remittance, and recollect well that
I felt not a little annoyed at this; the more so when, on picking
up a newspaper, I learned that Thackeray had sailed for
home. The day after he had gone, when there could be no
refusal, I received a certificate of deposit on his New York
bankers for an amount quite sufficient to meet any loss
incurred as he thought, on his behalf.[3]

[In 1859, Reed, who had been serving as American Minister
to China, was on his way home via London. He received a
hospitable letter, concluding, however, that 'of course you will
consort with bigger wigs than yours, always, W. M. Thackeray'
(*LPP*, IV, 136–7).] No 'bigger wigs' came between us. During
my fortnight in London – for I was hastening home after two
years absence – we saw him nearly every day. He came
regularly to our quarters, went with me to the Athenaeum –
that spot of brilliant association – where he pointed out the
eminent men of whom I had heard and read; and then he
would go to his working table in the Club library and write for
the *Cornhill*, to which he said he had sold himself to slavery for
two years. He would carry my son, a young man just of age, off
with him to see the London world in odd 'haunts'. I dined with
him twice – once at his modest house, No. 36, Onslow Square,
where we had the great pleasure of seeing his daughters, and
once at Greenwich, at a bachelor's dinner, where I made the
acquaintance, since ripened into intimacy, of another friend,
who will, I am sure, excuse this distant allusion to him. We
looked out on the Park and the river, where the *Great Eastern*
was lying before her first voyage, and talked of America and
American associations, and of the chance of his coming again
when the magazine slavery was at an end, and our last dinner
was over. I left London on the afternoon of 30 April 1859. Mr
and Miss Thackeray were at the Euston Square station to say
farewell. He took my son aside and, to his infinite confusion,
handed him a little *cadeau*, which I hope he will always cherish
with pride for the sake of the giver. 'We parted with a great

deal of kindness, please God, and friendly talk of a future meeting. May it happen one day, for I feel sure he was a just man.'

My pious duty is nearly done. On my return to America our correspondence, naturally enough, languished; each was much occupied; he with drudgery which was exhausting and engrossing. I often received kind messages, and sometimes apologies. After the Civil War began, no letter passed between us. I had not the heart to write, and I do not believe that he had; for I reject with emphasis the idea that his gentle nature could feel aught but horror at this war of brethren – 'brothers speaking the same dear mother tongue'. More than any Englishman of letters I have ever known, he was free from that sentimental disease of 'Abolitionism'.[4] His American novel, and his pictures of life in ancient days at Castlewood, on the Potomac, show this abundantly. His estimate of Mrs Stowe's evil-omened fiction, in one of the letters I have given, shows it.[5] He had been in the South, and met Southern ladies and gentlemen, the highest types of American civilisation. This I may say now in their hour of suffering and possible disaster. He had visited Southern homes, which the bloody hand of wanton outrage has since desecrated, and shared Southern hospitality, and no word, that I am aware of, ever fell from his lips, or his pen, which showed sympathy or approval of the crusade which has tumbled the American Union in bloody ruin.

NOTES

1. Reed's discreet way, of course, of referring to Isabella Thackeray.
2. 'The Ballad of Bouillabaisse', penultimate stanza.
3. Thackeray wrote, from on board the *Baltic*: 'I think it right to send back twenty-five per cent. to poor Hazard [the young bookseller]. Will you kindly give him the enclosed ...' (*LPP*, III, 601).
4. Reed's strong views on this matter ruined his career, after the victory of the North.
5. *Uncle Tom's Cabin*, he wrote to Reed in 1853, 'has done harm, by inflaming us [Englishmen] with an idea of our own superior virtue in freeing our blacks whereas you keep yours' (*LPP*, III, 293).